THE LIFE AND LEGEND
OF MICHAEL SCOT

An Enquiry into
The Life and Legend of
Michael Scot

By Rev. J. WOOD BROWN, M.A.

NEW ORLEANS: RARABI MANOR

2021

Published by
Arabi Manor Esoterica
A Rebel Satori Imprint

Design copyright 2022

ISBN: 978-1-60864-193-2 (hardcover)
978-1-60864-194-9 (paperback)

D. D. D.

ALMAE MATRI SUAE

EDINBURGENSI

HAUD IMMEMOR

AUCTOR

PREFACE

AFTER some considerable time spent in making collections for the work which is now submitted to the public, I became aware that a biography of Michael Scot was in existence which had been composed as early as the close of the sixteenth century. This is the work of Bernardino Baldi of Urbino, who was born in 1553. He studied medicine at Padua, but soon turned his attention to mathematics, especially to the historical developments of that science. Taking holy orders, he became Abbot of Guastalla in 1586, and in the quiet of that cloister found time to produce his work 'De le vite de Matematici' of which the biography of Scot forms a part. He died in 1617.

This discovery led me at first to think that my original plan might with some advantage be modified. Baldi had evidently enjoyed great advantages in writing his life of Scot. His time lay nearer to that of Scot by three hundred years than our own does. He was a native of Italy, where so large a part of Scot's life was passed. He had studied at Padua, the last of the great schools in which Averroës, whom Scot first introduced to the Latins, still held intellectual sway.

All this seemed to indicate him as one who was exceptionally situated and suited for the work of collecting such accounts of Michael Scot as still survived in the south when he lived and wrote. The purpose he had in view was also such as promised a serious biography, not entirely, nor even chiefly, occupied with the recitation of traditional tales, but devoted to a solid account of the philosopher's scientific fame in what was certainly one of the most considerable branches of science which he followed. It occurred to me therefore that an edition of Baldi's life of Scot, which has never yet been printed, might give scope for annotations and digressions embodying all the additional material I had in hand or might still collect, and that a work on this plan would perhaps best answer the end in view.

A serious difficulty, however, here presented itself, and in the end proved insuperable, as I was quite unable to gain access to the work of Baldi. It seems to exist in no more than two manuscripts, both of them belonging to a private library in Rome, that of the late Prince Baldassare Boncompagni, who had acquired them from the Albani collection. The Boncompagni library has been now for some time under strict seal, pending certain legal proceedings, and all my endeavours to get even a sight of the manuscripts were in vain. In these circumstances I fell back upon a printed volume, the *Cronica de Matematici overo Epitome dell'Istoria delle vite loro*, which is an abbreviated

form of Baldi's work and was published at Urbino
in 1707. The account of Michael Scot which it
gives is not such as to increase my regret that I
cannot present this biography to the reader in its
most complete form. Thus it runs: 'Michele
Scoto, that is Michael the Scot, was a Judicial
Astrologer, in which profession he served the
Emperor Frederick II. He wrote a most learned
treatise by way of questions upon the *Sphere* of
John de Sacrobosco which is still in common use.
Some say he was a Magician, and tell how he used
to cause fetch on occasion, by magic art, from the
kitchen of great Princes whatever he needed for his
table. He died from the blow of a stone falling on
his head, having already foreseen that such would be
the manner of his end.' Now Scot's additions to the
Sphere of Sacrobosco are among the more common
of his printed works, while the tales of his feasts
at Bologna, and of his sudden death, are repeated
almost *ad nauseam* by almost every early writer
who has undertaken to illustrate the text of Dante.
So far as we can tell, therefore, Baldi would seem to
have made no independent research on his own
account regarding Scot's life and literary labours,
but to have depended entirely upon very obvious
and commonplace printed authorities. To crown
all, he assigns 1240 as the *floruit* of Michael Scot,
a date at least five years posterior to that of
his death.! On the whole then there is little cause
to regret that his work on this subject is not more
fully accessible.

My study of the life and times of Scot thus resumed its natural tendency towards an independent form, there being no text known to me that could in any way supply the want of an original biography. It is for the reader to judge how far the boldness of such an attempt has been justified by its success. The difficulties of the task have certainly been increased by the want of any previous collections that could be called satisfactory. Boece, Dempster, and Naudé yield little in the way of precise and instructive detail; their accounts of Scot · fall to be classed with that of Baldi as partly incorrect and partly commonplace. Schmuzer alone seems by the title of his work[1] to promise something more original. Unfortunately my attempts to obtain it have been defeated by the great rarity of the volume, which is not to be found in any of the libraries to which I have access.

This failure in the department of biography already formed has obliged me to a more exact and extensive study of original manuscript sources for the life of Scot than I might otherwise have thought necessary, and has proved thus perhaps rather of advantage. It is inevitable indeed that a work of this kind, undertaken several ages too late, should be comparatively barren in those dates and intimate details which are so satisfactory to our curiosity when we can fall upon them. In the absence of these, however, our attention is naturally fixed, and not, as it seems to me, unprofitably, on what

---

[1] *De Michaele Scoto Veneficii injuste damnato*, Lipsiae, 1739.

is after all of higher or more enduring importance.
The mind is free to take a wider range, and in
place of losing itself in the lesser facts of an
individual life, studies the intellectual movements and gauges the progress of what was
certainly a remarkable epoch in philosophy, science,
and literature. The almost exact reproduction in
Spain during the thirteenth century of the Alexandrian school of thought and science and even
superstition; the part played by the Arab race
in this curious transference, and the close relation
it holds to our modern intellectual life—if the
volume now published be found to throw light
on subjects so little understood, yet so worthy of
study, I shall feel more than rewarded for the pains
and care spent in its preparation.

In the course of researches among the libraries
of Scotland and Italy, of England and France, of
Spain and Germany, I have received much kindness
from the learned men who direct these institutions.
I therefore gladly avail myself of this opportunity to
express my thanks in general to all those who have
so kindly come to my help, and in particular to
Signor Comm. G. Biagi, and Signor Prof. E.
Rostagno of the Laurentian Library; to Signore
L. Licini of the Riccardian Library; to the Rev.
Padre Ehrle of the Vatican Library; to Signor
Cav. Giorgi, and the Conte Passerini of the Casa-
natense; to Signor Prof. Menghini of the Vittorio
Emanuele Library, Rome; and to Signor Comm.
Cugnoni of the Chigi Library. I am also much

indebted to the kindness of Professor R. Foerster of Breslau; of Mr. W. M. Lindsay, Fellow of Jesus College, Oxford, and the Rev. R. Langton Douglas of New College, who have furnished me with valuable notes from the libraries of that university, and, not least of all, to the interest taken in my work by Mr. Charles Godfrey Leland, who has been good enough to read it in manuscript, and to favour me with curious material and valuable suggestions.

If the result of my studies should prove somewhat disappointing to the reader, I can but plead the excuse with which Pliny furnishes me, it is one having peculiar application to such a task as is here attempted : ' Res ardua,' he says, ' vetustis novitatem dare, novis auctoritatem, obsoletis nitorem, obscuris lucem, fastiditis gratiam, dubiis fidem, omnibus vero naturam, et naturae suae omnia.'

17 VIA MONTEBELLO,
    FLORENCE, *November 17th*, 1896.

CONTENTS

CHAPTER I

CHAPTER II

CHAPTER III

CHAPTER IV

CHAPTER V

CHAPTER VI

CHAPTER VII

CHAPTER VIII

CHAPTER IX

CHAPTER X

LIST OF ILLUSTRATIONS

CHAPTER I

BIRTHPLACE AND EARLY STUDIES OF MICHAEL SCOT

In the Borders of Scotland it is well known that any piece of hill pasture, if it be fenced in but for a little from the constant cropping of the sheep, will soon show springing shoots of forest trees indigenous to the soil, whose roots remain wherever the plough has not passed too deeply. Centuries ago, when nature had her way and was unrestrained, the whole south-eastern part of the country was covered with dense forests and filled with forest-dwellers; the wild creatures that form the prey of the snare and the quarry of the chase. In the deep valleys, and by the streams of Tweed and Teviot, and many another river of that well-watered land, stood the great ranks and masses of the oak and beech as captains and patriarchs of the forest, mingled with the humbler whitethorn which made a dense undergrowth wherever the sun could reach. On the heights grew the sombre firs; their gnarled and ruddy branches crowned with masses of bluish-green foliage, while the alders followed the water-courses, and, aided by the shelter of these secret valleys, all but reached the last summits of the hills, which alone, in many a varied slope and peak and swelling breast, rose eminent and commanding over these dark and almost unbroken woodlands.

A

Such was south-eastern Scotland in the twelfth century : a country fitted to be the home of men of action rather than of thought; men whose joy should lie in the chase and the conflict with nature as yet unsubdued, who could track the savage creatures of the forest to their dens, and clear the land where it pleased them, and build, and dwell, and beget children in their own likeness, till by the labours of generations that country should become pastoral, peaceful, and fit for fertile tillage as we see it now.

Already, at the early time of which we speak, something of this work had been begun. There were gaps in the high forest where it lay well to the sun : little clearings marked by the ridge and furrow of a rude agriculture. Here and there a baron's lonely tower raised its grey horn on high, sheltering a troop of men-at-arms who made it their business to guard the land in war, and in peace to rid it of the savage forest-creatures that hindered the hind and herd in their labour and their hope. In the main valleys more than one great monastery was rising, or already built, by the waters of Tweed and Teviot. The inmates of these religious houses took their share in the whole duty of peaceful Scottish men by following trades at home or superintending the labours of an army of hinds who broke in and made profitable the wide abbey lands scattered here and there over many a lowland county. All was energy, action, and progress : a form of life which left but little room for the enterprises of the mind, the conflicts and conquests which can alone be known and won in the world of thought within.

These conditions we know to have reared and trained generations of men well fitted to follow the pursuits of hardy and active life, yet they cannot have been so constraining as to hinder the birth of some at least who possessed an altogether different temper of mind and body. The lowland Scots were even then of a mixed race : the ancestry which tends more than any other to the production of life-eddies, where thought rather than activity naturally forms and dwells, while the current of the main stream sweeps past in its ordinary course. Grant the appearance of such natures here and there in these early times, and it is easy to see much in the only life then possible that was fit to foster their natural tendencies. The deep woodlands were not only scenes of labour where sturdy arms found constant employment, they were homes of mystery in which the young imagination loved to dwell ; peopling them with half-human shapes more graceful than their stateliest trees, and half-brutal monsters more terrible than the fiercest wolf or bear. The distant sun and stars were more than a heavenly horologe set to mark the hours for labour or vigil, they were an unexplored scene of wonder which patient and brooding thought alone could reach and interpret. The trivial flight and annual return of birds, tracing like the wild geese a mysterious wedge against the sky of winter, gave more than a signal for the chase, which was all that ordinary men saw in it. To these finer natures it brought the awakening which those know who have learned to ask the mighty questions—Why ? Whence ? and Whither ? demands which will not be denied till they have touched the heights and fathomed the depths of human life itself. *Our life is a bird,* said one in these early ages, *which flies by night, and, entering lighted hall at one end, swiftly passeth out at the other. So come we, who knoweth whence, and so pass we, who knoweth whither? From the darkness we come and to the darkness we go, and the brief light that is meanwhile ours cannot make the mystery plain.*

But though the nature of this primitive life in early Scottish days could not hinder the appearance of men of thought, and even helped their development as soon as they began to show the movements of active intellect, yet on the other hand Scotland had not reached that culture which affords such natures their due and full opportunity. Centuries were yet to pass before the foundation of St. Andrews as the first Scottish university. The grammar-schools of the country[1] were but a step to the studies of some foreign seat of learning. The churchmen who filled considerable positions at home were either Italians, or had at least been trained abroad, so that everything in those days pointed to that path of foreign study which has since been trodden by so many generations of Scottish students. The bright example of Scotus Erigena, who had reached such a high place in France under Charles the Bald, was an incitement to the northern world of letters. Young men of parts and promise naturally sought their opportunity to go abroad in the hope of finding like

---

[1] Some account of Scottish grammar-schools in the twelfth century will be found in Sir James Dalrymple's *Collections,* pp. 226, 255 (Advocates' Library, Edinburgh); also in Chalmers's *Caledonia,* vol. i. p. 76.

honourable employment, or, better still, of returning crowned with the honours of the schools to
occupy some distinguished ecclesiastical position in
their native country.

This then was the age, and these were the
prevailing conditions, under which Michael Scot
was born. To the necessary and common impulse
of Scottish scholars we are to trace the disposition
of the great lines on which his life ran its remarkable
and distinguished course. He is certainly one of
the most notable, as he is among the earliest,
examples of the student Scot abroad.

There can be little doubt regarding the nation
where he had his birth. Disregarding for a moment
the varying accounts of those who lived centuries
after the age of Scot himself, let us make a commencement with one whose testimony is of the very
highest value, being that of a contemporary. Roger
Bacon, the famous scientist of the thirteenth century, introduces the name of Michael Scot in the
following manner : ' Unde, cum per Gerardum
Cremonensem, et Michaelem Scotum, et Aluredum
Anglicum, et Heremannum (Alemannum), et Wil-
lielmum Flemingum, data sit nobis copia trans-
lationum de omni scientia.'[1] In this passage the
distinctive appellation of each author is plainly
derived from that of his native country. That
Bacon believed Michael to be of Scottish descent is
therefore certain, and his opinion is all the more
valuable since he was an Englishman, and not likely
therefore to have confused the two nations of Great
Britain as a foreigner might haply have done. To

---

[1] *Compendium Studii*, vol. i. p. 471, ed. Master of the Rolls. London,
Longmans, 1859.

the same purpose is the testimony of Guido Bonatti, the astrologer, who also belonged to the age of Bacon and Scot. ' Illi autem,' he says,[1] ' qui fuerunt in tempore meo, sicut fuit Hugo ab Alugant, Bene-guardinus Davidbam, Joannes Papiensis, Dominicus Hispanus, Michael Scotus, Stephanus Francigena, Girardus de Sabloneta Cremonensis, et multi alii.' Here also the significance of *Scotus*, as indicating nationality, is one that hardly admits of question. It was in all probability on these or similar authorities that Dempster relied when he said of Michael:[2] 'The name Scot, however, is not a family one, but national,' though he seems to have pressed the matter rather too far, it being plainly possible that *Scotus* might combine in itself both significations. In Scotland it might indicate that Michael belonged to the clan of Scott, as indeed has been generally supposed, while as employed by men of other nations, it might declare what they believed to have been this scholar's native land.

At this point, however, a new difficulty suggests itself. It is well known that the lowland Scots were emigrants from the north of Ireland, and that in early times *Scotus* was used as a racial rather than a local designation. May not Michael have been an Irishman? Such is the question actually put by a recent writer,[3] and certainly it deserves a serious answer. We may commence by remarking that even on this understanding of it the name is an indefinite one as regards locality, and might therefore have been applied to one born in Scotland

---

[1] Boncompagni *Vita di Gherardo Cremonense*, Roma, 1851, and the *De Astronomia Tractatus* x. of Guido Bonatti, printed at Bâle, 1550.
[2] *Historia Ecclesiastica*, xii. 494.
[3] In the last edition of Chambers's Encyclopædia, *sub nomine*.

just as well as if he had first seen the light in the
sister isle. So certainly is this the case that when
we recall the name of John Scotus we find it was
customary to add the appellative *Erigena* to determine his birthplace. At that time the separation
of race was much less marked than it had become
in Michael's day, and it seems certain therefore
that if *Michael Scotus* was thought a sufficient
designation of the man by Bacon and Bonatti, they
must have used it in the sense of indicating that he
came of that part of the common stock which had
crossed the sea and made their home in Scotland.
But to find a conclusive answer to this difficulty we
need only anticipate a little the course of our
narrative by mentioning here a highly curious fact
which will occupy our attention in its proper place.
When Michael Scot was offered high ecclesiastical
preferment in Ireland he declined it on the ground
that he was ignorant of the vernacular tongue of
that country.[1] This seems to supply anything that
may have been wanting in the other arguments we
have advanced, and the effect of the whole should
be to assure our conviction that there need be now
no further attempt made to deny Scotland the
honour of having been the native land of so distinguished a scholar.

Nor are we altogether without the means of
coming to what seems at least a probable conclusion
regarding the very district of the Scottish lowlands
where Michael Scot was born. Leland the antiquary
tells us that he was informed on good authority
that Scot came from the territory of Durham.[2]
Taken literally this statement would make him an

---

[1] See *infra*, ch. vii.   [2] Leland's work was published in 1549.

Englishman, but no one would think of quoting it
as of sufficient value to disprove the testimony of
Bacon and Bonatti who both believed Michael to
have been born in Scotland. If, however, there
should offer itself any way in which both these
apparently contending opinions can be reconciled,
we are surely bound to accept such an explanation
of the difficulty, and in fact the solution we are
about to propose not only meets the conditions of
the problem, but will be found to narrow very
considerably the limits of country within which the
birthplace of Scot is to be looked for.

The See of Durham in that age, and for long
afterwards, had a wide sphere of influence, extending
over much of the south-eastern part of the Scottish
Borders. Many deeds relating to this region of
Scotland must be sought in the archives that belong
to the English Cathedral. To be born in the
territory of Durham then, as Leland says Scot had
been, was not necessarily to be a native of England,
and the anonymous Florentine commentator on
Dante uses a remarkable expression which seems to
confirm this solution as far as Scot is concerned.
'This Michael,' he says, 'was of the Province of
Scotland';[1] and his words seem to point to that
part of the Scottish lowlands adjacent to the See
of Durham and in a sense its *province*, as subject to
its influence, just as Provence, the analogous part
of France, had its name from the similar relation
it bore to Rome. The most likely opinion therefore that can now be formed on the subject leads
us to believe that Scot was born somewhere in the

---

[1] *Comento alla Divina Commedia, Inf.*, canto **xx.** Bologna, Fanfani,
1866-74.

valley of the Tweed; if we understand that geographical expression in the wide sense which makes it equivalent to the whole of the south-eastern borders of Scotland.

Nor is this so contrary as might at first appear to the tradition which makes Scot a descendant of the family of Balwearie in Fife. Hector Boëce, Principal of Marischal College, Aberdeen, who first gave currency to the story,[1] could hardly have meant to imply that Michael was actually born at Balwearie. It is to be presumed that he understood *Scotus* to have been a family name; and the Scotts, who became of Balwearie by marriage with the heiress of that estate, did not enter into possession of it till long after the close of the twelfth century.[2] To call Michael a son of Balwearie in the genealogical sense, however, is in perfect agreement with the conclusion regarding his origin which we have just reached; for the original home of the Scotts who afterwards held that famous property as their *chef lieu*, lay by the upper streams of Tweed in the very district which every probability has already indicated to us as that of Michael's birthplace. In 1265 we find an entry of money paid by the Crown ' to Michael Scot and Richard Rufus who have occupied the waste lands at Stuth,' near Peebles.[3] Identification is here out of the question, as Michael the scholar, of whom we write, was by this time long in his grave, but the entry we have quoted shows that a family of this surname, who still used the Christian name of Michael, was flourishing in

[1] The *Scotorum Historia* of Boëce in which this statement appears was published at Paris in 1526.
[2] Between 1260 and 1280. See Cartulary of Dunfermline.
[3] Exchequer Rolls.

this part of Scotland during the second half of the thirteenth century.

It is to be remarked, too, that the Scottish tales of wonder relating to Michael Scot have a local colour that accords well with the other signs we have noticed. The hill which the sorcerer's familiar spirit cleaves in sunder is the triple peak of Eildon ; the water which he curbs is that of Tweed ; from Oakwood he rides forth to try the witch of Falsehope, and in Oakwood tower may still be seen the *Jingler's room* : a curious anachronism, for Oakwood is a building much more recent than the days of Michael Scot, yet one which fixes for us in a picturesque and memorable way the district of country where, according to the greatest number of converging probabilities, this remarkable man was born.

As to the date of his birth, it is difficult to be very precise. The probability that he died suddenly, and before he had completed the measure of an ordinary lifetime, prevents us from founding our calculations upon the date of his decease, which can be pretty accurately determined. A more certain argument may be derived from the fact that Scot had finished his youthful studies, made some figure in the world, and entered on the great occupation of his life as an author, as early as the year 1210.[1] Assuming then that thirty was the least age he could well have attained at the period in question, the year 1180 would be indicated as that of his birth, or rather as the latest date to which it can with probability be referred ; 1175 being in every way a more likely approximation to the actual time of this event.

[1] See *infra*, p. 55.

It is unfortunate that we find ourselves in the same position with regard to the interesting question of Scot's early education, having only the suggestions derived from probable conjecture to offer on this subject also. Du Boulay indeed, in his account of the University of Paris,[1] pretends to supply a pretty complete account of the schools which Scot attended, but, as he adds that this was the usual course of study in those days, we find reason to think that he may have been guided in his assertions, rather by the probabilities of the case, than by any exact evidence. Nor is it likely that any more satisfactory assurance can now be had on this point : the time being too remote and the want of early material for Scot's biography defeating in this respect all the care and attention that can now be given to the subject.

We know, however, that there was a somewhat famous grammar-school at Roxburgh in the twelfth century,[2] and considering the rarity of such an opportunity at so early a period, and the proximity of this place to the district in which Scot was born, we may venture to fancy that here he may have learned his rudiments, thus laying the foundation of those deeper studies, which he afterwards carried to such a height.

With regard to Durham, the matter may be considered to stand on firmer ground. The name of Michael Scot, as we have already seen, has for many ages been associated with this ancient Cathedral

[1] Bulaeus *Historia Univ. Paris.*, vol. iii. pp. 701, 702.

[2] Sir James Dalrymple's *Collections*, pp. 226, 255. There was also a school at Dryburgh, where Sibbald says Sacrobosco studied, but had Scot entered here he would hardly have been distinguished in later years as a man in close relation with another order—the Cistercian.

city by the Wear. If the question of his birthplace
be regarded as now determined in favour of Scotland, no reason remains for this association so convincing as that which would derive it from the fact
that he pursued his education there. The Cathedral
School of Durham was a famous one, which no
doubt exerted a strong attraction upon studious
youths throughout the whole of that province. In
Scot's case the advantages it offered may well have
seemed a desirable step to further advances; his
means, as one of a family already distinguished from
the common people, allowing him to plan a complete
course of study, and his ambition prompting him to
follow it.

The common tradition asserts that when he left
Durham, Scot proceeded to Oxford. This is not
unlikely, considering the fame of that University,
and the number of students drawn from all parts of
the land who assembled there.[1] The only matters,
however, which offer themselves in support of this
bare conjecture are not, it must be said, very convincing. Roger Bacon shows great familiarity with
Scot, and Bacon was an Oxford scholar, though his
studies at that University were not begun till long
after the time when Scot could possibly have been
a student there. It is quite possible, however, that
the interest shown by Bacon in Scot's labours and
high reputation—not by any means of a kindly sort
—may have been awakened by traditions that were
still current in the Schools of Oxford when the

---

[1] Not excepting the north. 'Morebatur eo tempore (c. 1180)
apud Oxenfordiam studiorum causa clericus quidam Stephanus nomine
de Eboracensi regione oriundus,' *Acta Sanctorum*, Oct. 29, p. 579. At
the exodus in 1209, no less than three thousand students are said to
have left Oxford.

younger student came there. Near the end of his life, Scot visited in a public capacity the chief Universities of Europe, and brought them philosophic treasures that were highly thought of by the learned. It seems most probable, from the terms in which Bacon speaks of this journey,[1] that it may have included a visit to Oxford. This might of course be matter of mere duty and policy, but one cannot help observing how well it agrees with the tradition that these schools were already familiar to Scot. As a recognised alumnus of Oxford, he would be highly acceptable there, being one whose European fame shed no small lustre upon the scene of his early studies.

As to Paris, the next stage in Scot's educational progress, the historian of that University becomes much more convincing when he claims for *Lutetia* the honour of having contributed in a special sense to the formation of this scholar's mind. For here tradition has preserved one of those sobriquets which are almost invariably authentic. Scot, it seems, gained here the name of *Michael the Mathematician,*[2] and this corresponds, not only with what is known concerning the character of his studies, but also with the nature of the course for which Paris was then famous. There is another circumstance which seems to point strongly in the same direction. Every one must have noticed how invariably the name of Scot is honoured by the prefix of *Master.* This is the case not only in his printed works, but also in popular tradition, as may be seen in the

---

[1] *Opus Majus,* ed. Jebbi, pp. 36, 37. The words are 'Tempore Michaelis Scoti, qui, annis 1230 transactis, apparuit, deferens librorum Aristotelis partes aliquas,' etc. See *infra,* ch. viii.
[2] See Anderson, *Scottish Nation, sub nomine.*

well-known rhyme :—' Maister Michael Scot's man.'[1]
A Florence manuscript, to which we shall presently
refer more fully, throws some light upon the meaning of this title, by describing Scot as that scholar,
' who among the rest is known as the chief Master.'[2]
It is matter of common knowledge, that this degree
had special reference to the studies of the *Trivium*
and *Quadrivium,* being the scholastic crown reserved
for those who had made satisfactory progress in the
liberal arts.   Scot then, according to the testimony
of early times, was the supreme Master in this
department of knowledge.   But it is also certain
that Paris was then recognised as the chief school
of the *Trivium* and *Quadrivium,* just as Bologna had
a like reputation for Law, and Salerno for Medicine.[3]
We are therefore warranted to conclude that Michael
Scot could never have been saluted in European
schools as ' Supreme Master,' had he not studied
long in the French capital, and carried off the highly
esteemed honours of Paris.

Another branch of study which tradition says
Scot followed with success at Paris was that of
theology.   Du Boulay declares, indeed, that he
reached the dignity of doctor in that faculty, and
there is some reason to think that this may actually
have been the case.   There can be no doubt that
an ecclesiastical career then offered the surest road
to wealth and fame in the case of all who aspired to
literary honours.   That Scot took holy orders[4] seems
very probable.   He may well have done so even
before he came to Paris, for Bacon makes it one of

---

[1] *Lay of the Last Minstrel,* Note Y.   See *infra,* ch. x.
[2] See *infra,* p. 18.   [3] Romance of *Elinando.*
[4] He probably joined the Cistercian Order.

his reproaches against the corruption of the times, that men were ordained far too readily, and before they had reached the canonical age : from their tenth to their twentieth year, he says.[1] It is difficult to verify Dempster's assertion that Scot's renown as a theologian is referred to by Baconthorpe the famous Carmelite of the following century.[2] This author was commonly known as the *Princeps Averroïstarum*. If he really mentions Michael, and does not mean Duns Scotus, as there is some reason to suspect, his praise may have been given quite as much on the ground of profane as of religious philosophy. On the other hand we find abounding and unmistakable references to Scripture, the Liturgy, and ascetic counsels in the writings of Scot, from which it may safely be concluded that he had not merely embraced the ecclesiastical profession as a means of livelihood or of advancement, but had seriously devoted himself to sacred studies. It is true that we cannot point to any instance in which he receives the title of doctor, but this omission may be explained without seriously shaking our belief in the tradition that Scot gained this honour at Lutetia. During the twelfth century the Bishop of Paris forbade the doctors of theology to profess that faculty in any other University.[3] Scot may well, therefore, have been one of those philosophical divines who taught *entre les deux ponts*, as the same statute commanded they should, though in other lands and during his after-life, he came to be known simply

---

Compendium Studii, p. 425.

[2] In the printed edition of Dempster, the reference is ' lib. 3 sententiarum, quaest. iii.,' but I have not been able to verify it.

[3] *Hist. Litt. de la France*, vol. ix. p. 65.

as the 'Great Master': the brightest of all those choice spirits of the schools on which Paris set her stamp.

At this point we may surely hazard a further conjecture. Bacon tells us that in those days it was the study of law, ecclesiastical and civil, rather than of theology, which opened the way to honour and preferment in the Church.[1] Now Paris was not more eminently and distinctly the seat of arts than Bologna was the school of laws.[2] May not Michael Scot have passed from the French to the Italian University? Such a conjecture would be worth little were it not for the support which it undoubtedly receives from credible tradition. Boccaccio in one of his tales[3] mentions Michael Scot, and tells how he used to live in Bologna. Many of the commentators on the *Divine Comedy* of Dante dwell on the theme, and enrich it with superstitious wonders.[4] It would be difficult to find a period in the scholar's life which suits better with such a residence than that we are now considering. On all accounts it seems likely that he left Paris for Bologna, and found in the latter city a highly favourable opening, which led directly to the honours and successes of his after-life.

He was now to leave the schools and enter a wider sphere, not without the promise of high and enduring fame. A child of the mist and the hill, he had come from the deep woods and wild outland life of the Scottish Border to what was already no inconsiderable position. He knew Paris, not, need

---

[1] *Opus Majus*, p. 84.   [2] *Elinando*.
[3] *Decamerone*, viii. 9.   [4] See *infra*, chap. x.

it be said, the gay capital of modern days, but Paris
of the closing years of the twelfth century, *Lutetia
Parisiorum* : her low-browed houses of wood and
mud ; her winding streets, noisome even by day,
and by night still darker and more perilous ; her vast
Latin Quarter, then far more preponderant than
now—a true cosmopolis, where fur-clad barbarians
from the home of the north wind sharpened wits
with the Latin races haply trained in southern
schools by some keen-browed Moor or Jew.   And
Paris knew him, watched his course, applauded
his success, crowned his fame by that coveted
title of *Master*, which he shared with many others,
but which the world of letters made peculiarly his
own by creating for him a singular and individual
propriety in it.   From Paris we may follow him
in fancy to Bologna, yet it is not hard to believe
he must have left half his heart behind, enchained
in that remarkable devotion which Lutetia could
so well inspire in her children.[1]   Bologna might
be, as we have represented it, the gate to a new
Eden, that of Scot's Italian and Spanish life, yet
how could he enter it without casting many a
longing glance behind to the Paradise he had
quitted for ever when he left the banks of the
Seine ?

[1] The MS. of Scot's *Physionomia* in the Vatican Library (*Fondo
della Regina di Svezia* 1151, saec. xvi ?) has joined to it some extravagant
lines in praise of the Parisian schools, where the writer compares them to
Paradise.   There is no reason to suppose Scot wrote these verses, but
they fully support the statement made in the text.

CHAPTER II

SCOT AT THE COURT OF SICILY

ALL tradition assures us that the chief occupation of Scot's life was found at the Court of Frederick II., King of Sicily, and afterwards Emperor of Germany: a Prince deservedly famous, not only for his own talent, but for the protection and encouragement he afforded to men of learning. A manuscript in the Laurentian Library,[1] hitherto unnoticed in this connection, seems to throw some light upon the time and manner of this employment: points that have always been very obscure. The volume is a collection of *Occulta*, and at p. 256 we find the following title, 'An Experiment of Michael Scot the magician.' What follows is of no serious importance: such as it has we shall consider in speaking of the Master's legendary fame. The concluding words, however, are of great interest, especially when we observe that this part of the manuscript, though written between 1450 and 1500, is said[2] to have been copied 'from a very ancient book.' The colophon runs thus: 'Here endeth the necromantic experiment of the most illustrious doctor, Master[3] Michael Scot, who among other scholars is known as the supreme

---

[1] Pl. lxxxix. *sup.* cod. 38.   See Appendix, No. I.
[2] See p. 244 of the MS.   [3] *Domini Magistri.*

Master; who was of Scotland, and servant to his most distinguished chief Don Philip,[1] the King of Sicily's clerk;[2] which experiment he contrived[3] when he lay sick in the city of Cordova.   Finis.'

Taking the persons here named in the order of their rank, we notice first the great Emperor Frederick II., the patron of Michael Scot.   It is worth remark that he is styled simply 'King of Sicily,' a title which belongs to the time previous to 1215, when he obtained the Imperial crown. This is a touch which seems to give high originality and value to the colophon.   We may feel sure that it was not composed by the fifteenth century scribe, who would certainly have described Frederick in the usual style as Emperor and Lord of the World. He must have copied it, and everything leads one to suppose that he was right in describing the source from which he drew as ' very ancient.'

Next comes Don Philip, whom we have rightly described as the clerk of Sicily, for the word *coronatus* in its mediæval use is derived from *corona* in the sense of the priestly tonsure, so that *Philippus coronatus* is equivalent to *Philippus clericus*.[4]   Of this distinguished man we find many traces in the historical documents of the period.[5]   Two deeds passed the seals of Sicily in the year 1200 when the King, then a boy of five years old, was living under the care of his widowed mother the Queen Constantia. These are countersigned by the royal notary, who is described as ' Philippus de Salerno, notarius et fidelis noster scriba.'   His name is found in the

---

[1] *Philipo.*   [2] *Coronato.*   [3] *Destinavit sibi.*
[4] See Ducange, *sub voce.*
[5] Huillard-Bréholles, *Hist. Dip. Frid. II.*, vol. i. pp. 44, 68, 242, 255.

same way, apparently for the last time, in 1213.
This date, and the particular designation of Philip
the Notary as 'of Salerno,' connect themselves very
naturally with the title of a manuscript belonging
to the De Rossi collection.[1] It is as follows : ' The
Book of the Inspections of Urine according to the
opinion of the Masters, Peter of Berenico, Constantine Damascenus, and Julius of Salerno ; which
was composed by command of the Emperor
Frederick, Anno Domini 1212, in the month of
February, and was revised by Master Philip of
Tripoli and Master Gerard of Cremona at the
orders of the King of Spain,' etc.   The person
designed as Philip of Salerno was very likely to be
put in charge of the revision of a medical treatise,
and as he disappears from his duties as notary for
some time after 1213 we may suppose that it was
then he passed into the service of the King of Spain.
This conjecture agrees also with the mention of
Cordova in the Florence manuscript, and with other
peculiarities it displays, such as the spelling of the
name *Philippus* like *Felipe*, and the way in which
the title *Dominus* is repeated, just as *Don* might
be in the style of a Spaniard.   There is, in short,
every reason to conclude that Philip of Salerno and
Philip of Tripoli were one and the same person.
We may add that Philip was the author of the first
complete version in Latin of the book called *Secreta
Secretorum*, the preface of which describes him as a
clericus of the See of Tripoli.   As will presently
appear, Michael Scot drew largely from this work
in composing one of his own ;[2] another proof that
in confronting with each other these three names—

[1] No. 354.   [2] See *infra*, p. 37.

Philippus coronatus or clericus; Philippus de Salerno, and Philippus Tripolitanus—and in concluding that they belong to one and the same person, we have a reasonable amount of evidence in our favour.

From what has just been said it is plain that three distinct periods must have composed the life of Philip so far as we know it: the first when he served as an ecclesiastic in Tripoli of Syria or its neighbourhood; the second when he came westward, and, not without a certain literary reputation, held the post of Clerk Register in Sicily; the last when Frederick sent him, in the height of his powers and the fulness of his fame, to that neighbouring country of Spain, then so full of attraction for every scholar. In which of these periods then was it that Michael Scot first came into those relations with Philip of which the Florentine manuscript speaks? The time of his residence in Spain, likely as it might seem on other accounts, would appear to be ruled out by the fact that it was too late for Philip to be then described as servant of the *King of Sicily*. Nor did he hold this office, so far as we can tell, until he had left Tripoli for the West. We must pronounce then for the Sicilian period, and precisely therefore for the years between 1200 and 1213. This conclusion, however, does not hinder us from supposing that the relation then first formally begun between Michael and Philip continued to bind them, in what may have been a friendly co-operation, during the time spent by both in Spain.

The period thus determined was that of the King's boyhood, and this opens up another line of argument which may be trusted not only to confirm

the results we have reached, but to afford a more
exact view of Scot's occupation in Sicily. Several
of his works are dedicated to Frederick, from which
it is natural to conclude that his employment
was one which brought him closely in contact
with the person of the King. When we examine
their contents we are struck by the tone which Scot
permits himself to use in addressing his royal
master. There is familiarity when we should expect
flattery, and the desire to impart instruction instead of the wish to display obsequiousness. Scot
appears in fact as one careless to recommend himself for a position at Court, certain rather of one
which must have been already his own. What can
this position have been?

A tradition preserved by one of the commentaries on Dante[1] informs us that Michael Scot was
employed as the Emperor's tutor, and this explanation is one which we need feel no hesitation in
adopting, as it clears up in a very convincing way
all the difficulties of the case. His talents, already
proved and crowned in Paris and Bologna, may well
have commended him for such a position. The
dedication of his books to Frederick, and the
familiar style in which he addresses the young prince,
are precisely what might be expected from the pen
of a court schoolmaster engaged in compiling
manuals *in usum Delphini.*[2] Nay the very title of
'Master' which Scot had won at Paris probably
owed its chief confirmation and continued employment to the nature of his new charge. Since the
fifth century there had prevailed in Spain the habit

---

[1] L'Anonimo Fiorentino, *Comento alla Divina Commedia.* Bologna,
Fanfani, 1866-74.
[2] See especially the preface to the *Physionomia.*

of committing children of position to the course of
an ecclesiastical education.[1] They were trained by
some discreet and grave person called the *magister
disciplinae*, deputed by the Bishop to this office.
Such would seem to have been the manner of
Frederick's studies. His guardian was the Pope ;
he lived at Palermo under charge of the Canons of
that Cathedral,[2] and no doubt the ecclesiastical
character of Michael Scot combined with his
acknowledged talents to point him out as a suitable
person to fill so important a charge. It was his
first piece of preferment, and we may conceive that
he drew salary for his services under some title
given him in the royal registry. This would explain
his connection with Philip, the chief notary, on
which the Florentine manuscript insists. Such
fictitious employments have always been a part of
court fashion, and that they were common in Sicily
at the time of which we write may be seen from
the case of Werner and Philip de Bollanden, who,
though in reality most trusted and confidential
advisers of the Crown, were known at Court as the
chief butler and baker, titles which they were proud
to transmit to their descendants.[3]

It was at Palermo, then, that Michael Scot
must have passed the opening years of the thirteenth
century ; now more than ever ' Master,' since he was
engaged in a work which carried with it no light
responsibility : the early education of a royal youth
destined to play the first part on the European
stage. The situation was one not without advan-

---

[1] Smith's *Dictionary of Christian Antiquities, sub voce* ' Magister.'
[2] From August 1200 to January 1208. See Amari, *Storia dei
Musulmani di Sicilia.*
[3] See the *Hist. Dip. Frid., passim.*

tages of an uncommon kind for a scholar like Scot, eager to acquire knowledge in every department. Sicily was still, especially in its more remote and mountainous parts about Entella, Giato, and Platani, the refuge of a considerable Moorish population, whose language was therefore familiar in the island, and was heard even at Court ; being, we are assured, one of those in which Frederick received instruction.[1] There can be little doubt that Scot availed himself of this opportunity, and laid a good foundation for his later work on Arabic texts by acquiring, in the years of his residence at Palermo, at least the vernacular language of the Moors.

The same may be said regarding the Greek tongue : a branch of study much neglected even by the learned of those times. We shall presently produce evidence which goes to show that Michael Scot worked upon Greek as well as Arabic texts,[2] and it was in all probability to his situation in Sicily that he owed the acquisition of what was then a very rare accomplishment. Bacon, who deplores the ignorance of Greek which prevailed in his days, recommends those who would learn this important language to go to Italy, where, he says, especially in the south, both clergy and people are still in many places purely Greek.[3] The reference to *Magna Grecia* is obvious, and to Sicily, whose Greek colonies preserved, even to Frederick's time and beyond it, their nationality and language. So much was this the case, that it was thought necessary to make the study of Greek as well as of Arabic part of Frederick's education. We can hardly err

---

[1] Amari.   [2] See *infra*, pp. 26, 59, and ch. vi.
[3] *Compendium Studii*, p. 434.

in supposing that Scot profited by this as well as
by the other opportunity.

In point of general culture too a residence at
Palermo offered many and varied advantages. Rare
manuscripts abounded, some lately brought to the
island, like that of the *Secreta Secretorum*, the
prize of Philip the Clerk, which he carried with
him when he came from Tripoli to Sicily, and
treasured there, calling it his 'precious pearl';[1]
others forming part of collections that had for some
time been established in the capital. As early as
the year 1143, George of Antioch, the Sicilian
Admiral, had founded the Church of St. Maria della
Martorana in Palermo, and had enriched it with a
valuable library, no doubt brought in great part
from the East.[2] A better opportunity for literary
studies could hardly have been desired than that
which the Prince's Master now enjoyed.

The society and surroundings in which Michael
Scot now found himself were such as must have
communicated a powerful impulse to the mind.
The Court was grave rather than gay, as had
befitted the circumstances of a royal widow, and
now of an orphan still under canonical protection
and busied in serious study, but this allowed the
wit and wisdom of learned men free scope, and thus
invited and encouraged their residence. Already,
probably, had begun that concourse and competition
of talents, for which the Court of Frederick was
afterwards so remarkable. Amid delicious gardens
at evening, or by day in the cool shade of court-
yards : those *patios* which the Moors had built so
well and adorned with such fair arabesques, all that

---

[1] See the preface to the *Secreta*. [2] Amari. See *infra*, p. 83.

was rarest in learning and brightest in wit, held
daily disputation, while the delicate fountains played
and Monte Pellegrino looked down on the curving
beauties of the bay and shore. A strange contrast
truly to the arcades of Bologna, now heaped with
winter snow and now baked by summer sun ; to the
squalor of mediæval Paris, and much more to the
green hillsides and moist forest-clad vales of southern
Scotland. Here at last the spirit of Michael Scot
underwent a powerful and determining influence
which left its mark on all his subsequent life.

As royal tutor, his peculiar duty would seem to
have been that of instructing the young Prince in
the different branches of mathematics. This we
should naturally have conjectured from the fact
that Scot's fame as yet rested entirely upon the
honours he had gained at Paris, and precisely in
this department of learning; for 'Michael the
Mathematician' was not likely to have been called
to Palermo with any other purpose. We have
direct evidence of it however in an early work
which came from the Master's pen, and one which
would seem to have been designed for the use of
his illustrious pupil. This was the *Astronomia*, or
Liber Particularis, and in the Oxford copy,[1] the
colophon of that treatise runs thus : ' Here endeth
the book of Michael Scot, astrologer to the Lord

---

[1] Bibl. Bodl. mss. Canon Misc. 555 ; cod. memb. in 4to ff. 97, saec.
xiv. ineunt., with a portrait of Michael Scot in one of the initials. The
preface opens thus :—' Cum ars astronomie sit grandis sermonibus
philosophorum.' The book begins :—' Cronica Grece Latine dicitur series
ut temporis temporum sicut dominorum,' and closes thus :—' De exposi-
tione fundamenti terrae volentes hic finere secundum librum quem
incepimus in nomine Dei, Cui ex parte nostra sit semper grandis laus et
gloria, benedictio et triumphus in omnibus per infinita saecula saeculorum Amen.' Other mss. of the *Astronomia* are found at Milan, Bibl.
Ambros. L. 92, *sup. cum figuris* ; and at Munich, see Halm and Meyer's
Catalogue, vol. ii. part i. p. 156, No. 1242, saec. xviii.

Frederick, Emperor of Rome, and ever August; which book he composed in simple style[1] at the desire of the aforesaid Emperor. And this he did, not so much considering his own reputation, as desiring to be serviceable and useful to young scholars, who, of their great love for wisdom, desire to learn in the Quadrivium the Art of Astronomy.' The preface says that this was the second book which Scot composed for Frederick.

The science of Astronomy was so closely joined in those times with the art of Astrology, that it is difficult to draw a clear distinction between them as they were then understood. The one was but the practical application of the other, and in common use their names were often confused and used interchangeably. We are not surprised then to find the title of Imperial Astrologer given to Michael Scot in the colophon to his *Astronomia*; he was sure to be employed in this way, and the fact will help us to determine with probability what was the *first* book he wrote for the Emperor, that to which the *Liber Particularis* was a sequel. For there is actually extant under Scot's name an astrological treatise bearing the significant name of the *Liber Introductorius*.[2] This title agrees exceedingly well with the position we are now inclined to give it, and an examination of the preface confirms our

---

[1] 'Quasi vulgariter.'

[2] Bodl. MS. 266, chart. in fol. saec. xv. 218 leaves; Bibl. Nat. Paris, Nouv. acq. 1401; the Escorial has another MS. of this work on paper, in writing of the fourteenth century. The *Liber Introductorius* commences thus: 'Quicumque vult esse bonus astrologus'—an expression which betrays the churchman in Scot. It closes with these words: 'finitur tractatus de notitia pronosticorum.' Extracts from the *Liber Introductorius* are found in the MS. Fondo Vaticano 4087, p. 38, ro. and vo., MS. in fol. chart. saec. xvi., and in the Bibl. del Seminario Vescovile, Padua, MS. 48, in fol. chart. saec. xiv.; also Bibl. Ambros, Milan, MS. I. 90.

conjecture in a high degree. It commences thus:
'Here beginneth the preface of the *Liber Introductorius* which was put forth by Michael Scot,
Astrologer to the ever August Frederick, Emperor
of the Romans, at whose desire he composed it concerning astrology,[1] in a simple style[2] for the sake
of young scholars and those of weaker capacity, and
this in the days of our Lord Pope Innocent IV.'[3]
One cannot help noticing the close correspondence
between this and the colophon of the *Astronomia*.
The two treatises were the complement each of the
other. They must have been composed about the
same time, and were doubtless meant to serve as
text-books to guide the studies of Frederick's youth.
That this royal pupil should have been led through
astrology to the higher and more enduring wonders
of astronomy need cause no surprise, for such a
course was quite in accordance with the intellectual
habits of the age. It may be doubted indeed
whether the men of those times would have shown
such perseverance in the observations and discoveries
proper to a pure science of the heavens, had it
not been for the practicable and profitable interest
which its application in astrology furnished. Astronomy, such as it then was, formed the last and
highest study in the Quadrivium.[4] It was here that
Scot had carried off honours at Paris, and now in
his *Liber Introductorius* and *Astronomia*, we see

---

[1] The Paris MS. reads 'in Astronomia,' a good example of the confusion mentioned above.   [2] 'Leviter.'

[3] This is a mistake common to both the MSS. Innocent IV. did not
begin to reign till 1243, when Scot was long in his grave. Innocent III.,
who was Pope from 1198-1216, is the person meant. He was guardian
to Frederick II. during his minority.

[4] According to the line: 'Lingua, Tropus, Ratio, Numerus, Tonus,
Angulus, Astra,' in which the Trivium and Quadrivium were succinctly
and memorably expressed.

him imparting the ripe fruits of that diligence to his
royal charge, whose education, so far as regarded
formal study, was thereby brought to a close.

In the year 1209, when Frederick was but
fourteen years of age, the quiet study and seclusion
in which he still lived with those who taught him
was brought to an abrupt and, one must think,
premature conclusion. The boy was married, and
to a lady ten years his senior, Constance, daughter
of the King of Aragon, and already widow of the
King of Hungary. It is not hard to see that such
a union must have been purely a matter of arrangement. The Prince of Palermo, undergrown and
delicate as he was,[1] promised to be, as King of
Sicily and possibly Emperor, the noblest husband of
his time. Pope Innocent III., his guardian, foresaw
this, and chose a daughter of Spain as most fit to
occupy the proud position of Frederick's wife, queen,
and perhaps empress. Had the wishes of Rome
prevailed at the Court of Aragon from the first,
this marriage would have taken place even earlier
than it did. The delay seems to have been owing,
not to any reluctance on the part of the bride's
parents, but solely to the doubt which of two sisters,
elder or younger, widow or maid, should accept the
coveted honour.

It was in spring, the loveliest season of the year
in that climate, that the fleet of Spain, sent to bear
the bride and her suite, rose slowly over the sea
rim and dropped anchor in the Bay of Palermo.
Constantia came with many in her company, the
flower of Catalan and Provençal chivalry, led by her
brother, Count Alfonso. The Bishop of Mazara,

---

[1] His mother was nearly fifty years old at his birth.

too, was among them, bearing a commission to represent the Pope in these negotiations and festivities. And now the stately Moorish palace, with its courtyard, its fountains, and its gardens, became once more a scene of gaiety, as—in the great hall of forty pillars, beneath a roof such as Arabian artists alone could frame, carved like a snow cave, or stained with rich and lovely colour like a mass of jewels set in gold—the officers of the royal household passed solemnly on to offer homage before their Prince and his bride. In the six great apartments of state the frescoed forms of Christian art: Patriarchs in their histories, Moses and David in their exploits, and the last wild charge of Barbarossa's Crusade,[1] looked down upon a moving throng of nobles and commons who came to present their congratulations, while the plaintive music of lute, of pipe, and tabor, sighed upon the air, and skilful dancers swam before the delighted guests in all the fascination of the voluptuous East.

What part could Michael Scot, the grave ecclesiastic, and now doubly the 'Master' as Frederick's trusted tutor, play in the gay scene of his pupil's marriage? For many ages it has been the custom among Italian scholars, the attached dependants of a noble house, to offer on such occasions their homage to bride and bridegroom in the form of a learned treatise; any bookseller's list of *Nozze* is enough to show that the habit exists even at the present day. This then was what Scot did; for there is every reason to think that the *Physionomia*, which he composed and dedicated to Frederick, was produced and presented at the time of the royal marriage. No date suits this publication so well as 1209, and

[1] See the description of this palace in the poem by Peter of Eboli.

nothing but the urgent desire of Court and people that the marriage should prove fruitful can explain, one might add excuse, some passages of almost fescennine licence which it contains.[1] We seem to find in the advice of the preface that Frederick should study man, encouraging the learned to dispute in his presence what may well have been the last word of a master who saw his pupil passing to scenes of larger and more active life at an unusually early age, and before he could be fully trusted to take his due place in the great world of European politics.

The *Physionomia*, however, is too important a work to be dismissed in a paragraph. Both the subject itself, and the sources from which Scot drew, deserve longer consideration. The science of physiognomy, as its name imports, was derived from the Greeks. Achinas, a contemporary of the Hippocratic school, and Philemon, who is mentioned in the introduction to Scot's treatise, seem to have been the earliest writers in this department of philosophy. It was a spiritual medicine,[2] and formed part of the singular doctrine of *signatures*, teaching as it did that the inward dispositions of the soul might be read in visible characters upon the bodily frame. The Alexandrian school made a speciality of physiognomy. In Egypt it attained a further development, and various writings in Greek which expounded the system passed current during the early centuries of our era under the names of

---

[1] Zurita says that Sancia, the Queen Dowager of Aragon, claimed the crown of Sicily for her son Fernando, in case there were no heir of Frederick ii. by Constance.

[2] See on this whole subject three most learned and satisfactory works by Prof. R. Foerster of Breslau — *De Arist. quae feruntur physiognomonicis recensendis*, Kiliae, 1882 ; *De trans. lat. physiognomonicorum*, Kiliae, 1884 ; and especially his *Scriptores Graeci Physiognomonici*, Teubner, 1894.

Aristotle and Polemon. Through the common channel of the Syriac schools and language it reached the Arabs, and in the ninth century had the fortune to be taken up warmly by Rases and his followers, who made it a characteristic part of their medical system. From this source then Scot drew largely; chapters xxiv.-xxv. in Book II. of his *Physionomia* correspond closely with the *De Medicina ad Regem Al Mansorem* [1] of Rases. [2]

Among ancient texts on physiognomy, however, perhaps the most famous was the *Sirr-el-asrar*, or *Secreta Secretorum*, which was ascribed to Aristotle. Its origin, like that of other pseudo-Aristotelic writings, seems to have been Egyptian. When the conquests of Alexander the Great had opened the way for a new relation between East and West, Egypt, and especially its capital, Alexandria, became the focus of a new philosophic influence. The sect of the Essenes, transported hither, had given rise to the school of the Therapeutae, where Greek theories developed in a startling direction under the power of Oriental speculation. The Therapeutae were sun-worshippers, and eager students of ancient and occult writings, as Josephus [3] tells us the Essenes had been. We find in the *Abraxas* gems, of which so large a number has been preserved, an enduring memorial of these people and their system of thought. [4]

---

[1] A *Physionomia* ascribed to Al Mansour himself was commented on by Jacopo da Samminiato. It is preserved in the Bibl. Naz. of Florence, MS. XX. 55.   [2] See Book II. chap. xxvi. *et seq.*

[3] B. J. II. 8. § 6. See also the Church Histories of Neander (i. 61, 83) and Kurtz (i. 65).

[4] The word Ἀβράξας read numerically gives the total of 365 = the number of days in which the sun completes his circle through the twelve signs. In this way it is equivalent to *Mithras*. These gems often bear the figure of a cock = the sun-bird, not without reference to Æsculapius. They were worn to recover or preserve health.

The preface to the *Sirr-el-asrar* affords several matters which agree admirably with what we know of the Therapeutae. The precious volume was the prize of a scholar on his travels, who found it in the possession of an aged recluse dwelling in the *penetralia* of a sun-temple built by Æsculapius.[1] All this is characteristic enough, and when we examine the substance of the treatise it appears distinctly Therapeutic. Much of it is devoted to bodily disease, to the regimen of the health, and to that science of physiognomy which professed to reveal, as in a spiritual diagnosis, the infirmities of the soul. The ascription of the work to Aristotle, Alexander's tutor, seems quite in accordance with this theory; in short, there is no reason to doubt that it first appeared in Egypt, where it probably formed one of the most cherished texts of the Therapeutae.

The preface to the *Sirr-el-asrar* throws light not only upon the origin of the treatise but also upon its subsequent fortunes. It is said to have been rendered from the Greek into Chaldee or Syriac,[2] and thence into Arabic, the usual channel

---

[1] This reminds one of the somewhat similar introduction to the alchemy of Crates, which speaks of a youth called Rissoures, the scion of a family of adepts, who made love to a maid-servant of Ephestelios, chief diviner in the Temple of Serapis at Alexandria, thus inducing her to steal the book and fly with him. The tradition of discovery is common to both legends, but the Crates has a colour of worldly passion and the Sirr-el-Asrar a shade of ascetic practice which agrees admirably with what we know of the Therapeutae. *Crates* is probably Democritus. The Arabic version was due to Khalid ben Yezid, and bears the title of *Kenz el Konouz*, or treasure of treasures. It is found in MS. 440 of Leyden. In a later chapter we shall recur to this subject with the view of showing that alchemy as well as physiognomy owed much to the Therapeutic philosophy.

[2] The printed copy—in fol. Venice, Bernardinus de Vitalibus, s. a. but probably 1501—reads 'romanam,' which would be neo-Greek or Romaic.

by which the remains of ancient learning have
reached the modern world.   The translator's name
is given as Johannes filius Bitricii, but this can
hardly have been the well-known Ibn-el-Bitriq,
the freedman of Mamoun.   To this latter author
indeed, the *Fihrist*, composed in 987, ascribes the
Arabic version of Aristotle's *De Cælo et Mundo*,
and of Plato's *Timaeus*, so that his literary
faculty would seem to accord very well with
the task of translating the *Sirr-el-asrar*.   But
Foerster has observed[1] that we find no trace of
this book in Arabian literature before the eleventh
century.   Now the famous Ibn-el-Bitriq lived in the
ninth, as appears from several considerations.   His
works were revised by Honain ibn Ishaq (873),
and, if we believe in the authenticity of the *El
Hawi*, where he is mentioned by name, then he
must have belonged to an age at least as early
as that of Rases who wrote it.   In these perplexing
circumstances, Foerster gives up the attempt to
determine who may have been the translator of
the *Sirr-el-asrar*, contenting himself with the conjecture that some unknown scholar had assumed
the name of El Bitriq to give importance to the
production of his pen.   We may be excused,
however, if we direct attention to two manuscripts
of the British Museum[2] which do not seem to
have been noticed by those who have devoted
attention to this obscure subject.   One of these,
which is written in a hand of the thirteenth
century, informs us that the man who transcribed

---

[1] See on this whole subject the excellent remarks of Foerster in his
treatise *De Aristotelis quae feruntur Secretis Secretorum*, Kiliae, 1888,
pp. 22-25.

[2] Wright's *Cat. of the Syriac MSS.*, Nos. 250 and 366.

it was a certain Said Ibn Butrus ibn Mansur, a
Maronite priest of Lebanon in the diocese of
Tripolis, a prisoner for twelve years in the place
where the royal standards were kept (? at Cairo),
who was released from that confinement in the
time of *al Malik an Nazir*. The other—a mere
fragment—contains a notice of the priest Yahyā,
or Yuhannā, ibn Butrus, who died in the year
1217 A.D. It is not unlikely that some confusion
might arise between the names Patrick and Peter,
often used interchangeably. 'Filius Patricii' then
may have been no assumed designation, but the
equivalent of Ibn Butrus, the real name of this priest
of Tripoli, who was perhaps the translator of the
Sirr-el-asrar at the close of the twelfth century.

Those chapters of the *Sirr-el-asrar* which relate
to regimen were translated into Latin by Johannes
Hispalensis. Jourdain identifies this author with
John Avendeath, who worked for the Archbishop
of Toledo between the years 1130 and 1150.[1] But
Foerster shows that caution is needed here.[2] The
Latin version was dedicated to Tarasia, Queen of
Spain. A queen of this name certainly lived con-
temporaneously with John Avendeath, but she
was Queen of Portugal. Another Tarasia, however,
was Queen of Leon from 1176 to 1180. We may
observe that this latter epoch agrees well enough
with the lifetime of Ibn Butrus, who died in 1217,
and we find trace of another Johannes Hispanus,
who was a monk of Mount Tabor in 1175. Such
a man, who from his situation in Syria could
scarcely have been ignorant of Arabic, and whose
nationality agrees so well with a dedication to

---

[1] *Recherches*, pp. 117, 118.   [2] *Op. cit.* pp. 26, 27.

the Queen of Spain, and who was a contemporary
of Tarasia of Leon, may well have translated the
Sirr-el-asrar into Latin. That part of the book
thus made public in the West appeared under
the following title : ' De conservatione corporis
humani, ad Alexandrum.' It is found in several
manuscripts of the Laurentian Library in Florence.[1]

Soon afterwards, and probably in the opening
years of the thirteenth century, the whole book
was published in a Latin version by the same
Philippus Clericus, with whom we have already
become acquainted. We may recall the fact that
he belonged to the diocese of Tripoli, as Ibn
Butrus also did, and as Johannes Hispanus was
also a monk of Syria, these three scholars are seen
to be joined by a link of locality highly increasing
the probability that they actually co-operated in
the publication of this hitherto unknown text.
In his preface, Philip speaks of the Arabic manuscript as a precious pearl, discovered while he
was still in Syria. This leads us to think that
his work in translating it was done after he had
left the East, and possibly in the course of his
voyage westward. We know that the Hebrew
version of Aristotle's *Meteora* was produced in
similar circumstances. Samuel ben Juda ben
Tibbun says he completed that translation in the
year 1210, while the ship that bore him from
Alexandria to Spain was passing between the
isles of Lampadusa and Pantellaria.[2] However
this may be, Philip of Tripoli dedicated his version
of the *Sirr-el-asrar*, which he called the *Secreta*

---

[1] Viz., P. xiii. sin. cod. 6 ; P. xxx. cod. 29 ; and P. lxxxix. *sup.*
cod. 76. There is also one at Paris, Fonds de Sorbonne, 955.

[2] See the MS. of the Laurentian Library, p. lxxxviii. cod. 24.

Secretorum, to the Bishop under whom he had
hitherto lived and laboured : ' Guidoni vere de
Valentia, civitatis Tripolis glorioso pontifici ' : a
name and title little understood by the copyists,
who have subjected them to strange corruptions.[1]

It is highly in favour of our identifying, as
we have already done, Philip of Tripoli, the
translator of the *Secreta*, with Philip of Salerno,
the Clerk Register of Sicily, that we find Michael
Scot, who stood in an undoubtedly close relation
to the Clerk Register, showing an intimate acquaintance with the *Secreta Secretorum*. Foerster has
given us a careful and exact account of several
passages in different parts of the *Physionomia* of
Scot, which have their correspondences in the
works of Philip, so that it is beyond question that
the Latin version of the *Secreta* was one of the
sources from which Scot drew. Before leaving
this part of the subject, we may notice that translations of Philip's version into the vernacular
languages of Italy, France, and England were
made at an early date, both in prose and verse.[2]

---

[1] By transposition ' G. de Valentia vere civitatis,' etc. (Bibl. Naz.
Flor. xxv. 10, 632) ; by corruption ' vere de violentia ' (Barberini MS.),
or ' grosso pontifici ' (Fondo Vaticano, 5047). This bishop has not yet
been identified.

[2] MSS. of the *Secreta Secretorum* are found in Florence, Bibl. Naz.,
xxv. 10, 632, chart. saec. xv. ; Bibl. Laur. (S. Crucis) xv. sin. 9 ; Rome,
Fondo Vaticano, 5047 ; Oxford, Bibl. Bod. Can. Misc., 562 ; Troyes and
St. Omer, *v.* Cat. MSS. des Depart., vol. ii. pp. 517, 518, and iii. 295 ;
Berne, v. Sinner's Cat., vol. iii. p. 525. It is interesting to note that the title
of this last MS. is *Physionomia*, just as the *Physionomia* of Scot is called
De Secretis in the editions of 1584 and 1598. This confirms the relation
between his work and that of Philippus Clericus. MSS. of the Italian
version of the *Secreta Secretorum* are found at Florence, Bibl. Riccard.,
Q. I. xxii. 1297 ; R. I. xx. 2224 ; L. I. xxxiv. 108. The first of these
is dated 1450. In the Bibl. Naz., Florence, there is another, and a
similar one of the *Physionomia Aristotelis*. In the Chigi Library of
Rome there is a MS., chart. saec. xvii., with the curious title : ' Migel
franzas, auctor obscurioris nominis, ad *Physionomiam* Aristotelis Com-

The English version of the *Secreta* came from the hand of the poet Lydgate.

Another treatise of the same school, to which Scot was also indebted, is to be found in the *Physionomia* ascribed, like the *Secreta*, to Aristotle. The Latin version of this apocryphal work was made, it is said, directly from a Greek original, by Bartholomew of Messina. This author wrote for Manfred of Sicily, and at a time which excludes the notion that Scot could have seen or employed his work. Yet several passages in the preface to Book II. of Scot's *Physionomia* have evidently been borrowed from that of the Pseudo-Aristotle. As no Arabic version of the treatise is known to exist, the fact of this correspondence is one of the proofs on which we may rely in support of the conclusion that Scot must have known and used the Greek language in his studies.

The last two chapters of Book I. in the *Physionomia* of Scot show plainly that he had the Arabic version of Aristotle's *History of Animals* before him as he wrote. We shall recur to this matter when we come to deal with the versions which Scot made expressly from these books. Meanwhile let us guard against the impression naturally arising from our analysis of the *Physionomia*, that it was a mere compilation. Many parts of the work show no correspondence with any other treatise on the subject that is known to us, and these must be held as the results of the author's

mentarium.' It is numbered E. vi. 205, and consists of 326 pages. The *Secreta Secretorum* with the *De Mineralibus* was printed at Venice (? 1501), by Bernardinus de Vitalibus, and a new version by G. Manente, comprehending the *Morals* and the *Physionomia* as well as the *Secreta*, issued from the same place in 1538. It was printed in 4to by Tacuino da Trino.

own observations. The arrangement of the whole
is certainly original, nor can we better conclude our
study of the *Physionomia*, than by giving a compre-
hensive view of its contents in their order. The
work is divided into three books, each having its
own introduction. The first expounds the mysteries
of generation and birth, and reaches, as we have
already remarked, even beyond humanity to a considerable part of the animal world so much studied
by the Arabians. The second expounds the signs
of the different complexions, as these become visible
in any part of the body, or are discovered by
dreams. The third examines the human frame
member by member, explaining what signs of the
inward nature may be read in each. The whole
forms a very complete and interesting compendium
of the art of physiognomy as then understood, and
must have seemed not unworthy of the author, nor
unsuitable as an offering to the young prince, who
by marriage was about to enter on the great world
of affairs, where knowledge of men would henceforth
be all-important to his success and happiness. The
book attained a wide popularity in manuscript, and
the invention of printing contributed to increase its
circulation in Europe :[1] no less than eighteen editions

[1] MSS. of the *Physionomia* : Oxford, Bibl. Bod. MSS. Canon. Misc. 555
(with the *Liber Particularis*) saec. xiv. ; Milan, Bibl. Ambros. L 92 *sup.*
(with the *Liber Particularis*) ; Padua, Bibl. Anton. xxiii. 616, chart. saec.
xvii ; Vatican, Fondo della Regina 1151 perhaps saec. xvi. Printed
editions : 1477 perhaps double ; 1485 Louvain and Leipsic ; 1499 s. l.
and five or six others of this century in 4to, s. l. et a ; 1508 Cologne,
Venice, and Paris, the last in 8vo ; 1514 Venice 8vo ; 1515 s. l. ; 1519
Venice 8vo ; 1584 Lyons 24mo along with the *Abbreviatio Avicennae*
and the *De animalibus ad Caesarem* under the general title of *De
Secretis Naturae* ; 1598 Lyons, *De Secretis Naturae* cum tractatu *De
Secretis Mulierum* Alberti Magni ; 1615 Frankfort 8vo ; 1655 and 1660
Amsterdam 12mo. Editions of the Italian version appeared at Venice
in 1533, 8vo, and 1537. During the sixteenth century an edition of the
Latin text in 8vo appeared from the press of Pietro Gaudoul without date.

are said to have been printed between 1477 and 1660.[1]

In the copy preserved at Milan, the *Physionomia* is placed immediately after the *Astronomia*, or *Liber Particularis*. A similar arrangement is found in the Oxford manuscript. This fact is certainly in favour of the view we have adopted, and would seem to fix very plainly the date and relation of these works. They stand beside the *Liber Introductorius*, and, together with it, form the only remains we have of Scot's first literary activity, being publications that were called out in the course of his scholastic duty to the King of Sicily. The *Liber Introductorius* opens this series. It is closely related by the nature of its subject-matter to the *Astronomia*, or *Liber Particularis*, while the *Physionomia* forms a fitting close to the others with which it is thus associated. In this last treatise Michael Scot sought to fulfil his charge by sending forth his pupil to the great world, not wholly unprovided with a guide to what is far more abstruse and incalculable than any celestial theorem, the mystery of human character and action.

In presenting the *Physionomia* to Frederick, Scot took what proved a long farewell of the Court; for many years passed before he saw the Emperor again. The great concourse of the Queen's train, together with the assembly of Frederick's subjects at Palermo, bred a pestilence under the dangerous heats of spring. A sudden horror fell on the masques and revels of these bright days, with the death of the Queen's brother, Count Alfonso of

---

[1] *Histoire Littéraire de la France.* The list given above will show that this statement rather falls short of the truth than exceeds it.

Provence, and several others, so that soon the fair gardens and pleasant palace were emptied and deserted as a place where only the plague might dare to linger. The King and Queen, with five hundred Spanish knights and a great Sicilian following, passed eastward; to Cefalù first, and then on to Messina and Catania, as if they could not put too great a distance between themselves and the infected spot. Meanwhile Michael Scot, whose occupation in Palermo, and indeed about the King, was now gone, set sail in the opposite direction and sought the coast of Spain. Whether the idea of this voyage was his own, was the result of a royal commission, or had been suggested by some of the learned who came with Queen Constantia from her native land, it is now impossible to say. It was in any case a fortunate venture, which did much, not only for Scot's personal fame, but for the general advantage in letters and in arts.

CHAPTER III

In following the course which Michael Scot held in his voyage to Spain, we approach what was beyond all doubt the most important epoch in the life of that scholar. Hitherto we have seen him as the student preparing at Paris or Bologna for a brilliant future, or as the tutor of a youthful monarch, essaying some literary ventures, which justified the position he held in Sicily, and recommended him for future employment. But the moment was now come which put him at last in possession of an opportunity suitable to his training and talents. We are to see how he won in Spain his greatest reputation in connection with the most important literary enterprise of the age, and one which is indeed not the least remarkable of all time.

The part which the Arabs took in the intellectual awakening of Europe is a familiar theme of early mediæval history. That wonderful people, drawn from what was then an unknown land of the East, and acted on by the mighty sense of religion and nationality which Mohammed was able to communicate, fell like a flood upon the weak remains of older civilisations, and made huge inroads upon the Christian Empire of the East. Having reached this point in their career of conquest they became

42

in their turn the conquered, not under force of arms indeed, but as subdued by the still vital intellectual power possessed by those whom they had in a material sense overcome. In their new seat by the streams of the Euphrates they learned from their Syrian subjects, now become their teachers, the treasures of Greek philosophy which had been translated into the Aramaic tongue. Led captive as by a spell, the Caliphs of the Abassid line, especially Al Mansour, Al Rachid, and Al Mamoun, encouraged with civil honours and rewards the labours of these learned men. Happy indeed was the Syrian who brought to life another relic of the mighty dead, or who gave to such works a new immortality by rendering them into the Arabic language.

Meanwhile the progress of the Ommiad arms, compelled to seek new conquests by the defeat they had sustained in the East from the victorious Abbassides, was carrying the Moors west and ever westward along the northern provinces of Africa. Egypt and Tripoli and Tunis successively fell before their victorious march ; Algiers and Morocco shared the same fate, and at last, crossing the Straits of Gibraltar, the Moors overran Spain, making a new Arabia of that western peninsula, which in position and physical features bore so great a likeness to the ancient cradle of their race.

It is true indeed that long ere the period of which we write the Moorish power in the West had received a severe check, and had, for at least a century, entered on its period of decay. The battle of Tours, fought in 732, had driven the infidels from France. The Christian kingdoms of Spain itself had rallied their courage and their forces, and, in a scene of chivalry, which inspired many a tale and song, had freed at least the northern provinces of that country from the alien power. But weapons of war, as we have already seen in the case of the Arabs themselves, are not the only means of conquest. The surest title of the Moors to glory lies in the prevailing intellectual influence they were able to exert over that Christendom which, in a political sense, they had failed to subdue and dispossess. The scene we have just witnessed in the East was now repeated in Spain, but was repeated in an exactly opposite sense. The mental impulse received from the remains of Greek literature at Bagdad now became in its turn the motive power which not only sufficed to carry these forgotten treasures westward in the course of Moorish conquest, but succeeded, through that nation, in rousing the Latin races to a sense of their excellence, and a generous ambition to become possessed of all the culture and discipline they were capable of yielding.

The chief centre of this influence, as it was the chief scene of contact between the two races, naturally lay in Spain. During the ages of Moorish dominion the Christians of this country had lived in peace and prosperity under the generous protection of their foreign rulers. To a considerable extent indeed the Moors and Spaniards amalgamated by intermarriage. The language of the conquerors was familiarly employed by their Spanish subjects, and these frequented in numbers the famous schools of science and literature established by the Moors at Cordova, and in other cities of the kingdom. Proof of all this remains in the public acts of the Castiles, which continued to be written in Arabic as late as the fourteenth century, and were signed by Christian prelates in the same characters ;[1] in the present language of Spain which retains so many words of eastern origin ; but, above all, in the profound influence, now chiefly engaging our attention, which has left its mark upon almost every branch of our modern science, literature, and art.

This result was largely owing to a singular enterprise of the twelfth century with which the learned researches of Jourdain have made us familiar.[2] Scholars from other lands, such as Constantine, Gerbert, afterwards Pope Sylvester ii., Adelard of Bath, Hermann, and Alfred and Daniel de Morlay, had indeed visited Spain during that age and the one which preceded it, and had, as individuals, made a number of translations from the Arabic, among which were various works in medicine and mathematics, as well as the first version of the Koran. But in the earlier half of the twelfth century, and precisely between the years 1130 and 1150, this desultory work was reduced to a system by the establishment of a regular school of translation in Toledo. The credit of this foundation, which did so much for mediæval science and letters, belongs to Don Raymon, Archbishop of Toledo and Primate of Spain. This enlightened and liberal churchman was by origin a French monk, born at Agen, whom Bernard, a previous Primate, had brought southward in his train, as he returned from a journey

[1] See Ticknor's *History of Spanish Literature*, p. 395.
[2] *Recherches sur l'âge et l'origine des trad. latines d'Aristote*, Paris, 1843, chap. iii. passim.

beyond the Pyrenees. Don Raymon associated with himself his Archdeacon, Dominicus Gundisalvus, and a converted Jew commonly known as Johannes Hispalensis or John of Seville, whom Jourdain has identified with Johannes Avendeath: this latter being in all probability his proper name. These formed the heads of the Toledo school in its earliest period, and the enterprise was continued throughout the latter half of the century by other scholars, of whom Gherardus Cremonensis the elder was probably the chief. Versions of the voluminous works of Avicenna, as well as of several treatises by Algazel and Alpharabius, and of a number of medical writings, were the highly prized contribution of the Toledo school to the growing library of foreign authors now accessible in the Latin language.

It is probable that when Michael Scot left Sicily he did so with the purpose of joining this important enterprise. His movements naturally suggest such an idea, as he proceeded to Toledo, still the centre of these studies, and won, during the years of his residence there, the name by which he is best known in the world of letters, that of the chief exponent of the Arabo-Aristotelic philosophy in the West.

The name and fame of Aristotle, never quite forgotten even in the darkest age,[1] and now known and extolled among Moorish scholars, formed indeed the ground of that immense reputation which Arabian philosophy enjoyed in Europe. The Latin schools had long been familiar with the logical writings of Aristotle, but the modern spirit, soon to show

[1] The bones of Aristotle were said to lie in the Mosque of Palermo, where they were highly reverenced. See *Charles III. of Naples*, by St. Clair Baddeley, London, 1894, p. 122.

itself as it were precociously in Bacon and Albertus
Magnus, was already awake, and under its influence
men had begun to demand more than the mere
training of the mind in abstract reasoning. Even
the application of dialectics to evolve or support
systems of doctrine drawn from Holy Scripture
could not content this new curiosity. Men were
becoming alive to the larger book of nature which
lay open around them, and, confounded at first by
the complexity of unnumbered facts in sea and sky,
in earth and air, they began to long for help from
the great master of philosophy which might guide
their first trembling footsteps in so strange and
untrodden a realm of knowledge. Nor was the hope
of such aid denied them. There was still a tradition
concerning the lost works of Aristotle on physics.
The Moors, it was found, boasted their possession,
and even claimed to have enriched these priceless
pages by comments which were still more precious
than the original text itself.

The mere hope that it might be so was enough
to beget a new crusade, when western scholars vied
with each other in their efforts to recover these lost
treasures and restore to the schools of Europe the
impulse and guidance so eagerly desired. Such
had, in fact, been the aim of Archbishop Raymon
and the successive translators of the Toledan school.
The important place they assigned to Avicenna
among those whose works they rendered into Latin
was due to the fact that this author had come to be
regarded in the early part of the twelfth century as
the chief exponent of Aristotle, whose spirit he had
inherited, and on whose works he had founded his
own.

The part of the Aristotelic writings to which
Michael Scot first turned his attention would seem
to have been the history of animals. This, in the
Greek text, consisted of three distinct treatises :
first the *De Historiis Animalium* in ten books ; next
the *De Partibus Animalium* in four books ; and
lastly, the *De Generatione Animalium* in five books.
The Arabian scholars, however, who paid great
attention to this part of natural philosophy and
made many curious observations in it, were accus-
tomed to group these three treatises under the
general title *De Animalibus*, and to number their
books or chapters consecutively from one to nineteen, probably for convenience in referring to them.
As Scot's work consisted of a translation from
Arabic texts it naturally followed the form which
had been sanctioned by the use and wont of the
eastern commentators.

At least two versions of the *De Animalibus* appeared from the pen of Scot. These have sometimes been confounded with each other, but are
really quite distinct, representing the labours of
two different Arabian commentators on the text of
Aristotle. We may best commence by examining
that of which least is known, the *De Animalibus ad
Caesarem*, as it is commonly called, and this the
rather that there is good reason to suppose it represents the first Arabian work on Natural History
which came into Scot's hands.

Nothing is known certainly regarding the author
of this commentary. Jourdain and Steinschneider
conclude with reason that the text must have been
an Arabic and not a Hebrew one, as Camus[1] and

---

[1] *Notices et extraits des Mss.*, vol. vi. p. 412.

Wüstenfeld[1] contend. No one, however, has hitherto ventured any suggestion throwing light on the personality of the writer. The colophon to the copy of Scot's version in the *Bibliotheca Angelica* of Rome contains the word *Alphagiri*, which would seem to stand for the proper name Al Faquir. But in all probability, as we shall presently show, this may be merely the name of the Spanish Jew who aided Michael Scot in the work of translation.

The expression 'secundum extractionem Michaelis Scoti,' which is used in the same colophon, would seem to indicate that this version, voluminous as it is, was no more than a compend of the original. The title of the manuscript too : ' Incipit flos primi libri Aristotelis de Animalibus' agrees curiously with this, and with the word *Abbreviatio* (*Avicennae*), used to describe Scot's second version of the *De Animalibus* of which we are presently to speak. Are we then to suppose that in each case the translator exercised his faculty of selection, and that the form of these compends was due, not to Avicenna, nor to the unknown author of the text called in Scot's version the *De Animalibus ad Caesarem*, but to Scot himself? The expressions just cited would seem to open the way for such a conclusion.

The contents of the *De Animalibus ad Caesarem* may be inferred from the Prologue which is as follows: ' In Nomine Domini Nostri Jesu Christi Omnipotentis Misericordis et Pii, translatio tractatus primi libri quem composuit Aristoteles in cognitione naturalium animalium, agrestium et marinorum, et in illo est conjunctionis animalium modus et modus generationis illorum cum coitu,

---

[1] *Die Uebersetz. Arabischer Werke*, Göttingen, 1877, p. 99.

D

cum partitione membrorum interiorum et apparen-
tium, et cum meditatione comparationum eorum, et
actionum eorum, et juvamentorum et nocumentorum
eorum, et qualiter venantur, et in quibus locis sunt,
et quomodo moventur de loco ad locum propter dis-
positionem presentis aetatis, aestatis et hiemis, et
unde est vita cuiuslibet eorum, scilicet modorum
avium, et luporum, et piscium maris et qui ambulant
in eo.' It seems tolerably certain that the substance of this prologue came from the Arabic
original, which must have commenced with the
ascription of praise to God so commonly employed
by Mohammedans : ' Bi–smilláhi–r–rahhmáni–r–
rahheém' (In the Name of God, the Compas-
sionate ; the Merciful).[1] The clumsiness of the
Latin, which here, as in the body of the work, seems
to labour heavily in the track of a foreign text,[2] adds
force to this assumption. The hand of Scot is seen,
however, where the name of our Saviour has been
substituted for that of Allah, and also in the closing
words, which ring with a strong reminiscence of the
eighth Psalm. The churchman betrays himself here
as in not a few other places which might be quoted
from his different writings.

By far the most interesting matter, however,
which offers itself for our consideration here, lies in
the comparison we are now to make between this
book and a former work of Scot, the De Physionomia.
This comparison, which has never before been attempted, will throw light on both these texts, but
has a special value as it affords the means of dating,

---

[1] See Lane's Modern Egyptians, vol. i. p. 197 note.
[2] We should remember, however, the Emperor's instructions to his
translators: 'verborum fideliter servata virginitate.' See his circular
of 1230 to the Universities.—Jourdain, Recherches, p. 133.

at least approximately, the composition of Scot's version of the *De Animalibus ad Caesarem*.

We have already remarked that the last two chapters of the first book of the *Physionomia* suggest that in compiling them the author had before him an Arabic treatise on Natural History. A natural conjecture leads us further to suppose that this may have been the original from which he translated the *De Animalibus ad Caesarem*, and this idea becomes a certainty when we pursue the comparison a little more closely. Take for example this curious passage from the *Physionomia* (Book I. chap. ii.): 'Incipiunt pili paulatim oriri in pectine unitas quorum dicitur femur . . . item sibi vox mutatur.' Its obscurity disappears when we confront it with the corresponding words in the *De Animalibus ad Caesarem*, and thus discover what was no doubt the original source from which Scot derived it : ' Incipiunt pili oriri in pectore *Kameon alkaratoki*, et in isto tempore mutatur vox eius.'[1] There is no need to extend the comparison any further than this significant passage. Doubt may arise regarding the depth and accuracy of Scot's knowledge of the Arabic tongue, the nature of the text that lay before him, or the reason he may have had for retaining foreign words in the one version which he translated in the other ; but surely this may be regarded as now clearly established, that some part of the first book of the *Physionomia* was derived by compilation from the same text which appeared in a Latin dress as the *De Animalibus ad Caesarem*, and that this source was an Arabic one.

This point settled, it becomes possible to establish

[1] *De Animalibus ad Caesarem*, chap. ix.

another. One of the copies of the *De Animalibus
ad Caesarem*[1] has the following colophon : 'Completus est liber Aristotelis de animalibus, translatus a magistro michaele in tollecto de arabico in
latinum.' Now if the version was made in Toledo,
it was probably posterior in date to the *Physionomia*.
This indeed is no more than might have been asserted on the ground of common likelihood; for,
when a compilation and a complete version of one
of the sources from which it was derived are both
found passing under the name of the same author,
it is but natural to suppose that the first was made
before the other, and that in the interval the author
had conceived the idea of producing in a fuller form
a work he had already partially published.

Resuming then the results we have reached, it
appears that Scot had met with this Arabic commentary on the Natural History of Aristotle while
he was still in Sicily, and had made extracts from
it for his *Physionomia*. Coming to Spain he probably carried the manuscript with him, and as his
version of the *De Animalibus ad Caesarem* seems to
have been the first complete translation he made
from the Arabic, and to have been published shortly
after he came to the Castiles, he may possibly have
begun work upon it even before his arrival there.
On every account, there being no positive evidence
to the contrary, we may conjecture that the *De
Animalibus ad Caesarem*, like the *Physionomia*,
belongs to the year 1209. If the latter work
appeared at Palermo in time for the royal marriage,
which took place in spring, the former may well

---

[1] Bibl. Laur. Pl. xiii. sin. cod. 9 in fol perg. This MS. was written
in 1266.

have been completed and published towards the end of the same year, when Scot had no doubt been already some time settled in Toledo.

The second form in which Michael Scot produced his work upon the Natural History of Aristotle was that of a version called the *Abbreviatio Avicennae*. The full title as it appears in the printed copy[1] is : ' Avicenna de Animalibus per Magistrum Michaelem Scotum de Arabico in Latinum translatus.' Like the *De Animalibus ad Caesarem* it consists of nineteen books, thus comprehending the three Aristotelic treatises in one work.

The name of *Ibn Sina* or Avicenna, the author of the Arabic original, is significant, as it enables us to connect in a remarkable way the present labours of Scot's pen with those which had in a past age proceeded from the school of translators at Toledo, and to place the *Abbreviatio* in its true relation with the system of versions which had been published there nearly a century before. We have already remarked that Don Raymon directed the attention of his translators to Avicenna as the best representative, both of Aristotle himself and of the Arabian wisdom which had gathered about his writings. A manuscript of great interest preserved in the library of the Vatican[2] shows what the labours of Gundisalvus, Avendeath, and their co-adjutors had been, and how far they had proceeded in the task of making this author accessible to Latin students. From it we learn that the *Logic*, the *Physics*, the *De Cœlo et Mundo*, the *Meta-*

---

[1] Fifteenth Century s. l. et a. in fol. pp. 54. There are also Venice editions of 1493 and 1509.

[2] Fondo Vaticano 4428 in fol. perg. saec. xiii. See a complete inventory of this MS. in Appendix II.

physics; the *De Anima*, called also *Liber sextus de Naturalibus*; and the *De generatione Lapidum* of Avicenna, had come from the school of Toledo during the twelfth century in a Latin dress. The last-named treatise was apparently a comment on the *Meteora* of Aristotle, and the whole belonged to that *Kitab Alchefâ*, which was called by the Latins the *Assephae*, *Asschiphe* or *Liber Sufficientiae*. This collection was said to form but the first and most common of the three bodies of philosophy composed by Avicenna. It represented the teaching of Aristotle and the Peripatetics, while the second expounded the system of Avicenna himself, and the third contained the more esoteric and occult doctrines of natural philosophy.[1] Of these the first alone had reached the Western schools.

It is plain then that until Michael Scot took the work in hand Toledo had not completed the Latin version of Avicenna by translating that part of the *Alchefâ* which concerned the Natural History of Animals. The *Abbreviatio Avicennae* thus came to supply the defect and to crown the labours of the ancient college of translators. This place of honour is actually given to it in the Vatican manuscript just referred to, where it follows the *De generatione Lapidum*, and forms the fitting close of that remarkable series and volume. Thus, while the *De Animalibus ad Caesarem* connects itself with the *Physionomia*, and with Scot's past life in Sicily, the *Abbreviatio Avicennae* joins him closely and in a very remarkable way with the whole tradition of the Toledo school, of which, by this translation, he at once became not the least distinguished member.

---

[1] See Roger Bacon, *Opus Majus*, p. 37.

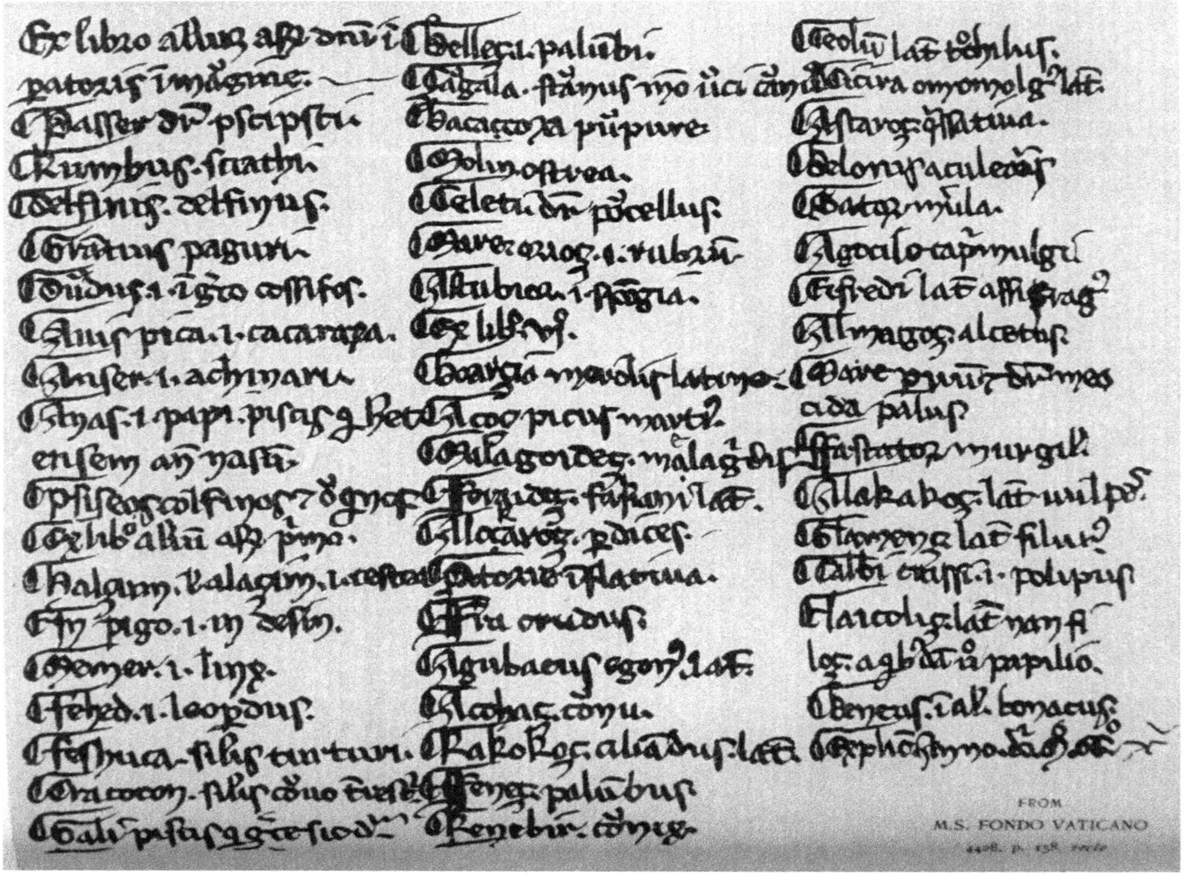

FROM
M.S. FONDO VATICANO
4408. p. 158 recto

The authority of this manuscript, now perhaps for the first time appealed to, is sufficient not only to determine the relation of Scot's work to that of the earlier Toledan school, but even, by a most fortunate circumstance, enables us to feel sure of the exact date when the translation of the *Abbreviatio* was made. For the colophon to the Vatican manuscript, brief as it is, contains in one line a fact of the utmost interest and importance to all students of the life of Scot. It is as follows: ' Explicit anno Domini m°c°c°x.'[1] The researches of Jourdain had the merit of making public two colophons from the manuscripts of Paris, containing the date of another and later work of Scot,[2] but since the days of that savant no further addition of this valuable kind has been made to our knowledge of the philosopher's life. The date just cited from the Vatican copy of the *Abbreviatio* shows, however, that further inquiry in this direction need not be abandoned as useless. We now know accurately the time when this version was completed, and find the date to be such as accords exactly with our idea that Scot must have quitted Sicily soon after the marriage of Frederick; for the year 1210 may be taken as a fixed point determining the time when he first became definitely connected with the Toledo school. It will be remembered that we anticipated this result of research so far as to use it in our attempt to conjecture the date of Scot's birth.[3]

Like the *De Animalibus ad Caesarem*, the *Abbreviatio Avicennae* bears a dedication to Frederick conceived in the following terms: ' *O Frederick,*

---

[1] P. 158 *recto*, the last line of the third column.
[2] *Recherches*, p. 133.   [3] See *ante*, p. 10.

*Lord of the World and Emperor, receive with
devotion this book of Michael Scot, that it may be
a grace unto thy head and a chain about thy neck.'* [1]
It will always be matter of doubt whether in this
address Scot appealed to a taste for natural history
already formed in his pupil before he left Palermo,
or whether the interest subsequently shown by this
monarch in studying the habits of animals was
awakened by the perusal of these two volumes. In
any case they must have done not a little to guide
both his interest and his researches. The chroniclers
tell us of Frederick's elephant, which was sent to
Cremona, of the cameleopard, the camels and
dromedaries, the lions, leopards, panthers, and rare
birds which the royal menagerie contained, and of
a white bear which, being very uncommon, formed
one of the gifts presented by the Emperor on an
important occasion. We hear too that Frederick,
not content with gathering such rarities under his
own observation, entered upon more than one curious
experiment in this branch of science. Desiring to
learn the origin of language he had some children
brought up, so Salimbene tells us, beyond hearing
of any spoken tongue. In the course of another
inquiry he caused the surgeon's knife to be ruth-
lessly employed upon living men that he might lay
bare the secrets and study the process of digestion.
If these experiments do not present the moral
character of the Emperor in a very attractive light,
they may at least serve to show how keenly he was
interested in the study of nature.

This interest indeed went so far as to lead

---

[1] There is an evident reference to Prov. i. 9 in these words which
accords well with Scot's usual style.

Frederick to join the number of royal authors by publishing a work on falconry.[1] In it he ranges over all the species of birds then known, and insists on certain rarities, such as a white cockatoo, which had been sent to him by the Sultan from Cairo. He thus appears in his own pages, not merely as a keen sportsman, but as one who took no narrow interest in natural history. Clearly the dedica- tion of the *De Animalibus* and the *Abbreviatio Avicennae* was no empty compliment as it flowed from the pen of Scot. He had directed his first labours from Toledo to one who could highly appreciate them, and to these works must be ascribed, in no small measure, the growth of the Emperor's interest in a subject then very novel and little understood.

As regards the *Abbreviatio Avicennae* indeed, we have actual evidence of the esteem in which Frederick held it. The book remained treasured in the Imperial closet at Melfi for more than twenty years, and, when at last the Emperor consented to its publication, so important was the moment deemed, that a regular writ passed the seals giving warrant for its transcription.[2] Master Henry of Colonia[3] was the person selected by favour of Frederick for this work, and, as most of the manuscripts of the *Abbreviatio* now extant have a colophon referring in detail to this transaction, we may assume that Henry's copy, made from that belonging to the Emperor, was the source from which all others have been derived.

[1] Printed, but very incompletely, at Augsburg in 1596 in 8vo.
[2] *Hist. Dip. Frid. II.* vol. iv. pt. i. pp. 381, 382.
[3] Can this have been *Cologna*, a village about four miles north of Salerno?

This Imperial original would seem to be more nearly represented by the Vatican copy[1] than by any other which remains in the libraries of Europe. From it we discover that the Arabic names with which the *Abbreviatio* abounds were given in Latin in the margin of the original manuscript, which Scot sent to the Emperor.[2] These hard words and their explanations were afterwards gathered in a glossary, and inscribed at the end of the treatise; an improvement which was probably due to Henry of Colonia. The glossary has, however, been quite neglected by later copyists, nor does it appear in the printed edition of the *Abbreviatio Avicennae*. The completeness with which it is found in the Vatican manuscript shows the close relation which that copy holds to the one first made by the Emperor's permission. The Chigi manuscript[3] seems to be the only other in which the glossary is to be found. It therefore ranks beside that of the Vatican, but is inferior to it as it presents the glossary in a less complete form.

The originality of the Vatican text perhaps appears also in the curious triplet with which it closes: 'Liber iste inceptus est et expletus cum adiutorio Jesu Christi qui vivit, etc.

> Frenata penna, finito nunc Avicenna
> Libro Caesario, gloria summa Deo
> Dextera scriptoris careat gravitate doloris.'[4]

Several other copies of the *Abbreviatio* have the first two lines, but this alone contains the third.

---

[1] Fondo Vaticano 4428.

[2] The words are: 'Ex libro animalium Aristotelis Domini Imperatoris in margine' (p. 158 *recto*) : see facsimile at p. 55.

[3] Bibl. Chisiana E viii. 251, at p. 41 bottom margin.

[4] P. 158, *recto* col. 1.

In the Chigi manuscript, the place of these verses is occupied by a curious feat of language :—

latinum	arabicum	sclauonicum	teutonicum	arabicum
Felix	el melic	dober	Friderich	salemelich.[1]

To whatever period it belongs, the writer's purpose was doubtless to recall to the mind the four nations over which Frederick II. ruled, and the splendid kingdoms of Sicily, Germany, and Jerusalem which he gathered in one under his imperial power.

In the Laurentian Library there is a valuable manuscript, written during the summer and autumn of 1266, for the monks of Santa Croce.[2] It contains the *De Animalibus ad Caesarem* ; the *Abbreviatio Avicennae*, and, as a third and concluding article, an independent version of the *Liber de Partibus Animalium*, corresponding, as has been said, to books xi.-xiv. of the other versions which the volume contains. Bandini, in the printed catalogue of the library, asserts that this third translation, unlike the two which precede it, was made from the Greek. This is probably correct, as it was only the Greek text which treated these four chapters of the Natural History as a distinct work. He further ascribes the version to Michael Scot, relying no doubt on the general composition of the volume, for this particular translation does not seem to contain any direct evidence of authorship. Thus the

---

[1] p. 164.

[2] Pl. xiii. sin. cod. 9. Other MSS. of the *Abbreviatio Avicennae* are these : Fondo Vaticano 7096 ; Fondo Regina di Svezia 1151 ; Bibl. Burgensis 8557 in 8vo memb. saec. xiii. vel xiv. ; Bibl. Pommersfeld, saec. xiv. ; Paris, Anc. Fonds 6443 ; Venice, Bibl. St. Marc. 171 memb. saec. xiv. (the same library has another MS. in 4to memb. saec. xiv., see the Catalogue by Valentinelli, vol. v. p. 58). Bologna, Bibl. Univ. 1340 in fol. chart. saec. xiv. doubtful ; Oxford, Bodl. MSS. Canon. Misc. 562 saec. xiv. et xv. ; Merton Coll. MS. 277 saec. xiv. ; All Souls MS. 72 saec. xiv.

doubt expressed by Jourdain in this matter[1] is not without reason, though the balance of probability would seem to incline in favour of Bandini's opinion; for such a volume can scarcely be assumed to have been a mere miscellany without clear evidence that the contents come from more than one author. Taking it for granted then that the *De Partibus Animalium* came from Scot's pen, then this is the third form in which his labours on the Natural History of Aristotle appeared.

In any case, however, his chief merit in this department of study belonged to Michael Scot as the exponent of the Arabian naturalists. It is difficult for any one who has not read the books in question to form an adequate idea of their contents, and still more of their style; even from the most careful description. We are made to feel that the task of the translator must have been a very difficult one. There is a concentration combined with great wealth of detail, and withal a constant nimble transition from one subject to another, seemingly remote, under the suggestion of some subtle connection, which result in a style almost baffling to one who sought to reproduce it in his comparatively slow and clumsy Latin.

No greater contrast could be imagined than that which separates such works from those which are the production of our modern writers on the same subject. Nor does this difference depend, as one might suppose, on the fact that a wider field of observation is open to us, and more adequate collections of facts are at our disposal. Rather is it the case that between ancients and moderns, between the eastern

[1] *Recherches*, p. 133.

and western world, there is an entirely different understanding of the whole subject. A different principle of arrangement is at work, and results in the wide diversity of manner which strikes us as soon as we open the *De Animalibus* or the *Abbreviatio*. We find ourselves in the presence of a system of ideas, more or less abstract, which a wealth of facts derived from keen and wide observation of the world of nature is employed to illustrate. There is a finer division than with us. The unit in these works is not the species nor even the individual, but some single part or passion. This the author follows through all he knew of the multitudinous maze of nature, comparing and discerning and recording with a *bizarrerie* which comes to resemble nothing so much as the fantastic dance of form and colour in a kaleidoscope.

'Birds,' says Avicenna,[1] ' have a way of life that is peculiar to themselves. Those that are long-necked drink by the mouth, then lift their head till the water runs down their neck. The reason of this is that their neck is long and narrow, so that they cannot satisfy their thirst by putting beak in water and straightway drinking. There is, however, a great difference between different birds in their way of drinking, and the mountain hog loveth roots to which his tusk helpeth, wherewith he turneth up the ground and breaketh out the roots. Six days or thereabout are proper for his fattening, wherein he drinketh not for three, and there are some who feed their hogs and yet will not water them for perchance seven days on end. And in their fatten-

---

[1] P. 13, *recto et verso*, in the undated fifteenth century edition of the *Abbreviatio*.

ing all animals are helped by moderate and gentle exercise, save the hog, who fatteneth lying in the mud, and that mightily, for thereby his pores are shut upon him so that he loseth nothing by evaporation. And the hog will fight with the wolf, and that is his nature, and cows fatten on every windy thing, such as vetches, beans, and barley, and if their horns be anointed with soft wax, straightway, even while still upon the living animal, they become soft, and if the horns of ox or cow be anointed with marrow, oil, or pitch, this easeth them of the pain in their feet after a journey.'

In another place[1] he continues : 'Some animals have teeth which serve them not save for fighting, and not for the mastication of their food. Such are the hog and the elephant, for the elephant's tusks are of use to him in this matter as we have said. And there are animals which make no use of their teeth save for eating or fighting, nay, I believe that every animal having teeth will fight with them upon occasion, and some there are whose teeth are sharp and stand well apart, so that they are therewith furnished to tear prey : such is the lion. And those animals that have need to crop their food, as grass and the like, from the ground, have level and regular teeth, and not long tusks or canines, which would hinder them from cropping; and since in some kinds the males are more apt to anger than the females, tusks have been given them that they may defend the females, because these are weaker in themselves and of a worse complexion, and this is true in a general way of all animals, even in those kinds that eat no flesh,

---

[1] *Ibid.* pp. 33 *verso*, 34 *recto*.

and need not their tusks for eating, but only for defence, such as boars, and this is the reason why they have the strength of which we have just spoken. It is the same with the camel, and so we pass to speak of this general truth as it appears with regard to all other means of defence. Hence hath the stag his horn and not the hind; the ram and not the ewe; the he-goat and not his female, and fish which eat not flesh have no need of teeth that are sharp.'

The city where these strange writings were deciphered and translated into Latin, being itself so strange and remote from the ways of modern life, had a certain poetic fitness as the scene where Michael Scot undertook his labours upon the Arabian authors. No passage of all their texts was more bizarre and tortuous than the mass of intricate lanes which formed then, as they form to-day, the thoroughfares of communication in Toledo. No hidden jewel of knowledge and observation could surprise and reward the translator in the midst of his tedious labours with a flash of sudden light and glory more unexpectedly delicious than that felt by the traveller, when, after long wandering in that maze and labyrinth, he finds a wider air; a stronger light beats before him, beckoning, and in a moment he stands in the full sunshine of the *plaza mayor*, with space to see and light to show the wonders of mind and hand, and all the toil of past ages in the fabric of the great cathedral.

Such as it now stands, the Cathedral of Toledo had not yet begun to rise above ground when Michael Scot had his residence there, but enough of the ancient city remains to show what Toledo must have been like in these early days. The splendid and commanding site, swept about by the waves of the Tagus; the famous bridge of Alcantara; the steep slope of approach crowned by ancient fortifications; and above all the massed and massive houses of the old town, so closely crowded together as hardly to give room for streets that should rather be called lanes; all this, beneath the unchanging sky of the south, recalls sufficiently what must have been the surroundings of Scot's life during ten laborious years. Even yet, where white-wash peels and stucco fails, strange records of that forgotten past reveal themselves in the walls and on the house fronts: sculptured stones of every age; bas-reliefs, arabesques; windows in the delicate Moorish manner of twin arches, and a central shaft with carved cornices, long built up and forgotten till accident has revealed them.

Here then, perhaps in some house still standing, the scholar come from Sicily made his home. The quiet courtyard is forgotten; the *azulejos* have disappeared from walls and pavement; the rich wood-work of the ceilings, still bearing dim traces of colour and gold, looks down on the life of another age; even the curious cedar book-chest has crumbled to dust, for all its delicate defence of ironwork spreading away like a spider's web from hinges and from lock. But the name and the fame endure, and the years which Michael Scot spent in Toledo have left a deep mark upon that and every succeeding age.

CHAPTER IV

THE ALCHEMICAL STUDIES OF SCOT

THE Moorish schools of Spain were famous, not only for their researches in natural history, but also for the interest they took in chemistry, then called alchemy: a name which sufficiently indicates the nation which chiefly pursued these studies, and the language that recorded their progress. The practical turn taken by alchemy, as the foundation of a scientific *materia medica* in minerals, is shown by the writings of Rases. This author, who belonged to the ninth and tenth centuries (860-940), produced a considerable work on medicine in which he devoted special attention to the diseases of children. Under his name appeared several alchemical writings, either his own or the productions of the school which followed his teaching and borrowed his name.

Michael Scot, as we know, had become familiar with the works of Rases while still in Sicily, and thought so highly of the *De Medicina* as to borrow thence for his treatise on physiognomy no fewer than thirty-one chapters relating to that subject.[1] It is a natural conjecture then which leads us to find in his acquaintance with this author's writings the starting-point of Scot's interest both in

[1] See *ante*, p. 32.

E

medicine and in alchemy. Leaving for the present what may hereafter be said of his name and fame as a physician, let us examine the origin and nature of his work as a student of the Arabian chemistry. We have reached what would seem to be the proper moment for such an inquiry. The treatises of Michael Scot on this subject are not dated indeed, but their form shows them to belong to the epoch of his work as a translator. They were therefore probably produced during the period of his residence at Toledo, and as there is a long interval, otherwise unaccounted for, between 1210, when the *Abbreviatio Avicenna* appeared, and the date of his next publication some seven years later, this blank cannot be better filled than by supposing that it was during these years he found time for the study of alchemy, and for the translation or composition of the writings in that branch of science which still bear his name.

In this, as in almost all his other studies, Michael Scot sat at the feet of Eastern masters. But the Arabians themselves had derived their chemical science, at least in its first principles and primitive processes, from still older peoples. If we are to understand the progress of human thought in this science we must trace it from the beginning, following again that beaten track of tradition by which not physiognomy and alchemy alone, but almost all the secrets of early times, have reached the modern world.

Primitive chemistry was closely connected with the still older art of metallurgy, out of which it arose by a natural process of development. Those who worked with ores soon discovered the secret of

alloys, whereby a considerable quantity of baser
metal, such as copper, lead or tin, could be added
to gold or silver, so as greatly to increase the bulk
of the whole without injuring either its appearance
or usefulness. The problem of the crown set before
Archimedes, and happily solved by that philosopher
in the bath, shows how dexterously alloys were
used by the Greeks, and what subtle means were
necessary for their detection.

M. Berthelot has reminded us[1] that the transmission of receipts for such processes from early
times to our own has been naturally and inevitably
secured by the unbroken continuity of practice in
the arts which gave them birth, and that they thus
passed safely from generation to generation, and
even spread from the tribes that originated them to
other and distant peoples. He cites in support of
this observation a papyrus of the third century,
preserved at Leyden, which, he says, contains what
are substantially the same directions as those of the
chief mediæval authorities in such matters: the
Mappae Clavicula and the *Compositiones ad Tingenda*.[2] These receipts are not unnaturally entitled 'How to make Gold,' and it is curious to
find in them the veritable starting-point of the

[1] *La Chimie au Moyen Age*, Paris, 1893. One cannot praise too
highly the interest and value of this monumental work. I am greatly
indebted to it for many of the facts and conclusions here repeated.

[2] The *Mappae Clavicula* (Key to Painting) belongs to the tenth
century; the *Compositiones ad Tingenda* is of the age of Charlemagne.
A MS. of the eighth century (not the ninth as Berthelot says) is extant
at Lucca (Bibl. Capit. Can. I. L.). Muratori has printed it in his
Antiquitates Italicae, ii. 364-87. It contains receipts for the colours
used in making *tesserae* for mosaic, for dyeing skins, cloth, bone, horn
and wood; for making parchment; for various processes such as gold
and silver beating and drawing, and the gilding of iron; for chryso-
graphy and the gilding of leather; 'quomodo eramen in colore auri
transmutetur,' 'operatio Cinnaberim,' a perfume for the hands called
lulakin, and for certain amalgams of gold and silver called *glutina*.

dreams which made so many a furnace smoke, and
so many a crucible glow during the course of
centuries, in the vain hope of effecting an actual
transmutation of substance.

Thus it was that in the first ages, long before
authentic record, in the dimness of early Egyptian
history, or of that still more ancient Pelasgic civili-
sation from which the pyramid-builders learned so
much, the germs of this science may already be
perceived. Only one source of genuine gold seems
then to have been known : the mines of Ophir. This
circumstance, by making the supplies of precious
metal small and uncertain, mightily encouraged the
art which taught men to counterfeit its appearance
in a colourable way. How this was done may be
judged of by the receipts themselves. The *Mappae
Clavicula*, for instance, has the following : 'To
make gold. Silver, one pound; copper, half-a-
pound ; gold, a pound; melt, etc.' Here indeed a
considerable proportion of the precious metal itself
was required, but there are other receipts which
dispense with any such admixture. It is said, for
example, that one hundred parts of copper and
seventeen of zinc joined in a state of fusion with
divers small proportions of magnesia, sal ammoniac,
quicklime, and tartar, yield an alloy which is fine
in grain and malleable, which may be polished and
used in damascening just as if it were the pure
gold that it has all the appearance of being. Such
then were the receipts which formed the hereditary
riches of the mighty clan of the *Smiths*. It is easy
to see how the famous 'powder of projection,' so
much sought in later times, was, in fact, but the
transfiguration of one of these formulae.

When, during the early centuries of the Christian era, the traditions of Greece found a new home in lower Egypt, and especially in Alexandria, they were profoundly influenced by the still more ancient philosophy of the East. We have already remarked this in the case of another science, that of physiognomy, but the same influence may also be traced in the modification it brought to the notions of primitive chemistry. The Chaldæans and Persians had long believed that the heavens influenced the earth, and were capable of producing strange effects in the lower spheres of being.[1] Their wise men considered that an individual connection could be established between the stars and the elements, the planets and the metals. It was in contact with this new doctrine and under its influence that there arose the hope, soon hardening into a settled belief, that the rules of art might be sufficient to effect an actual transmutation of the baser into the nobler metals, of copper into gold, and of tin or lead into silver.

This opinion must have been immensely heightened, and its authority reinforced, by the secrecy with which the receipts for alloying metals were guarded. These were handed down orally from father to son ; were not committed to writing till a comparatively late period, and even then remained for the most part the cherished treasures of temple guilds. On the well-known principle of the proverb, ' Omne ignotum pro magnifico ' this secrecy tended to confirm the impression that, however much had been communicated,

---

[1] See Chwolson, *Die Ssabier und der Ssabismus.* The Egyptians extended this correspondence to the members of the human body.

more remained untold, to await discovery by the
patient and undaunted chemist. The Therapeutæ
or Essenes were among the earliest representatives of this new tendency, as appears from the
testimony of Josephus,[1] who describes them as not
only devoted to ancient writings, but eager to in-
vestigate the properties of minerals. The chief
object of their inquiries, the maintenance of health
by medicines thus derived from the vegetable and
mineral kingdoms, is not only an early instance of the
connection between chemistry and pharmacy, but is
remarkable as the probable starting-point of the
search for the elixir of life : that other and nobler
dream which so much of the enthusiastic energy
of the mediæval alchemists was spent to realise.

The point of connection between these speculations of Eastern philosophy and the practice of the
primitive chemistry may with probability be sought
in the fire which of necessity played so large a part
in the operations of the metal-worker. Fire bore a
highly sacred character in the philosophy and religion of the East. This element, it soon came to be
thought by those whom Eastern speculation influenced, might be trusted not only to melt, to
calcine and to sublime in the vulgar way, but to
form the long-sought link of sympathy between the
stars of heaven, themselves compact of fire, and the
elements of earth, as these were subjected to its
piercing and transforming power. In its due employment the suspected connection between the
higher and lower worlds would become an accom-

---

[1] Σπουδάζουσιν ἐκτόπως περὶ τὰ τῶν παλαιῶν συγγράμματα, μάλιστα
τὰ πρὸς ὠφέλειαν ψυχῆς καὶ σώματος ἐκλέγοντες. Ἔνθεν αὐτοῖς πρὸς
θεράπειαν παθῶν ῥίζαι τε ἀλεξητήριοι καὶ λίθων ἰδιότητες ἐνερευνῶνται.
—Bell. Jud., ii. 8. § 6.

plished fact.   Thus, under the power of the planets,
in some favourable hour and fortunate conjunction,
the mighty work would be done : the philosopher's
stone discovered, the metals transmuted, and the
elixir of life produced.

It is highly curious to find this idea presented in
a novel and perhaps an exaggerated form by a writer
of the sixteenth century.   This was Fra Evangelista
Quattrami of Gubbio, *semplicista*, or master of the
still-room, to the Cardinal d'Este.   He wrote a
book entitled, *The true declaration of all the
metaphors, similitudes, and riddles of the ancient
Alchemical Philosophers, as well among the Chaldeans and Arabians as the Greeks and Latins.*[1]
According to this work, the potable gold ; the elixir
of life ; the quintessence, and the philosopher's
stone were nothing but fantastic names for the fire
itself which was used in distillation and other
chemical operations.   In this the Frate may possibly
have touched the true sense of Al Kindi at least,
who, in his commentary on the *Meteora*,[2] speaks of
fire as if it were the all in all of the alchemist.

While the primitive chemical practice followed
the progress of the arts which it served, the new
theory of alchemy, with the ever-growing tradition
of fantastic experiments arising out of it, found
different and less direct channels in its descent from
ancient to modern times.   It has been customary
to speak of the Arabs as if that nation had been the
chief means of transmitting the knowledge of Greek
doctrine to our mediæval scholars, but we now

---

[1] *Roma, Vincentio Accolti*, 1587.   My copy is the one presented by
the author to the great Aldrovandus of Bologna, with whom he seems to
have been on intimate terms.
[2] See the Paris MS. 6514, pp. 133-35.

know that there was a previous link in the chain of intellectual succession. This was supplied by the care and industry of the Syrian subjects of the early Caliphs, nor did their learned men play a less important part in the history of chemistry than in that of the other sciences. Sergius of Resaina, a scholar of the fifth century, was, it is said, the first Syrian who attempted to translate the Greek chemists, several of whom mention him by name. The chief development of this work belongs, however, to the ninth and tenth centuries, and its glory must ever remain with the great school of Bagdad. Chemical treatises composed by Democritus and Zosimus [1] were there and then rendered into Syriac, as may be seen by the manuscripts still preserved in the British Museum and at Cambridge.

It was not long before the Arabs themselves began to feel powerfully the intellectual impulse thus communicated to them in the heart of a country which they had made their own. Khaled ben Yezid ibn Moauia, who died in the year 708, is said by their historians to have been the first of that nation who devoted his attention to chemistry. In his case the filiation of doctrine would seem very plain, as he was the pupil of a Syrian monk named Mariannos. Djabar, the *Geber* of Western writers, followed in the same line of study, and from the ninth century there was a regular school of Arabian chemists whose labours may be studied in the manuscript collections of Paris and Leyden.

In the eleventh century appeared a curious phenomenon, in the shape of a. dispute among the Arabians of that day regarding the truth of the

---

[1] Of Pannopolis, a chemist of the fourth century.

tradition which pronounced the transmutation of metals possible. The unwearied but still unavailing experiments which had now been carried on through several ages, produced at last their inevitable effect in the shape of philosophic doubt, eagerly urged on the one part and as eagerly repelled on the other. The chemical school was now divided according to these opposite opinions, and each party in their writings sought to give weight to what they taught by borrowing in support of their arguments the names of the mighty dead. In this conflict it was left to the followers of Rases to sustain the affirmative and to assert the possibility of transmutation. These were the apologists for the past, and the advocates, in the name of their great master, of that hope which had inspired previous research and borne fruit in so many important discoveries.

The defence of the new doubt belonged on the other hand to the school of Al Kindi. This chemist lived and died during the ninth century. He was probably the earliest Arabian commentator on Aristotle, and seems to have paid special attention to the *Meteora* of that author. The treatise *De Mineralibus*, so often appended to the *Meteora* as a supplement, is ascribed to Al Kindi in the Paris manuscript.[1] It represents the alchemy of the time.

Between these two contending parties stood the school of Avicenna, which now occupied an intermediate position and doubted of the doubt. That this had not always been the opinion of Avicenna himself is plain, however, from a passage which occurs in his *Sermo de generatione lapidum*, where

[1] 6514.

the author unhesitatingly pronounces against the theory of transmutation. 'Those of the chemical craft,' he says, 'know well that no change can be effected in the different species of things, though they can produce the appearance of them : tinging that which is ruddy with yellow till it looks like gold, and that which is white with colour at their pleasure till the same effect is in great measure produced. Nay, they can also remove the impurity from lead, so that it looks like silver, though it be lead still, and can endue it with such strange qualities as to deceive men's senses, and this by the use of salt and sal ammoniac.'[1] Avicenna was evidently well acquainted with the secrets of art and held them at their proper value. Had his followers in the eleventh century done the same they would have supported the school of Al Kindi instead of taking a less definite position.

This view of the later Arabian schools and their differences is forced upon us by the fact, that works are extant under the names of Rases, Al Kindi, and Avicenna, which evidently belong to the eleventh century, the period when they first appeared, and could not therefore have been written by authors who lived at an earlier date. They are plainly the production of later chemists who followed more or less intelligently the doctrine of these great masters in alchemy. The artifice involved in this ascription of authorship is one which has always been common in Eastern literature.

We have a direct interest in observing that Spain was the country where these developments

[1] Fondo Vaticano, 4428, p. 114. This treatise is the same as the *De mineralibus* published along with the *De Secretis* at Venice (? 1501) by Bernardinus de Vitalibus.

of the later Arabian chemistry arose, contended and flourished. Spain, therefore, during the eleventh and twelfth centuries, became, by the attraction she offered to European scholars, the country where these theories first reached the Latin races, and began to find an entrance among them. M. Berthelot indeed, by a happy citation, has enabled us to fix, almost with certainty, the very moment of this important event. Robert Castrensis, the author alluded to, remarks : 'Your Latin world has not as yet learned the doctrine of Alchemy.' These words are taken from the preface to this author's version of the *Liber de Compositione Alchimiae*, and a colophon informs us that the translation was completed on the 11th of February 1182. We may add that the same year, corrected, however, in one copy to 1183, was the date of another of these versions of the Arabian chemistry : that of the treatise called *Interrogationes Regis Kalid, et responsiones Morieni.*[1] Here then we stand on the threshold of a new age, and find ourselves in presence of an intellectual movement which was certainly of the greatest importance, since in it we may trace the origin of our modern chemistry. The knowledge of what had already been gained by Greek and Arabian alchemists was the first step to independent research among the Latins. The closing years of the twelfth century saw that knowledge at last beginning to unfold itself in a form intelligible to the Western schools.

As in Bagdad during the ninth century, the

---

[1] Speciale MS. No. vi. See the work by Sac. I. Carini, *Sulle Scienze Occulte nel Medio Evo*, Palermo, 1872. 'Kalid Rex' was Khaled ben Yezid ibn Moauia, and 'Morienus' was Mar Jannos, his Syrian master.

palmy period of Syrian studies, so in Spain three hundred years later, the work was in its commencement essentially one of interpretation, and the first age of these labours was distinguished by the number of versions which were then produced. From 1182, through the whole of the following century, students laboured in the translation of Moorish books on chemistry. Only towards the close of this period did a tendency become apparent which led in the direction of improvement and innovation. The seed already sown had begun to bear fruit. The material thus derived from Eastern sources was now treated with a new freedom, enriched by the results of original experiment, and edited in forms which betray the influence of scholastic philosophy. The criticism, however, which would determine the precise point when this change began to be operative, and the extent to which it proceeded, attempts what is perhaps an impossible and certainly a difficult task. For it is a remarkable fact that no Arabic texts have been preserved to us which can be regarded as the originals from which these earlier Latin versions were made. This want is probably due to the widespread destruction which overtook the Moorish libraries of Spain.[1] That such originals did at one time exist, however, is made certain by the correspondence which the Latin translations show with those which have come down to us in another language, the Hebrew. The labours of these Latin translators during a hundred years may be found in the manifold collections of chemical

---

[1] *Gayangos*, i. 8. Eighty thousand books are said to have been burned in the squares of Granada alone.

treatises, containing some forty or fifty articles apiece, which were arranged and copied out at the beginning of the fourteenth century. These volumes became, after the invention of printing, the chief quarry whence were composed the *Ars Aurifera*; the *Theatrum Chemicum* of Zetzner, and the *Bibliotheca* of Manget.

We are now in a position to understand, not only the nature and progress of the work in which Michael Scot took part, but the exact development which alchemy had reached in his day, and therefore the relation which his chemical publications bore to the general direction of study in this department of science. The time and care which our survey of the field has demanded need not be thought ill spent. It has prepared the way for a more intelligent appreciation of Scot's labours as a chemist, and has furnished us with the means of coming to a true judgment regarding their authenticity and value.

To put the matter to the proof: we may begin by dismissing altogether from consideration a treatise which has long been attributed to Scot, and still appears in the most recent list of his works: the *Quaestio curiosa de natura Solis et Lunae*. It has probably received more attention than it deserves since it appeared under Scot's name in the *Theatrum Chemicum*.[1] The subject

---

[1] In the editions of 1622 and 1659, Argentorati. It has been stated that the *Quaestio Curiosa* is a chapter taken from the *Liber Introductorius* of Michael Scot. The alternative title of that work, *Judicia Quaestionum* would seem to favour this idea, and may in fact have suggested it. But an examination of the *Liber Introductorius* (MS. Bodl. 266), which I have caused to be made, proves that the statement referred to is without foundation. It was advanced in a paper read before the Scottish Society of Antiquaries by Mr. John Small, and printed in their *Proceedings*, vol. xi. p. 179.

of this treatise is indeed an alchemical one; for the *sun* and *moon* of which it speaks are not these heavenly bodies themselves, but, by an allegorical use common in the Middle Ages, and derived from the Eastern theories of sympathy already mentioned, stand for the nobler metals of gold and silver. A brief examination, however, shows that Scot could not have been the author. The very style suggests this conclusion; for it is distinctly scholastic, and proper therefore to a later age than that which aimed at the direct and simple reproduction of Eastern texts. It is satisfactory to find that this criticism, hardly convincing *per se*, is fully borne out by what occurs in the substance of the work itself. The author quotes from the *De Mineralibus* of Albertus. Now Albertus Magnus, by common testimony, produced this treatise after the year 1240, and we may anticipate what is afterwards to be told of Michael Scot's death so far as to say here that he had then been long in his grave. The *De Natura Solis et Lunæ* then must be ascribed to some other and later alchemist, who lived in the end of the thirteenth or the beginning of the fourteenth century. A more careful examination of the treatise than has been necessary for our purpose might succeed in fixing its date with greater precision, and might possibly throw some light upon the person of its true author.

Another work ascribed to the pen of Michael Scot, and one which seems likely to be authentic, is that contained in the Speciale Manuscript. This volume is one of those collections of alchemical tracts made in the fourteenth century to which we have already alluded. It belonged to the library of the Speciale family in Palermo, and has been made the subject of an interesting monograph by Carini.[1] No. 44 of this manuscript is entitled *Liber Magistri Miccaelis Scotti in quo continetur Magisterium*. The term *Magisterium*, or supreme secret of art, would seem to carry with it a certain reference to Aristotle, 'Il *Maestro* di color che sanno,' as Dante calls him.[2] Curious as the appearance of such a name in connection with alchemy may seem to us, it is certain that Aristotle held a high place in the chemical traditions of the Middle Ages. The *Meteora* afforded a text which lent itself readily to large commentaries by the Arabian chemists. The tract *De Mineralibus*, which we noticed when speaking of Al Kindi, was one of these commentaries, and it is easy to see how it became confused with the text which it illustrated so as in time to be considered the work of Aristotle himself. This, we may believe, was the ground on which so many alchemical works were afterwards published under the same mighty name.[3] An interesting example appears in the Speciale collection itself which contains the following title : *Liber perfecti Magisterii Aristotelis qui incipit cum studii solertis indigere*.[4] The treatise *Cum studii* is also found in the Paris manuscript,[5] where it is ascribed to Rases. To the school of Rases then we are

---

[1] See the note to p. 75 *supra*.   [2] *Inf.* iv. 131.

[3] In the *Theatrum* of Zetzner there is a tract : 'Aristoteles de perfecto Magisterio,' and the Bibl. Naz. of Florence has a MS., 'De Tribus Verbis,' ascribed to the same author.

[4] Sic pro *indagine*, v. cod. xvi. 142 of the Bibl. Naz. Florence, where this treatise is given to *Alfidius*, *i.e.* Al Kindi. In it occur the significant words : 'est (alchimia) de illa parte physice quae *Metheora* nuncupatur.'

[5] No. 6514.

inclined to attribute the works on the *Magisterium*,
and among the rest therefore, this treatise in the
Speciale Manuscript, which bears the name of
Michael Scot, seemingly because he translated it
from the Arabic. This conclusion is confirmed
when we notice the character of some of the chapter
headings as given by Carini ; for example : ' Qualiter
Venus mutatur in *Solem* ' ; and again, ' Transfor-
matio *Mercurii* in *Lunam*.' These show beyond all
doubt that the doctrine which Michael Scot published by means of this version was that held by
the school of Rases.

A curious question here offers itself for our consideration. In the times of Robert Castrensis
alchemy was as yet unknown to the Latins.
Michael Scot, as we shall presently see, described it
in one of his works as meeting with but a poor
reception at its first introduction among them.[1]
How then did it come to pass that in a few years
the theory of Rases became so popular in the West,
and continued for so many ages to direct the progress of chemical study among the European nations
with enduring power ? We find the explanation of
this sudden change in the fact that human thought
has always been subject to the tyranny of ruling
ideas. In our own day the place of direction is
filled by a doctrine of development which is eagerly
made use of in every department of knowledge. In
those earlier ages the same place seems to have
been held by a doctrine of *transformation*. This
idea ruled the thoughts of men like an obsession, in
whatever direction they turned their minds. We
see it in their superstitions, suggesting the wild

[1] ' Penitus denegatam,' see *infra*, p. 89.

tales of were-wolves and of other animal forms assumed at will by wizard and witch. We find it in religion, infusing a new meaning into the hyperbolical language of still earlier times, till, under this direction, there came to be fastened upon the Church a full-formed doctrine of Transubstantiation.[1] It is the operation of the same idea then that we are to remark also in the scientific sphere. As soon as the first shock of their surprise was over, the Latins greedily embraced a theory of chemical change which related itself so naturally to the prevailing habit of their minds, and which promised to show as operative in the mineral kingdom a law already conceived to hold good in the world of organic life.

The Riccardian Library of Florence possesses another of those volumes to which we have already referred : a collection of alchemical treatises formed in the end of the thirteenth or beginning of the fourteenth century.[2] Among these appears one called the *Liber Luminis Luminum*. It is said to have been translated by Michael Scot, and, as there is no reason to doubt this ascription, we have now the means of determining with some fulness and accuracy the lines on which the philosopher proceeded in his chemical researches.

The book opens with a preface somewhat scholastic,[3] and one which, on this ground as well as on others, is probably to be ascribed to Scot himself.

---

[1] It is remarkable in this connection that 'Transubstantiation' was finally imposed on the faithful by the Lateran council of 1215. The term had not been previously used in theology. This was the very epoch of Michael Scot and of the introduction of alchemy in the West.

[2] MS. Ricc. L. iii. 13. 119, p. 35vo.

[3] 'In quo talia continentur, Intencio, Causa Intencionis et Utilitas,' etc.

F

In this part of the work he informs us that he took as his basis in the following compilation a text called the *Secreta Naturae*. To it he added material derived from other sources, which seemed necessary in order to complete the doctrine of chemistry contained in the *Secreta*. In this way he endeavoured to present his readers with a full and practical body of Alchemy according to the teaching of the school to which he belonged.

In the study of a composite work, such as the *Liber Luminis* is thus declared to be, our first problem is naturally to determine and separate the original text from the additions which have been made to it. Which then are those parts of the *Liber Luminis* that represent the *Secreta Naturae*? Very fortunately the volume where the *Liber Luminis* is found contains another treatise that throws considerable light on the matter. This is the *Liber Dedali Philosophi*. The correspondences between that book and the *Liber Luminis* are so many, close, and verbal, that it is evident both have borrowed from the same source. This source can hardly have been other than the *Secreta Naturae*, so that a comparison of these two books such as is attempted in the Appendix [1] should go far to determine what that hitherto unknown text was.

The question of the chemical doctrine contained in the *Secreta* is an interesting one, and we shall return to it, but meanwhile, let us observe that the *Liber Luminis* contains hints which seem to carry us further still, and throw some light upon the source from which the *Secreta* was itself derived. One of the authors quoted is a certain 'Archelaus.'

[1] See Appendix, No. III.

Now there was a veritable chemist of this name who lived during the fifth century. This author wrote a treatise on his art in Greek verse. In later times his name seems to have become common property, as did so many others distinguished in alchemy, and to have been freely used by some who wrote long after his day. Thus the Riccardian manuscript itself contains no less than three books ascribed to this author : the *Liber Archelai Philosophi de arte alchimiae*,[1] called also in the margin *Practica Galieni in Secretis secretorum*;[2] the *Summula*, 'quam ego Archilaus transtuli de libro secretorum';[3] and finally the *Mappa Archilei nobilis philosophi*.[4]

The fact that these titles mention the *Secreta* is enough to show us that in following up the alchemy of the Pseudo-Archelaus, we are on the right track. As we proceed the traces become still more interesting and significant. The *Summula* offers the following curious passage : 'Et hoc feci amore Dei et cuidam compatri meo, qui pauper sint [*sic*] et infortunatus, et postea fortunatus fortuna bona et amore Imperatoris Emanuelis et Frederici.'[5]

The name Emanuel is found in other alchemical writings. The *De Perfecto Magisterio*, for example,

---

[1] Pp. 192vo-195vo.

[2] The Paris MS. 6514 has these words : 'Magister Galienus scriptor qui utitur in Episcopatu est alkimista et scit albificare eramen ita quod est album ut argentum commune.'

[3] Pp. 190ro.-192vo.   [4] Pp. 185vo-190ro.

[5] Manuel Comnenus reigned as Emperor of the East from 1143 to 1180, while Frederick I. was Emperor of the West from 1152 to 1190. This would seem to indicate the twelfth century as the time when these works of the Pseudo Archelaus were produced. It is curious to notice that Manuel was the Emperor who suffered defeat by sea at the hands of George of Antioch the Sicilian admiral (Gibbon, chap. lvi.) This brave seaman was the same who founded the library of the Martorana in Palermo (see above, p. 25), and enriched it with the literary spoils of his conquests. It is highly probable that it was in this way the scholars of Sicily became acquainted with the Byzantine alchemy.

which has been reprinted by Zetzner, embodies another work, the *Liber duodecim aquarum* which is expressly said to be taken from the 'Liber Emanuelis.' Pursuing the matter further still, we come to the *Liber Aristotelis* which commences, 'Cum de sublimiori atque precipuo.' The author of this treatise, we find, claims not only the *Liber duodecim aquarum* ('quae qualiter se habeant in libro quem XII. aquarum vocabulo descripsimus, prudens lector intelligere poterit'), but also, it would seem, the very one of which we are in search ('in libro secretorum a nobis dictum est'). Everything inclines us to the belief that we here touch the source from which the main part of the *Liber Luminis* was drawn, and this conclusion is not a little strengthened when we observe that the treatise 'Cum de sublimiori' is called the *Lumen Luminum* in the Riccardian copy.[1]

The *Secreta*, however, was not the only source from which the *Liber Luminis* and the *Liber Dedali* were drawn, and the assertion of the preface that the former was composed of extracts from many different philosophers is fully borne out when we examine the substance of the books themselves. A strain of Greek influence is to be traced, for example, in the names of Archelaus, Dedalus, Plato, and Hermes, as well as in the use of *ciatus* as an equivalent for the word 'cup,' and this reminds us strongly of the *Summula* with its reference to the Emperor Manuel. It is not impossible that Scot may have borrowed much from the Byzantine chemists of the twelfth century. With this notion agrees the passage of the *Liber Dedali* where

_____
[1] MS. Ricc. L. iii. 13. 119. pp. 19vo.-29ro.

Saracens are spoken of as foreigners. On the other hand, much had evidently been taken from Arabic sources, as is plain from the names given to several of the vessels used in alchemy, such as the *alembic* and *aludel*. Indeed, Unay and Melchia, who are quoted in the *Liber Luminis*, must have been Moors, for the corresponding passage of the *Liber Dedali* describes them as from ' Lamacha of the Saracens.' Both these texts agree in showing such familiarity with the process of refining sulphur that one is led to suppose the *Secreta*, their common original, may have been composed in Sicily. The *Liber Luminis* says of one of the alums that it is ' brought from Spain :' an expression agreeing well with the notion of a Sicilian author, who would naturally speak of Spain as a foreign land.

Leaving, however, these questions of origin and derivation, let us come to that of the chemical doctrine taught in the book which Michael Scot compiled, or at least translated. The title of the *Liber Luminis Luminum* is a significant one, and has a real relation to the contents of the work itself.[1] To discover the sense which it must be held

---

[1] Titles resembling this are not uncommon in the literature of alchemy. Thus the Paris MS. 6514 has two treatises, both called *Lumen Luminum* and both ascribed to Rases. The latter of these, the *Liber Lumen Luminum et perfecti Magisterii*, is that which has been printed by Zetzner in the *Theatrum Chemicum*, under the name of Aristotle. It contains, as we have already observed, the *Liber XII. aquarum* and other material derived from the *Liber Emanuelis*. The former treatise bearing the name of the *Liber Lumen Luminum* in the Paris MS. (pp. 113-120) is remarkable on account of the words with which it closes : 'explicit liber autoris invidiosi,' which Berthelot notes, but does not attempt to explain. The *Mappa* of the Pseudo-Archelaus mentions the 'Liber invidiosus' ('quia liber iste invidiosus est ab omnibus hominibus'), but what may be the true reading of the matter is found in the *Liber Dyabesi* or book of the distillation of the land-tortoise (MS. Ricc. p. 4ro.) where these words occur : 'Omnia ista pondera fuerunt occulta a philosophis, et dederunt nobis alia pondera . . . quia fuerunt invidiosi,' *i.e.* unwilling to make public the secrets of their art. In later days the title *Lumen Luminum* is found in use by Raymond Lull and his school.

to bear we have only to turn to the passage in which, speaking of alum, the author says: 'sicut illuminat pannos, ita illuminat martem ut recipiat formam lunae. Ut enim lana illuminatur ita et metalla illuminantur.'[1] A distinction is clearly present in the writer's mind between the substance and the form of the metals. He probably held that there existed but one common metallic substance, which assumed the appearance of iron, gold, or silver, according to the form which it had received. His employment of the title *Liber Luminis Luminum* was meant to indicate that the purpose of his book was that of teaching the student how metals might best be purified and improved. Their inferiority, when of the baser kind, he conceived as an impurity, manifesting itself in the imperfect forms of lead, iron, tin, and copper. He believed that this being removed or changed by art, they might be made to shine with the lustre and indeed possess the only distinctive quality of gold and silver. That we have rightly read the meaning of this title seems plain from a curious spelling which may be noticed in the *Liber Dedali*. 'Illuminantur' there appears as 'aluminantur.' The chemistry taught in these books did in fact prescribe the use of alum as a great means of purifying and refining the metals.

The preface of the *Liber Luminis* closes with a brief summary of the chapters which compose the work itself. The first of these deals with the different salts used in this chemistry: common salt; rock salt; alkali; sal ammoniac; nitre and others. The second treats in like manner of the various

---

[1] *Liber Luminis Luminum*, ii. 1.

kinds of alum, the third describes the vitriols, and
the fourth the powders or spirits, by which we are to
understand those minerals which are capable of
being sublimed or made volatile, such as sulphur,
arsenic, and mercury. Two supplementary chapters,
the one on the preparation of the salts, alums, and
vitriols, and the other on that of the remaining
class of chemicals, complete the whole book. This
supplement seems genuinely such, as it is not mentioned in the general contents, as these appear in
the preface. Perhaps we do not err if we suppose it to have embodied the result of Scot's own
experiments in alchemy.

It is indeed the practical nature of the alchemical
doctrine taught in the *Liber Luminis* which strikes
us most strongly when we read this book. A large
part of it is taken up with exact descriptions of the
minerals, according to their various forms and the
countries from which they were derived. The rest
consists of receipts for their employment in refining
metals. Whatever we may think of the validity
and use of these processes, we cannot fail to notice
that they are described in a perfectly straightforward
and simple style. Here are none of the mysteries,
the riddles and ridiculous allegories so common in
chemical works written at a later time. The truth
of the matter may probably be that, in following
the doctrine here set forth, Michael Scot and the
alchemists of his time did obtain results which were
then so surprising, as to excuse a certain exaggera-
tion in those who described them. Tests that could
touch and reveal the real nature of the metals under
any change of outward appearance were not then so
well known as now. Copper that had been made to

shine like gold, or to assume the appearance of
silver, was practically gold or silver to those who had
no means of discovering that the real nature of the
metal itself remained unchanged. Thus then are to
be understood the assertions of the *Liber Luminis*
regarding transmutation. They are plainly made
in all good faith, and depend on the doctrine already
mentioned, which held that the differences between
the metals were an affair of the superficial form
rather than of the underlying substance. To
change the appearance of one metal to that of
another, was therefore to effect a real transmutation : the only one conceivable by the philosophers
of that time. When the *Liber Luminis* speaks of
giving copper ' a good colour,' or preparing iron to
' receive the appearance (*formam*) of silver,' these
expressions reveal with frank sincerity the conceptions of this alchemy and the results it endeavoured
to obtain.

One other alchemical work attributed to the pen
of Michael Scot remains to be noticed ; the *De
Alchimia,* contained in a manuscript of Corpus
Christi College, Oxford.[1] Tanner in his *Bibliotheca*
has noticed this work in the following terms :
' Chymica quaedam ex interpretatione Michaelis
Scoti dedicata Theophilo regi Scotorum. Corpus
Christi MS. 125. In eodem codice MS. fol. est haec
nota " Explicit tractatus magistri Michaelis Scoti
de aelchali," huius vero tractatus, a priore diversi,
hoc tantum fol. extat.' This account is erroneous
in several particulars. ' Scotorum ' should be
' Saracenorum,' and ' de aelchali ' is a misreading of
' de alkimia,' as a glance at the manuscript informs

[1] Corpus Christi MS. cxxv. pp. 116-119.

us. Nor is it the case that we have here to deal
with two distinct works. The last leaf, to which
Tanner more particularly refers (fol. 119, old
numeration), shows a hand of the fourteenth century,
and forms the only remainder of the original. The
rest of the manuscript (fol. 116-118) has been
supplied by a scribe of the fifteenth century, but
the whole is perfectly continuous, as appears plainly
when we notice that the first words of the original
(fol. 119 *recto*), 'et cum siccatus,' have also been
written by the later scribe at the bottom of page
118 *verso*.

In spite of the highly suspicious dedication,
'Theophilo Regi Saracenorum,' several reasons
incline us to regard the *De Alchimia* as, in substance at least, a genuine work of Michael Scot.
To begin with, it clearly belongs to a very early
period ; for, in the opening words of his preface,
the author describes alchemy as a science, noble
indeed, but as yet neglected and contemned by the
Latins ('apud Latinos penitus denegatam'). In
the same sentence we find him referring to the
secreta naturae, just as Scot does in the *Liber
Luminis*, and declaring his purpose to furnish the
world with a commentary on it in the work he now
attempts ('secreta naturae intelligentibus revelare').
In the opening paragraph of the book itself he
seems to refer plainly to the *Liber Luminis* as a
work written by him ('notitia de salibus vel salium
prout in aliquo libro a me translato dixi'). Nor
should we overlook the distinctly ecclesiastical tone
which is to be observed in the *De Alchimia*. Part
of the preface is conceived almost in the form of a
prayer, commencing thus : 'Creator omnium rerum

Deus qui cuncta ex nihilo condidit,' and in at least one passage, a well-known text of Scripture is reproduced ('et haec est res quae erigit de stercore pauperem et ipsum regibus equiparat'). This style is a noticeable characteristic of all the works of Michael Scot.

On the other hand, the *De Alchimia* shows several doubtful features which, on the supposition that it came from Scot's pen, can only have been due to some interference with the text at a subsequent time. Such is the dedication to Theophilus, King of the Saracens, which we have already noticed, and the latter part of the preface shows a turgid passage ('hic est puteus Salomonis et fimi acervus, et hic est fons in quo latet anguis cuius venenum omnia corpora interficit,' etc.) that strongly recalls the fancies of the later alchemy.

The body of the work, however, is no doubt genuine, and offers matters of considerable interest. The first of these is perhaps the distinction drawn here between the greater and the lesser mystery (magisterium) of alchemy. The former, it seems, was the transmutation of *Venus* into the *Sun*; that is, of copper into gold. The latter comprehended the fixation of mercury and its transmutation into the *Moon*, or silver.

We soon notice too that the author addresses himself not, as one would at first expect, to 'Theophilus,' but to a certain Brother Elias ('tibi Fratri Helya')—another proof, if any were needed, that the dedication to the apocryphal King of the Saracens was due to some other and later hand. 'Brother Elias,' however, was far from being a merely imaginary personage. He was an Italian,

born (for accounts vary) either at Bivillo near
Assisi, Cellullae or Ursaria near Cortona, or in Pied-
mont. In 1211 he joined the Order of St. Francis,
then just formed, thus becoming one of its earliest
members. His history as a Franciscan was rather
an eventful one. On the death of St. Francis
in 1226 he succeeded the Founder as General of
the Order, but was deposed by the Pope in 1230
on some suspicion that he favoured schism among
his brethren. The Order re-elected him in 1236,
but he was finally removed from office by Gregory
three years later, and profited by the occasion
to join himself openly to the party of the Emperor.
For this he suffered excommunication in 1244, and
was not restored to the privileges of the Church till
1253, when he lay on his death-bed at Cortona.
There is no doubt that he had the reputation of
possessing skill in alchemy, as a treatise is extant
called the *Liber Fratris Eliae de Alchimia*.[1] This
renown would not tend to his honour in religion.
It seems indeed to invest with a cruel and pointed
meaning the words used by the Pope on the
occasion of his first deposition.[2] He is said to have
been sent in early days on an embassy to the
Emperor of the East. Perhaps this may have been
the occasion when he first acquired a taste for those
chemical studies which that nation still pursued.
Michael Scot addresses him in the *De Alchimia* as a
pupil (' Et ego, Magister Michael Scotus, sum opera-
tus super solem, et docui te, Fr. Elia, operari et tu

---

[1] In MS. Ricc. L. iii. 13, 119, No. 37.
[2] See on the whole subject the *Annales Minorum* of Wadding,
especially vol. i. p. 109. In vol. ii. p. 242, we find the reproof addressed
by the Pope to Fra Elias. The words referred to above are these :
' mutari color optimus auri ex quo caput (*i.e.* Franciscus) erat compactum.'

mihi saepius retulisti te instabiliter multis viabus operasse'), while at the same confessing that he was not above learning some of the secrets of art from the well-known Franciscan. This relation between two such distinguished men has not hitherto been noticed, and is certainly a curious point in the history of the times.

The *De Alchimia* presents several features which distinguish it from the *Liber Luminis*. One of these is an early passage which refers to the correspondence between the metals and the planets, and explains that when the latter are named we must understand that the former are intended. Near the end of the treatise a description of the *materia chemica* occurs, but it would seem as if this had been written to supplement that given in the *Liber Luminis*, for it deals, not with salts, alums, vitriols, or volatile substances, but with the different varieties of what the author calls 'gummae,' which, however, are mineral substances ;[1] and with 'tuchia' in all its various kinds.

Many words and phrases, however, might be cited to show how the strain of doctrine observable in the *Liber Luminis* is continued with scarcely any change in the *De Alchimia*. We have hardly read a line in the first receipt before we meet with the expression 'sanguinem hominis rufi' recalling the 'sanguinem hominis rubei' of the *Liber Luminis*. The 'pulvis bufonis' indeed is here replaced by another ingredient derived from the animal kingdom, the 'sanguis bubonis'; but, reading a little further, we find the familiar 'urina taxi'

---

[1] For example, 'quaedam gumma quae invenitur in alumine de pluma, et ista gumma est rubea, et gumma quae invenitur in alumine rubeo et ista gumma est preciosa et bona valde.' The word becomes intelligible when read as 'gemma.'

again recommended as an almost universal solvent and detergent. Evidently both works proceeded from one and the same alchemical school. The number of Arabian chemists[1] cited in the *De Alchimia* seems to show that if these books came from a Greek source it was not that of ancient times, but some Byzantine school that had borrowed much from Eastern alchemists.

To give a substantial idea of the *De Alchimia* let us translate one of the formulae which it contains : 'Medibibaz the Saracen of Africa used to change lead into gold [in the following manner]. Take lead and melt it thrice with caustic ('comburenti'), red arsenic, sublimate of vitriol, sugar of alum, and with that red tuchia of India which is found on the shore of the Red Sea, and let the whole be again and again quenched in the juice of the *Portulaca marina*, the wild cucumber, a solution of sal ammoniac, and the urine of a young badger. Let all these ingredients then, when well mixed, be set on the fire, with the addition of some common salt, and well boiled until they be reduced to one-third of their original bulk, when you must proceed to distil them with care. Then take the marchasite of gold, prepared talc, roots of coral, some carcha-root, which is an herb very like the *Portulaca marina*; alum of cumae something red and saltish, Roman alum and vitriol, and let the latter be made red; sugar of alum, Cyprus earth, some of the red Barbary earth, for that gives a good colour; Cumaean earth of the red sort, African

---

[1] Such as 'Yader saracenus,' 'Arbaranus,' 'Theodosius saracenus,' 'Medibibaz,' and 'Magister Jacobus Judaeus.' The name of the place 'halaph' which is probably Aleppo, and of the herb 'carcha' point in the same direction.

tuchia, which is a stone of variegated colours and being melted with copper changeth it into gold; Cumaean salt which is . . . ; pure red arsenic, the blood of a ruddy man, red tartar, *gumma* of Barbary, which is red and worketh wonders in this art; salt of Sardinia which is like . . . Let all these be beaten together in a brazen mortar, then sifted finely and made into a paste with the above water. Dry this paste, and again rub it fine on the marble slab. Then take the lead you have prepared as directed above, and melt it together with the powder, adding some red alum and some more of the various salts. This alum is found about Aleppo ('Alapia'), and in Armenia, and will give your metal a good colour. When you have so done you shall see the lead changed into the finest gold, as good as what comes from Arabia. This have I, Michael Scot, often put to the proof and ever found it to be true.'

If such a receipt is valuable as indicating the chemical practice of those days, it is no less interesting as it throws light upon the life and occupations of Scot. He must have set up a complete chemical laboratory at Toledo, with crucibles for the melting of metals, and alembics for the distillation of the substances which his art required him to mix with them. His situation was one very favourable to these pursuits, not only because Spain was one of those countries where the doctrine of alchemy made its greatest progress, and attracted most powerfully the concourse of foreign adepts, but also from the facility with which the necessary *materia chemica* could there be procured. The *sierras* of that country were full of mineral wealth of all kinds, especially quicksilver, which was one

of the substances most frequently chosen to become
the subject of the transmuter's art. In the *Alpu-
jarras*, a mountainous district lying under the soft
climate of Granada, grew plenty of these rare herbs
employed in alchemy, as they were also in the
medicine of the Arabians. Ibn Beithar of Malaga
describes them in his botanical thesaurus, and
it is said that after the Moors had lost that fair
kingdom their herbalists, even as late as our
own times, made yearly journeys from Africa to
gather in these hills the plants which ancient
science taught them to value highly. But the
days of the ' ultimo sospiro del Moro ' were yet in
the far future, and meanwhile Michael Scot in his
laboratory at Toledo could easily command all these
treasures for the purposes of experiment. Nor was
it in vain that he fanned his fires, and watched the
metals melt and the menstruum distil in the process
of the lesser or greater mystery. If he never saw
Venus blush into the true substance of *Sol*, or
Mercury, the fickle and obstinate, congeal into
a veritable *Luna*, his chemical practice, and the records in which he has embodied it, mark none the
less true and significant a moment in the history
of scientific progress.

CHAPTER V

THE alchemy of the thirteenth century, to the progress of which Michael Scot contributed not a little, bore a close relation to the opinions then entertained in another branch of science : that of astronomy. We have already noticed how chemistry, as practised in Egypt, was largely influenced by Eastern theories regarding the stars and their power over earthly elements. That this connection and sympathy was still a matter of common belief at the time Scot wrote is not only probable but can readily be established by direct evidence. The treatise ' Cum studii solertis indagine,' already referred to,[1] has a curious passage which bears directly on the point in question. We find in the preface the following remarkable statement : ' For the art of alchemy belongs to the deeper and more hidden physics, and in particular to that division thereof which . . . is called the lower astronomy.' It is plain then that no chemist could in those days be considered fully competent for the task he undertook unless to a knowledge of the customary theories and processes of his art he added some acquaintance with the mysteries of the heavenly spheres as well.

To Michael Scot, even before he came to

---

[1] Bibl. Naz. Flor. MS. xvi. 142, see *supra*, p. 79.

Toledo, the science of astronomy was already a beaten path. His progress in mathematical studies naturally led him to this, the highest sphere in which they could be exercised. At the court of Frederick he had made many an observation and cast many a horoscope. In the *Liber Introductorius* and *Liber Particularis* he had produced two manuals expounding in a popular way the twin sciences of astrology and astronomy; publications which no doubt reproduced pretty exactly the teaching he had given to the Emperor.

In Spain he not only kept up his interest in this subject but lost no opportunity of improving his past acquirements. He was constantly on the watch for new astronomical works. He read them, not only as a student eager to extend his knowledge, but as a translator anxious to find the opportunity of adding to the resources of other scholars by the production of some important book in a Latin dress.

As a resident in Toledo, Scot found himself very favourably situated for such studies. That city was now indeed to become what may be called the classic ground of Moorish astronomy. A Spanish author would have us believe that there presently assembled there an incredible number of astronomers drawn, not only from all parts of Spain, but from France as well, and especially from Paris. The king himself is said to have presided over this congress. The works of Ptolemy, with the commentaries of Montafan and Algazel, were translated into Latin for the use of those scholars who did not understand Arabic. Discussions were held in the Alcazar of Galiana upon the various theories of the heavenly bodies and their movements. These labours, which commenced in 1218, and are said to have lasted till 1262, resulted in a more exact series of observations than had hitherto been made. They were published, and became generally known as the *Tables of Toledo*.[1]

It was in such a direction indeed that the line of true progress lay. As alchemy rose into a real chemistry rather by the practice of the laboratory than by the theory of the schools, so it was with regard to astronomy. The scheme of Ptolemy with its various modifications necessarily held the field, imperfect and erroneous as it was, till wider and more exact observations, such as those for which the wise king of Castile thus provided had, in the course of after ages, furnished adequate ground for the magical and illuminative speculations of Copernicus, Galileo, and Newton.

Favourable, however, as Scot's situation in Toledo undoubtedly was, much of what we are considering lay beyond his reach, being yet in the womb of the future. The Moorish astronomers, and he doubtless with them, felt far from satisfied with the Ptolemaic system as expounded in the *Almagest*. While no one as yet ventured to interfere with its fundamental conception of the earth as the centre of the universe, every fresh observation, by bringing into view more of the delicacy and subtlety of the heavenly movements, made additions and modifications of that theory constantly necessary. Hence arose a series of Arabian works on the *sphere*, each superseding that which had preceded it, and reflecting the last results

---

[1] Romanus de Higuera, a very doubtful authority.

obtained with the astrolabe. Such a line of progress could not but lead to the time when the Ptolemaic theory no longer lent itself by any modification to the full explanation of ascertained facts. Then and then only arose the new astronomy of the sixteenth and seventeenth centuries, which is thus seen to be vitally connected, even in its highest reach and most splendid developments with the now forgotten theories of the Moorish schools.

Considering then the epoch at which he lived, and the incomplete material which existed in his days for a true science of the heavens, Michael Scot did all that could be reasonably expected of him. He sat at the feet of those who were then the best authorities on this subject. He used his opportunities at Toledo to make the last and most subtle theories of the Moors intelligible to those less fortunate scholars whose attention these must otherwise have escaped.

His services to astronomy appeared in the Latin version which he made from a treatise on the *Sphere* lately composed by Alpetrongi. This author's name is said to have been, in its Arabic form, Nur-ed-din el Patrugi. Munk, in his *Mélanges*, tells us that the latter designation was derived from a village called Petroches lying a little to the north of Cordova.[1] The Latins corrupted the name in different ways, so that among them it became *Avenalpetrandi*, *Alpetrongi*, or *Alpetragius*. The astronomer who bore it flourished about the year 1190, and is said to have been a renegade, and a

[1] This village gave name to another Moorish writer, Abu Gafar Ahmed ben Abd-el-Rahman ben Mohammed, also surnamed el Bitraugi. He died in 1147 and his fame survives as that of the author of an encyclopedia of science.

scholar of the celebrated Ibn Tofail, the author of the curious Sufic romance called *Hay Ibn Yokhdan*.

In the preface to his book on the *Sphere* Alpetrongi begs to be excused if he has ventured to differ from the tradition of the ancients in his theory of the heavenly movements, and especially from Ptolemy the great master of this science. His apology reminds us that it may be well to examine more exactly than we have yet done the various advances which had been made up to this time by the Arabian astronomy.

As early as the ninth century the mathematicians of that nation had simplified the problems of the circle by discovering the way of measurement by sine and tangent instead of by the chord. This improvement is ascribed to Albategni who lived between the years 877 and 929. Calculation was soon made still easier by the invention of algebra. The year 820 is given as the age of Mohammed ben Moussa, surnamed Al Khowaresmi, who had the honour of this important discovery. From the surname of this mathematician the Latins afterwards formed by corruption their common noun *Algorisma* or *Algorithmus*, from which our word arithmetic is derived.

These improved methods of calculation were soon applied to astronomy. Al Mamun, whose reign commenced in the year 813, summoned an assembly of scholars learned in that science. They met in the great Babylonian plain, having chosen that place as suitable for their observations, and measured the declination of the ecliptic, which they determined to be 23° 33″. About the same time the secular motion of the heavens began to attract attention. Albategni corrected the observations of Ptolemy here, and showed that the retrograde movement amounted to one degree, not in a century as the Greek philosopher had said, but in a shorter period which is variously stated as sixty-six or seventy years. Alfargan repeated this calculation, and amended that relating to the declination of the ecliptic, which he computed at 23° 35".

This was the progress and these the data which led the Moorish astronomers to abandon the earlier and simpler theories of the *sphere* as inconsistent with ascertained facts. They were aware of motions among the heavenly bodies not to be explained by the mere supposition that round the earth as a centre moved the concentric spheres on the axes of their poles. It is true that even Ptolemy himself had felt something of this difficulty and had endeavoured to meet it by a theory of eccentrics and epicycles. As knowledge increased, however, this primitive explanation was felt to be cumbrous and unsatisfactory. Aboasar[1] and Azarchel gained fame by boldly striking out in new paths, and later Moorish astronomers eagerly followed the lead thus given them, each adding some modification of his own.

Thus then we return to the preface of Alpetrongi prepared to understand his position when he declares himself obliged to depart from previous traditions. He proceeds to avow himself a scholar of Azarchel, but when we examine his work we find that the theory he proposes differs considerably even from that taught by his immediate master.

---

[1] For the unfavourable judgment of Mirandola on this astronomer, see *infra*, p. 143.

It was one which, through the labours of Michael
Scot, as translator of Alpetrongi, exercised no small
influence on the study of astronomy among the
Latins, and we may well spend a moment in considering the chief features which it presents.

One of the most important problems which
called for solution at the hands of the Moorish
astronomers was that of the recession of the
heavenly bodies, by which, when observed at
sufficient intervals of time, they were seen to fall
short of the positions they might have been
expected to reach. This recession, as we have
remarked already, had been very accurately studied,
and computed as exactly as the methods of the
time allowed; but a reason for so remarkable a
phenomenon was yet to seek. Alpetrongi boldly
declared that the eastward motion was apparent
only and not real. He explained that the source
of power lay in the *primum mobile* or ninth sphere;
that lying outside the sphere of the fixed stars.
From hence the force producing circular motion
was derived to the eighth, and so to the inferior
spheres; each handing on a part of the impulse
to that which lay beneath it. In the course of
transmission, however, the prime force became
gradually exhausted. Thus, said Alpetrongi, it
happens that each sphere moves rather more
slowly than the one above it, and so the apparent
recession is accounted for in a way which shows it
to be relative only and not absolute.

Another matter which exercised the minds of
those who studied the heavens was the difference
of elevation which the heavenly bodies showed
according to the seasons of summer and winter.

The sun, for example, at noonday of the summer solstice stood, they saw, at his highest point in the heavens, while he sank to his lowest on the shortest day of winter. Between these extremes he held gradually every intermediate position, and as he was meanwhile supposed to be moving in a circular path round the earth, his course came to be conceived of as a spiral alternately rising and declining. How was this spiral motion to be explained?

Each sphere, said Alpetrongi, has its own poles, which differ from those of the *primum mobile*, and thus each, while following the motion of the ninth sphere, accomplishes at the same time another revolution about its own proper poles. From the combination of these two movements arises one of the nature of a spiral which fully accounts for the seeming deviations of the heavenly bodies to north or south.[1]

Such were the contributions of this philosopher to the astronomy of his time. They were the fruit, he assures us, of patient study of the ancients, and specially of Aristotle and his commentators. He offered them to his age as a distinct improvement on the cumbrous theories of Ptolemy, and as an advance even upon that of Azarchel, whom, in the main, he acknowledges as his master in science. Antiquated and childish as his explanations may seem to us, we cannot help feeling that he had at least grasped firmly some of the chief problems of the sky. He stood in the line of that inquiry and patient progress which have issued in the marvellous discoveries of later times.

Scot's version of the *Sphere* of Alpetrongi has

[1] See the excellent account in Munk.

reached us accompanied by the date of its composition ; a distinction which belongs to only one
other among his translations, that of the *Abbreviatio
Avicennae*. M. Jourdain had the merit of being
the first who drew attention to this fortunate
circumstance,[1] and he did so by quoting the colophons of two manuscripts of the *Sphere* discovered
by him in the Paris library.[2]   One of these closes
thus : ' Praised be Jesus Christ who liveth for ever
throughout all time:[3] on the eighteenth day of August,
being Friday, at the third hour, *cum aboleolente*,[4]
in the year one thousand two hundred and fifty-
five.' The other gives the date thus : ' The year of
the Incarnation of Christ twelve hundred and
seventeen.' These two epochs coincide exactly, as
the apparent difference arises from the date being
expressed in the first manuscript according to the
era of Spain.   It is therefore doubly certain that
Scot's version of the *Sphere* of Alpetrongi was made
in the year 1217.[5]

In completing this translation Michael Scot
anticipated by one year only the great astronomical congress which the King of Castile presently
caused to assemble at Toledo.   It may very possibly
therefore have been one of the versions prepared
with a view to this great occasion and designed for
the use of the Latin astronomers who might come

---

[1] *Recherches*, p. 133.

[2] These are *Ancien Fonds* 7399 and *Fonds de Sorbonne* 1820.

[3] ' Qui vivit in aeternum per tempora.'

[4] There is a copy in the Barberini library (ix. 25 in fol. chart. saec.
xv.) which reads ' cum abuteo leñite.'   Another at Paris, MSS. lat. 1665
(olim Sorbonicus) has ' c. Abuteo Levite.'   It would be rash to conjecture the sense of this curious phrase.   It is evidently a sign of time,
and perhaps astrological

[5] The Barberini MS. (ix. 25) gives 1221 as the date of the version,
but the consensus of the other copies shows this to be a mistake.
Almost all the MSS. mention that the work was done at Toledo.

there. Certain it is that the author was not less fortunate in this than in his previous literary ventures. The text was well chosen, the time of publication opportune, and the *Sphere* of Alpetrongi as it came from Scot's hand had a wide circulation and influenced profoundly the astronomical beliefs of the day.[1]

[1] See the references made to this work of Scot by Albertus Magnus and Vincent of Beauvais.

CHAPTER VI

SCOT TRANSLATES AVERROËS

WE have already noticed how the commentaries of Avicenna on Aristotle had been translated into Latin at Toledo during the twelfth century, and how Michael Scot had completed that work by his version of the books relating to Natural History. Since the beginning of the thirteenth century, however, another Arabian author of the first rank had become the object of much curiosity in Europe. This was the famous Averroës of Cordova, whose history might fill a volume, so full was it of romantic adventure and literary interest.[1] He was but lately dead, having closed a long and laborious life on the 10th of December 1198, at Morocco, where his body was first laid to rest in the cemetery outside the gate of Tagazout. Born at Cordova in 1126, his name was closely associated with that of his native city, so that after three months had elapsed his corpse was brought thither from Africa, and given honourable and final burial in the tomb of his fathers at the cemetery of Ibn Abbas.

Two reasons combined to raise the fame of Averroës among the Latins, and to inspire them with a high curiosity regarding his works. He was

---

[1] For the life and opinions of Averroës, see the excellent monograph *Averroës et l'Averroïsme*, which Renan published at Paris in 1866. I have drawn largely upon it in composing this chapter.

known to have devoted his life to the study and exposition of Aristotle ; then, as for many ages, the idol of the Christian schools. His philosophy was further understood to embody the strangest and most daring speculations regarding the origin of the universe and the nature of the soul. For these he had suffered severely at the hands of the Moslem orthodox. They had proscribed his works and compelled him to leave his employment and pass the most precious years of his life in exile.

These common impressions regarding Averroës were in the main correct. His labours had appeared in three forms ; a paraphrase, and a lesser and greater commentary on the books of Aristotle, and the philosophy which these writings contained was undoubtedly Manichæan, if not in a measure Pantheistic. Like that of all the Arabian philosophers, to whose teaching Averroës gave its final and most characteristic form, this doctrine was really Greek : the Aristotelic scheme of the universe as it had been conceived anew by Porphyry of Alexandria. At the foundation lay a mighty Duality : that of the opposing powers of Good and Evil. With the notion of exalting Him above the possibility of blame, God, the Centre of the Universe, about whom all revolves, was declared to be the Absolute and unconditional Being ; while over against Him was set Matter, also eternal, from which, in its stubborn resistance to the Divine Will, all evil had arisen. Any direct action of Deity upon matter could not be thought of; so the interval between them was conceived of as occupied by several Emanations proceeding from God, among which we may notice those of the Divine Wisdom and the

Divine Power. This Wisdom was said to be impersonal; one common to all intelligent creatures; the Light that lighteneth every man that cometh into the world. This Power was regarded as supreme, seated high above the spheres, and, through the *Primum Mobile*, entering into touch with matter and deriving its force downward from one heavenly circle to another till it reaches earth itself.

The origin of created beings was a problem which received much attention from Averroës. His ideas on this subject will be seen when we come to speak of the important digression he wrote under the title of *Quaestiones Nicolai Peripatetici*.[1] In every man he perceived the existence of a passive intellect or reason, in relation to which the other Heavenly Intelligence, or Divine Wisdom, presented itself to him as the Active Reason: that in whose motions Thought was always accompanied by Power. The one was Impersonal and Eternal, the other individual and perishable, yet Averroës taught that a close relation subsisted between them, and a consequent sympathy and attraction, in which the passive intelligence strove to unite itself with the active and thus achieve eternity and immortality.[2]

This union was known as the *ittisal* : the supreme object of the wise man's desire, and in connection with it emerged for the first time a distinction between Averroës and his predecessors. Ibn Badja, with whom he held the closest relation, had pro-

---

[1] See *infra*, p. 128. Nicolas Damascenus was born B.C. 64.
[2] This was purely Alexandrian doctrine : 'enseñaron Plotino, Porfirio y Iamblico, que, en la union extatica, el alma y Dios se hacen uno, quedando el alma como aniquilada por el *golpe intuitivo*.' Pelayo, *Heterodoxos Españoles*, vol. ii. p. 522.

posed a course of moral discipline as the best way
of attaining the *ittisal*: the same ascetic practice
which Ibn Tofail so remarkably illustrated and commended in his mystical romance *Hay Ibn Yokhdan*.
Gazzali on the other hand, who was the sceptic of
these schools, boldly declared that the *ittisal* was
only to be reached by an intellectual and spiritual
confusion attained in the *zikr*, or whirling dance of
the Dervishes. It was left then for Averroës to
vindicate once more the validity of human reason,
and this he did by proclaiming that science, rightly
understood, was the true way of entering into intellectual communion with the Deity. All, however,
agreed in teaching that the soul of man was but
an individual and temporary manifestation of the
Divine, from which it had proceeded, and into
which it would again be absorbed.

It is plain that the way to this consummation
proposed by Averroës had much in common with
the ancient theories of the Alexandrian Gnosis.
The Albigenses and other sects of the time,
especially that called the Brotherhood of the Holy
Ghost, had already done much to familiarise the
West with these essentially Eastern speculations.
A taste for such flights of the mind had been
formed, and, as soon as it became known that a
new teacher had arisen to advocate a theory of this
kind among the Moors, Christianity too was alive
with curiosity to know what the doctrine of Averroës
might be.

In these circumstances the anathema of the
Church proved powerless to restrain so strong an
impulse of the human spirit. The Council of Paris
in 1209 had sounded the first note of warning and

of censure. In 1215 Robert de Courçon published a statute in that university by which the name of *Mauritius Hispanus*, understood by Renan to mean Averroës, was associated with those of David of Dinant and Almaric of Bena the French Pantheists of the day, and all men were warned to have nothing to do with their writings under pain of censure. In spite of these enactments five years had not passed since the date of the latter proclamation, before the commentaries of Averroës were rendered into Latin and the secrets of his remarkable philosophy laid open to the scholastic world.

The credit of this bold and successful enterprise belongs, it would be hard to say in what proportions, to the Emperor Frederick II. and to Michael Scot his faithful servant. Frederick had indeed every reason to feel an interest in the works of Averroës. His mind was naturally keen and of a speculative cast. He showed little inclination to subject his curiosity to the restraints of custom or ecclesiastical authority, and was thus at least as likely as any of the wise and noble of his day to indulge his passion for what promised to be both original and curious. We are to remember also that he stood in close relation with the peculiar religious opinions already noticed, which were then so prevalent both in south-eastern France and the adjoining parts of Spain. His brother-in-law, who died so suddenly at Palermo, was Count of Provence, and, whatever place the unfortunate Alphonso may have held with regard to the heresy so common in his dominions, we may feel sure that among the host of Provençal knights who formed his train when he came to Sicily there must have been some at least who were adherents of the Albigensian party. No religious opinion ever made so striking a progress among the wealthy and noble as this, and none was ever commended in a way more fit to win the sympathy and interest of a youthful monarch inclined to letters and gallantry. The doctrine of the Albigenses was in fact a late revival of the *Gnosis* of Alexandria. It flattered the pride of those who desired distinction even in their religion. Its representatives and advocates were no repulsive monks or sour ascetics but men of birth and breeding, who excelled in manly exercises, and were famous for their success in the courts of love and in the *gay saber*. It would not have been wonderful if Frederick himself had become an Albigensian. He is known to have caught a taste for Provençal poetry if nothing more, and it is certain that he remained, to the close of his life, and even beyond it, a grateful and sympathetic figure among those who, after the great persecution, still represented Albigensian doctrine.[1] Something of this may have been due to the influence of his wife Constantia, whose father, Don Pedro of Aragon, had fallen gallantly in 1213 under the walls of Murel, during an expedition in which he led the Spanish chivalry to aid the

---

[1] Albertus Stadensis speaks of a heretical sect which appeared at Halle in 1248. They abused the clergy, the monastic orders and the Pope, but their preachers exhorted them to pray for the Emperor Frederick and his son Conrad, *qui perfecti et justi sunt.* Among the Albigenses and Cathari generally the word *perfecti* was used in a technical sense to indicate those who had been received into complete fellowship as opposed to the *credentes* who were still on probation. As applied therefore to the Emperor and his son it would seem to indicate at least certain leanings to these opinions on Frederick's part. This might explain the action he certainly took in trying to detach the Sicilian clergy from the see of Rome and to set up a national or imperial church in which he pretended to the earthly headship.

Counts of Toulouse and Foix the champions of the Albigensian party.

The probability that the Emperor had early felt an interest in Averroës is confirmed by a curious statement of Gilles de Rome,[1] who tells us that the sons of the Moorish philosopher received a cordial welcome from Frederick and lived in honour at his Court. Renan indeed finds reason to doubt the truth of this statement,[2] yet we may remember that the chronicler could not in any case have ventured upon it unless the Emperor's sympathy for Averroës had been matter of common knowledge.

As to Michael Scot we may feel sure that he was every whit as eager as his master could be to honour the philosopher's memory and to gain a nearer acquaintance with his writings. The manuscript in the Laurentian library to which we have already referred[3] speaks, it will be remembered, of a visit paid by Scot to the city of Cordova. It is not difficult to determine with a high degree of probability the reason that may have led him thither. Had he lived three hundred years earlier indeed, the fame of Cordova as a centre of learning might well have proved a sufficient attraction to account for this journey. In the tenth century that city shone as the seat of a great Jewish school: one of those lately transferred to Spain from the eastern cities of Pombeditha and Sura. The Caliph Hakim, under whose protection this change took place, gave royal encouragement to the learned men who came to Cordova. Thousands of students assembled

[1] *Opera*, p. 102.
[2] *Averroës*, pp. 28, 254, 291.   [3] See *ante*, p. 18.

in the great Mosque, and Hakim collected for their use a magnificent library which was said to contain four hundred thousand volumes. Al Mansour, however, who succeeded to Hakim's throne, fell under the influence of orthodox scruples. He burnt much of the great library, and the rest perished at the disastrous sack of Cordova in the following century. The ruin of the Rabbinical academies was completed a little later by the cruel edict of Abd-el-Mumen, who expelled the Jews from his realm. The most famous teachers of Cordova and Lucena then betook themselves to Castile. Alphonso VII. received them kindly and gave them liberty to settle in his capital. These events took place before 1150, and from that date the ancient schools which had given such fame to Cordova and Lucena became one of the chief attractions of Toledo.

The sole glory which Cordova still retained in the days when Scot visited it was the memory of departed greatness, and of Averroës, whose fame must yet have endured as a living tradition in the place of his birth and burial. We may therefore believe that it was as a pilgrim to the shrine of that illustrious name that the traveller came hither. As he wandered amid the countless columns of the great Mosque, or stayed his steps by the tomb of Ibn Abbas, he must have found a melancholy pleasure in recalling the mighty past, when these aisles were crowded with eager students and when, still later, the last scion of the Cordovan schools had appeared in the person of the Master whose writings were now the object of so much curiosity. It is quite possible that something of a practical purpose may have combined with these sentiments

H

to determine the direction of Scot's journey. Twenty years had not passed, we must remember, since the body of Averroës was laid in its last resting-place. What if those who directed and composed the solemn funeral procession from Morocco to Cordova had brought with them the books which the philosopher was engaged in completing at the time of his death? The hope of a great literary discovery could hardly have been absent from the mind of Michael Scot as he travelled southward to seek the white walls of the Moorish city.[1]

There is no reason to think that the story of the spell framed by Scot at Cordova was literally and historically true ; it seems to belong rather to the department of his legendary fame as a necromancer. Yet, read as a parable, this conjuration is not without interest and perhaps importance. It professes to compel the appearance of spirits from the nether deep, and to command an answer to any question the sage or student might choose to ask. A slight effort of fancy will find here the picturesque representation of Scot's mental and physical state while at Cordova, and especially under the stress of the illness from which we are assured he then suffered.[2] What wonder if, in the vertigo of fever, he felt prisoned with swimming brain in magic circles ; or is it strange that one so intent upon the doctrine of the departed Averroës should, in the height of his delirium, have planned to force

---

[1] This inquiry was afterwards interpreted to Scot's disadvantage and in a way that heightened his necromantic fame. See *infra*, ch. ix.

[2] See Appendix, No. i. Averroës had maintained in opposition to Galen that the best of all climates was that of the fifth terrestrial region : that in which Cordova was situated.—*Colliget*, ii. 22. Michael Scot can hardly have shared this opinion.

the grave itself, and summon the dead philosopher to tell the secret of his lost works? Something of the Greek δεινότης, something terrible, superhuman almost, we discover in a spirit so fully roused and determined, and if we have read rightly the mind of Scot, no wonder that he and the Emperor were fully at one in regard to what they had to do. We have no means of knowing which of the two first conceived the idea of translating the works of Averroës: as master and servant they fairly share the fame of that great enterprise. It was one which demanded, not only means, talent, and unwearied labour, but high courage as well, considering the suspect character of that philosophy and the censures under which it already lay. In the event indeed this proved to be a matter highly creditable to those who promoted it, but one which carried serious and far-reaching consequences both for Michael Scot and for the Emperor himself in the ecclesiastical and political sphere.

When Scot returned to Toledo it was not with the purpose of attempting single-handed a task for which not only time, but the co-operation of several scholars, was evidently necessary. There is reason to think that the Emperor's commission conveyed some instruction to this effect; for, as a matter of fact, we know that at least two other hands were associated with Scot in the translation of Averroës.

One of these was Gerard of Cremona, not of course the Cremonese who died in 1187, but the younger scholar of the same name, perhaps a son or nephew of the elder. He is distinguished as Gherardus *de Sabloneta* Cremonensis. The Victorine manuscript[1] supplies evidence that he contributed to the work in which Michael Scot was now engaged.

It is not impossible that Philip of Tripoli may have joined in the new enterprise. His name does not indeed appear in any of the manuscripts which contain the Latin Averroës, but we have seen that he was certainly in Spain about this time and even at work with Gerard of Cremona.[2] His intimate relation to Michael Scot is also beyond question, and, upon the whole, it seems reasonable to suppose that the Emperor may have engaged him to help in the work now going forward.

However this may have been as regards the exact details of time and persons, we may regard it as a matter now for the first time brought to light and established, that in the years between 1217 and 1223 there existed a college of translators in Toledo just such as that which had done so much excellent work there a century before. In the new school Frederick II. held the honourable place of patron, as Archbishop Raymon had done in his day, while Michael Scot and Gerard of Cremona aided each other in completing the version of Averroës as Dominicus Gundisalvus had lent his help to form that of Avicenna. This view of the matter should be found very interesting, not only in itself, but with regard to the conclusions arrived at by Jourdain, whose discoveries in the literary history of the twelfth century it so remarkably repeats and extends to the following age.

This correspondence between the earlier and later schools of Toledo is even more close and exact than we have yet observed. It appears also in the

---

[1] St. Victor, 171.　　　[2] De Rossi MS. 354. See *ante*, p. 20.

fact that a Jewish interpreter was attached to each, and rendered important service as a member of the college. Under Don Raymon this place was held by Johannes Avendeath, or Johannes Hispalensis as he is commonly called, who worked along with the Archdeacon. 'You have then,' says Avendeath, addressing the Archbishop, 'the book which has been translated from the Arabic according to your commands: I reading it word by word into the vernacular (Spanish), and Dominic the Archdeacon rendering my words one by one into Latin.'[1] The same division of labour seems to have been followed in the new school which Frederick promoted. The Emperor drew the attention of these learned men to Averroës, and signified his desire that a version of this author should be prepared like that which had been made from Avicenna. Michael Scot and Gerard of Cremona were responsible, the former probably in a special sense, both for the general conduct of the undertaking, and, in particular, for the accuracy of the Latin. Now these scholars also, like their predecessors, availed themselves of the help of a Jewish interpreter. This was one Andrew Alpha-girus, who seems to have taken the same part that Avendeath had formerly done, by translating the Arabic of Averroës into current Spanish, which Scot and his coadjutor then rendered into Latin.

Such at least appear to be the suggestions which offer themselves naturally to one who peruses the colophon to the copy of the *De Animalibus ad Caesarem* preserved in the *Bibliotheca Angelica*

---

[1] See preface to the *De Anima* of Avicenna, MSS. Fondo Vaticano 4428, p. 78vo, and 2089, p. 307ro. Jourdain has reprinted this preface in his *Recherches*, p. 449, from the MSS. Fonds de Sorbonne 1793 and Ancien Fonds 6443.

of Rome. Thus it runs: 'Here endeth the book of Aristotle concerning animals, according to the abbreviation of Michael Scot Alphagirus.' The form of expression is curious, but may be exactly matched from the versions produced by the earlier Toledan translators: that is, if we are to believe Bartolocci. This author, in the first volume of his *Bibliotheca Rabbinica*, mentions a manuscript of the Fondo Urbinate in the Vatican which, he says, contains the four books of Avicenna on Physics translated by 'Johannes Gundisalvi.' This name has evidently, like that of 'Scoti Alphagiri,' been formed by composition from those of the two translators, *Johannes* Avendeath and Dominicus *Gundisalvi* who aided each other in the work.[1]

As to the personality of Alphagirus, the only ground of conjecture seems to be that supplied by Romanus de Higuera, who, speaking of the learned men assembled in 1218 at Toledo for the astronomical congress, mentions that one of them was 'el Conhesso Alfaquir' of Toledo.[2] The place, the date, and the similarity of name, are all in favour of our supposing these two to be one and the same person. Nay further, as Alfaquir was of Toledo, and did not need to be summoned thither in 1218, there is no reason why he should not, as the 'Alphagirus' of 1209, have assisted Michael Scot in producing the *De Animalibus* for Frederick.

It is from a remark made by Roger Bacon that we know the first name of the Toledan interpreter

[1] Bibl. Rabb. i. p. 7. 'Eiusdem Avicennae Physicorum lib. iv., Magistro Johanne Gunsalui et Salomone interpretibus, No. 449,' *i.e.* of the Fondo Urbinate.

[2] Bibl. Española, ii. pp. 643-4. 'Conhesso' may be a mistake for *converso*. There is reason to think that Andrew had embraced the Christian faith.

to have been Andrew, and that he was a Jew.
Bacon gives us this information in no kindly spirit,
but in order to lead up to the bitter conclusion
that Scot's work was not original, but borrowed
from one whose labours and just fame he had
appropriated. 'Michael Scot,' he says, 'was ignorant of languages and science alike. Almost all
that has appeared in his name was taken from a
certain Jew called Andrew.'[1]

A sufficient answer to this serious accusation
may be found in what we already know of the
literary fashions of the day, and, in particular, of
the traditional methods of work pursued by the
Toledan translators. It was precisely thus that
the Archdeacon Gundisalvus had used the aid of
Avendeath. A little later too, we find the same
system adopted in the translation of the Koran
promoted by Peter the Venerable. That ecclesiastic
thus expresses himself in sending a copy of his book
to St. Bernard : 'I had it translated by one skilled
in both tongues ; Master Peter of Toledo ; but since
he was not as much at home in the Latin, and did
not know it as well as the Arabic, I appointed one
to help him . . . Brother Peter our Notary.' To
his Koran Peter the Venerable joined a *Summa
Brevis* of the Christian controversy with the Mohammedans. This work also came from the pen of
Master Peter, and with regard to it he makes the

---

[1] 'Michael Scotus, ignarus quidem et verborum et rerum, fere
omnia quae sub nomine ejus prodierunt, ab Andrea quodam Judaeo
mutuatus est.'—*Opus Majus.* In his *Compendium Studii*, a much later
work, Bacon repeats the accusation in a milder form : 'Michael Scotus
ascripsit sibi translationes multas. Sed certum est quod Andreas quidam
Judaeus plus laboravit in his.' It has been conjectured that Andrew
was a convert to Christianity, *v.* Renan, who cites the preface to Jebb's
edition of the *Opus Tertium* of Bacon. It is curious at any rate that
the name given him was that of Scotland's patron saint.

following remarks : ‘By giving elegance and order
to what had been rudely and confusedly stated by
him (*i.e.* by Master Peter) he (*i.e.* Brother Peter
the Notary) has completed an epistle, or rather a
short treatise, which, as I believe, will be very useful to many.’[1]

This correspondence throws a clear light upon
the case of Michael Scot in regard to the charge of
plagiarism. Like Master Peter, he was familiar with
both the Latin and the Arabic language. His weak
point, however, we may suppose to have made itself
felt with regard to the latter, which he probably
knew better in its colloquial than its literary
form, and this must have been the reason why
he availed himself of the aid of a Spanish Jew
to secure the accuracy of his work. Such col-
laboration seems to have produced nearly all the
previous versions which came from Toledo, and it
is obvious that the honour due to the various con-
tributors who combined in forming these translations can only be determined by those who have
it in their power to make a careful and unprejudiced
valuation of their individual labours in each case.
We may gravely doubt whether this was what
Bacon did before he sat down to pen his sharp
censure on Michael Scot. Certainly such an
estimate is now out of the question. We can only
affirm the undoubted fact that the critic was wrong
when he said Scot did not know Arabic. The
contrary appears, not only from the probability we
have already drawn from his Sicilian residence, but
by actual testimony of a very honourable kind.[2]

---

[1] Bibl. Max. Vett. Patrum, Lugduni, 1677, vol. xxii. p. 1030.
[2] The letter, namely, of Pope Gregory ix.

Nor must we forget to notice that the openness with which this copartnery was carried on affords a proof that no deceit could have been thought of in the matter. Considering the past history of the Toledan School, it must have been taken for granted that every version which came from thence under the name of a Christian scholar owed something to the care of his Moorish scribe.

Even had we not been able to make such an appeal to the use and wont of the times in vindication of Scot's method of work, might not a little consideration of what was natural and inevitable in such a task have served to explain what Bacon found so objectionable? The scholars from distant lands who came to Toledo could not, as a rule, afford to spend much time there, and were anxious to use every moment of their stay to the best advantage. They naturally therefore secured on their arrival the services of a Jew or Moor for the purpose of learning Arabic. Needing a knowledge of that tongue not so much in its colloquial as its literary dialect, they must have been engaged from the first in the study of a text rather than in conversing with their teachers. What then could have been more suitable than that these scholars should begin by attacking the very books of which they desired to furnish a Latin version? This method had the merit of gaining two objects at once. The students learned to read Arabic, following the text as it was translated to them by the interpreter. Writing in Latin from his vernacular, and polishing as they wrote, they engaged from the day of their arrival in the very work of translation which had brought them to Spain. It is plain too that any modification of this method which the case of Michael Scot might demand would depend on the knowledge of Arabic he already possessed. It must therefore have been such as left him more and not less credit in the result of his labours than that which commonly belonged to the Christian translators in Toledo.

The whole matter of these versions, and of the fame belonging to Michael Scot in connection with them, seems to receive some further light when we compare the Toledan practice with that which distinguished the most famous schools of painting. It would surely be a strange freak of criticism which should deny to any of the great masters his well-earned fame because of the ground on which it was raised, or the numerous scholars whom it attracted to his studio. Yet we know well what this relation between the master and his school implied in the palmy days of pictorial art. There were apprentices who stretched canvas, mixed colours, and pricked and pounced designs. There were pupils, to whom, according to their talents and proficiency, varied parts of the execution were assigned. To the master alone belonged the oversight and responsibility of the whole. Giving a general design, were it only in a sketch from his hand, he watched the progress of the work with jealous eye, and caught the decisive moment to interpose by executing with his own pencil such parts of the painting as might give a distinctive character, a *cachet*, to the whole. Not till he was satisfied that the desired effect had been secured might the picture leave his studio, and who shall say that he did wrong to sign his name to works produced in such a way? Thus, at any rate, have the highest reputations in the world of art risen into their deserved and enduring fame.

Now, as it is certain that the Toledan School pursued similar methods in their literary labours, right requires that the reputation of its members should be judged by the same canons of criticism which we apply without hesitation to pictorial art. His own day unhesitatingly gave Scot the chief credit in the version of Averroës without inquiring too curiously what parts had been executed by the Cremonese, or other scholars, and what share belonged to Andrew the Jew. It may make us the more ready to accept this verdict and adopt it as our own when we remember the intellectual qualities of the Emperor for whom this work was done. It is certainly out of the question to suppose that a reputation in letters, such as Michael Scot undoubtedly enjoyed at the court of Frederick II., could have been gained by any but legitimate and honourable means.

Coming to an examination then of the various versions which came from the new Toledan School, we find that two of them expressly bear to have been the work of Scot himself. The first of these is the treatise commencing 'Maxima cognitio naturae et scientiae.' It is the commentary of Averroës on the *De Coelo et Mundo* of Aristotle,[1] and Scot has prefaced it by an introduction conceived as follows: 'To thee, Stephen de Pruvino, I, Michael Scot, specially commend this work, which I have rendered into Latin from the sayings of

[1] Paris, Fonds de Sorbonne 924, 950; St. Victor, 171; Navarre, 75; Venice, St. Mark, vi. 54; Fondo Vaticano, 2184, 2089, p. 6ro.

Aristotle. And should Aristotle have delivered somewhat in an incomplete form concerning the fabric of the world in this book, thou mayest have what is wanting to complete it from that of Alpetragius which I have likewise rendered into Latin; and, indeed, it is one with which thou art well acquainted.' As we know when the version of Alpetrongi on the *Sphere* was produced, this fortunate reference to that previous work enables us to determine, at least approximately, that of the *De Coelo et Mundo*, and hence of these translations of Averroës in general. The year 1217 is the first limit, before which they cannot have appeared, and 1223 is the last; for by that time Michael Scot had already left Spain. Between these two dates then, and probably nearer the former than the latter, must his labours and those of his coadjutors have been devoted to this important work.

Stephanus de Provino has been happily identified by M. Bourquelot with a somewhat notable ecclesiastic of the Church of Nôtre Dame du Val de Provins, whose name occurs in various documents dated between the years 1211 and 1233. Renan conjectures that he may be the same as a certain Etienne de Rheims, who, it seems, was born at Provins.[1] Perhaps he is the *Stephanus Francigena* of Guido Bonatti.[2] Scot's friendship with him, to which the dedication of the *De Coelo et Mundo* bears witness, was probably begun in their student days at Paris.

[1] See 'Proviniana' in the *Feuille de Provins* for 7 Février 1852; also the *Hist. Litt. de la France*, xvii. 232; the Bibl. Imp. Colb. *Suite du Reg. Princ. Campan*, *III*. 50ro. and 199vo.; and the letters of Gregory IX., anni v. 9 kal. Maii (1231 or 1232), anni vii. kal. Feb., and 3 kal. Martii in the collection of Laporte du Theil.

[2] See *ante*, p. 6.

The second version bearing the name of Scot is that which commences with the words : 'Intendit per subtilitatem demonstrare ;' being the commentary of Averroës on the *De Anima* of Aristotle.[1] In the Victorine manuscript this treatise offers a curious title : 'Here beginneth the Commentary of the Book of Aristotle the Philosopher concerning the Soul, which Averroës commented on in *Greek*, and Michael Scot translated into Latin.'

In the same manuscript the version of Averroës's Commentary on the various books which compose the *Parva Naturalia* of Aristotle is ascribed to Gerard of Cremona. Renan observes that this ascription does not occur in any other copy, and supposes it to have been a mistake. He seems influenced in this conclusion by the fact that Gerard of Cremona died in 1187. It is curious to find such an eminent scholar forgetful of the existence of a younger Cremonese ; and he is not alone in this error, for it has been repeated even of late years. Yet in 1851 Prince Baldassare Boncompagni had distinguished well between the elder and younger Gerard of Cremona in an excellent monograph on the subject.[2] Even had this work not been published, the learned world had already reason enough to suspect the truth. In a well-known passage of his *Compendium Studii*,[3]

---

[1] Paris, Sorbonne, 932, 943 ; St. Victor, 171 ; Ancien Fonds, 6504 ; Venice, St. Mark, vi. 54.

[2] *Vita di Gherardo Cremonense*, Roma, 1851. The distinction between the elder and younger Gerard had been noticed by Flavio Biondo (1388-1463) ; by Zaccharia Lilio (*obiit c.* 1522) and by Giulio Faroldo in the sixteenth century. I have found the same accuracy in the *Risorgimento d'Italia* of the Abate Saverio Bettinelli, which appeared at Bassano in 1786 (vol. i. p. 81). Only foreigners, therefore, seem to have overlooked it.

[3] *Compendium Studii*, p. 471.

Roger Bacon speaks of Gerard of Cremona as a contemporary of Michael Scot, Alured of England, William the Fleming, and Herman the German, adding that those who were still young had nevertheless known Gerard, who was the eldest of this company of scholars. Now the *Compendium Studii* is commonly assigned to the year 1292, but even if we carry this passage back to 1267, when the most of Bacon's works were written, it still appears evidently impossible that any one still young in that year could have seen a man who died in 1187. Boncompagni, as we have said, explains the difficulty by acquainting us with the younger Gerard, called *de Sabloneta* Cremonensis. He was undoubtedly a contemporary of Michael Scot, and the De Rossi manuscript, already referred to,[1] shows that he was in Spain about this time. There is therefore no reason to distrust the testimony of the Victorine codex when it gives Gerard the honour of having translated Averroës on the *Parva Naturalia*. In accomplishing this work he vindicated his right to the place we have already ventured to assign him as a member of the Toledan College.

The manuscript collections where the *De Coelo et Mundo*, the *De Anima*, and the *Parva Naturalia* of Averroës are found in a Latin dress, contain also versions of several other commentaries by the same author: those concerning the *De Generatione et Corruptione*, the four books of the *Meteora*, the *De Substantia Orbis*, and the *Physica* and *Metaphysica* of Aristotle.[2] We may safely ascribe them to the Toledo College. They were translated either by

---

[1] No. 354 ; see *ante*, pp. 20, 116.
[2] See the list of MSS. already given, p. 123.

Michael Scot, Gerard of Cremona, or some other scholar who worked under these masters.

Renan, relying on the authority of Haureau,[1] has shown good reason to believe that at least the commentaries on the *Physica* and *Metaphysica* in their Latin versions came from the pen of Scot. Albertus Magnus, in a passage of high censure, delivers himself in the following terms : ' Vile opinions are to be found in the book called *Quaestiones Nicolai Peripatetici.* I have been wont to say that the author of it was not Nicholas but Michael Scot, who in very deed knew not natural philosophy, nor rightly understood the books of Aristotle.'[2] The doctrine thus condemned is undoubtedly that of Averroës on the *Physica* and *Metaphysica*. A manuscript of the Paris library has a treatise commencing thus : ' Haec sunt extracta de libro Nicolai Peripatetici,' and it seems that a close correspondence exists between this and a certain digression in the commentary by Averroës on the twelfth book of the Metaphysics. This digression, says Renan, often occurs in the manuscripts as a separate treatise called ' Sermo de quaestionibus quas accepimus a Nicolao et nos dicemus in his secundum nostrum posse.' These words have been omitted from the printed editions of the Commentaries of Averroës, and thus the identity of this treatise with the book censured by Albertus Magnus was not recognised till Haureau discovered it.

The only result then of this sharp criticism is to assure us that the versions of the *Physica* and *Metaphysica* must also be reckoned to the credit

[1] *De la Philosophie Scolastique*, i. 470.   [2] *Opera*, ii. 140.

of Michael Scot. For undoubtedly the opinions to
which Albert took such exception were those of
Averroës, and not of the translator. But if so,
then what becomes of the censure passed upon
Scot? The truth is that if he was more original
than Bacon gave him credit for, on the other hand
he escapes the force of Albert's blame by proving
to have been less original than the latter critic had
supposed. His was indeed a hard case. He could
not form versions from the Arabic but either he
was accused of plagiarism or else held up to the
indignation of Christianity as if he had been the
author of the opinions he rendered into Latin.
This steady determination to find fault overreaches
itself. We begin to discover in it the bitter fruit
of some *odium philosophicum*, and of that envy
which even a just reputation seldom fails to excite.

Some curiosity may be felt with regard to the
doctrine contained in the *Quaestiones Nicolai Peripatetici* which gave ground for such adverse opinions.
M. Renan's *résumé* of this treatise is clear and
sufficient,[1] and we may reproduce it here, as it will
afford a useful supplement to the account already
given of the philosophy of Averroës. 'As to the
origin of the different kinds of being,' says Averroës,
' there are two exactly opposite opinions, as well as
others occupying an intermediate position. The
one explains the world by a theory of development,
the other by creation. Those who hold the former
say that generation is nothing but the outcome and
in a sense the multiplication of being; the Agent,
according to this hypothesis, doing no more than
extricate being from being and make a distinction

---

[1] *Averroës*, p. 108.

between them,[1] so that the Agent, thus conceived, has the function of a mere motive power. As to those who hold the hypothesis of creation, they say that the Agent produces being without having any recourse to pre-existent matter. This is the view taken by our *Motecallemin*, and by the followers of the Christian religion: for example, by Johannes Christianus (Philopon), who asserts that the possibility of creation lies in the Agent alone.'

'The intermediate views may be reduced to two only, though the first of these admits several subdivisions which show considerable differences. These opinions agree in affirming that generation is only a change of substance; that all generation implies a subject; and that everything begets in its own likeness. The first opinion asserts, however, that the part of the Agent is to create form, and to impress it upon already existent matter. Some of those who hold this view, as Ibn Sina,[2] make an entire separation between matter in generation and the Agent, calling the latter the *source of form*, while others, among whom we may notice Themistius and perhaps Alfarabi, maintain that the Agent is in some cases conjoined with matter, as when fire produces fire, or man begets man; and in others separate from it, as in the generation of creeping things and plants, *i.e.* those not produced from seed,[3] which all owe their being to causes that are unlike themselves.'

'The third theory is that of Aristotle, who holds that the Agent produces at once both form

[1] See *Metaphysica*, xii. 334.
[2] Avicenna. See *Destruction of Destruction*, iii. 350.
[3] The doctrine of spontaneous generation, common among the Arabian Philosophers, and specially taught by Ibn Tofail.

and substance, by impressing motion on matter, and begetting a change therein which rouses its latent powers to action. In this way of thinking the function of the Agent is only to make active that which already existed potentially, and to realise a union between matter and form. Thus all creation is reduced to motion of which heat is the principle. This heat, shed abroad in the waters and in the earth, begets both the animals and the plants which are not produced by seed. Nature puts forth all these both orderly and with perfection, just as if guided by a controlling mind; though nature itself has no intelligence. The proportions and productive power which the elements owe to the motion of the sun and stars are what Plato called by the name of *Ideas*. According to Aristotle the Agent cannot create forms, for in that case something would be produced from nothing.

'It is, in fact, the notion that forms could be created which has led some philosophers to suppose that forms have a substantive existence of their own, and that there is a separate source of these. The same error has infected all the three religions of our day,[1] leading their divines to assert that nothing can produce something. Starting from this principle our theologians have supposed the existence of one Agent producing without intermediary all kinds of creatures; an Agent whose action proceeds by an infinity of opposite and contradictory acts done simultaneously. In this way of thinking it is not fire that burns, nor water that moistens; all proceeds by a direct act of the

---

[1] This is a notable saying which may well have given rise to the legend of a book *De Tribus Impostoribus*. It was certainly one of the *foeda dicta* blamed by Albertus Magnus.

Creator. Nay more, when a man throws a stone, these teachers attribute the consequent motion not to the man but to the universal Agent, and thus deny any true human activity.

'There is even a more astounding corollary of this doctrine; for if God can cause that which is not to enter into being, He can also reduce being to nothing; destruction, like generation, is God's work, and Death itself has been created by Him. But in our way of thinking destruction is like generation. Each created thing contains in itself its own corruption, which is present with it potentially. In order to destroy, just as to create, it is only necessary for the Agent to call this potentiality into activity. We must in short maintain as co-ordinate principles both the Agent and these potential powers. Were one of the two wanting, nothing could exist at all, or else all being would reduce itself to action; either of which consequences is as absurd as the other.'

We cannot wonder that Albertus Magnus, and all who held the Christian faith, were alarmed by doctrine of this kind and fiercely opposed it. The orthodox beliefs of Christians, Jews, and Mohammedans alike were declared false by this bold writer, whom several expressions which we have embodied in the above summary show clearly to have been Averroës, and not Michael Scot. In one passage indeed we seem to discover what may have suggested the widely spread fable that Frederick ii., or Scot, or some other of their company and party, had produced an atheistic work called *De Tribus Impostoribus*. The imputation was a false one, yet most natural were the feelings of prejudice which the publication of this philosophy aroused against the great Emperor and Michael Scot who had acted as his agent in the matter.

Pursuing our investigation of the works which came from the Toledan College we discover that these were not confined to the books of Aristotle already noticed, but that the translators took a wider range in their labours. The Venice manuscript of Aver-roës,[1] besides the *De Coelo et Mundo*, the *De Anima*, the *Meteora*, the *De Substantia Orbis*, the *De Generatione et Corruptione*, and the *Parva Natura-lia*, contains several other treatises that deserve attention. Two of these were compositions of Averroës; the one a commentary on the book of Proclus, *De Causis*, then commonly ascribed to Aristotle,[2] and the other an independent work, as it would seem, bearing the following title: 'Qualiter intellectus naturalis conjungitur Intelligentiae abstractae,' in short a treatise on the *ittisal*. The volume also contains the Latin version of a book by the Rabbi Moses Maimonides, entitled 'De Deo Benedicto, quod non est Corpus, nec Virtus in Corpore.'[3] Maimonides, like Averroës, was a native of Cordova, and hence no doubt arose the interest that was felt in his works by the Toledan translators.

That the Venice manuscript is to be understood

---

[1] St. Mark, vi. 54 *memb. saec.* xiv. The *De Substantia Orbis* is said to have been completed by Averroës in Morocco in 1178.

[2] Also Fondo Vaticano, 2089, p. 1, with commentary by Alfarabius.

[3] This title recalls a passage in the *De Anima* of Averroës as reproduced by Pendasius: 'Si intellectus esset numeratus ad numerum individuorum, esset aliquod hoc (*i.e.* aliquod particulare) determinatum, *corpus aut virtus in corpore.* Si hoc esset, esset quid intellectum potentia.'

as a collection of the versions which came from that school appears plainly in the dedication to Stephen of Provins. This is generally prefixed to the *De Coelo et Mundo*, thus forming an introduction to the versions which follow; but here it has been placed at the end of the volume, occurring immediately after the short article *De Vita Aristotelis* which closes the whole series. We may see in this fact a certain probability that some at least of these additional versions may have been the work of Michael Scot himself. Nor will the five years which he spent at Toledo appear too scant a space of time for the production of the whole body of the Latin Averroës and something more, when we remember the ample and able assistance he enjoyed in the prosecution of his labours as a translator.

There is one other version of which we must speak before leaving the subject which has engaged our attention so long. The library of St. Omer contains a manuscript collection of the works of Aristotle in Latin which was written during the thirteenth century.[1] The fly-leaf at the commencement of this volume shows the same handwriting as the other pages, and has proved upon examination to be the last relic of a work which has unfortunately perished. What that work was may be seen from the closing words, which are as follows: 'Here end the *Nova Ethica* of Aristotle, which Master Michael Scot translated from the Greek language into the Latin.' This colophon opens a curious question. Are we to consider that the scribe wrote *Greek* when he should rather have said *Arabic*? It was by a mistake of such a kind that

---

[1] No. 620. See *Cat. Gen. des Bibl. des Dep.* vol. iii. Paris, 1855.

the writer of the Victorine manuscript asserted that Averroës had commented on the *De Anima* in *Greek*.[1] Taking it in this way the version of the *Nova Ethica* would fall into line with the others which Scot and Gerard of Cremona composed at Toledo. But it deserves notice that none of the manuscript collections usually considered to contain the work of that school comprises among its contents the *Nova Ethica*. We know, further, that a Latin version of the Ethics with the commentary of Averroës was made from the Arabic by Hermannus Alemannus.[2] This work was completed on the third of June 1240, and we can hardly suppose that it would have been entered on if Michael Scot had already accomplished the same task but twenty years earlier. These facts and considerations make it very unlikely that the St. Omer fragment represents a version of the Arabic text.

Assuming then the literal truth of this interesting colophon, we are confirmed in the conclusion to which an examination of the *De Partibus Animalium* in the Florence manuscript has already inclined our minds.[3] Michael Scot, it must now be held, did not confine his studies altogether to the Arabian authors, but undertook to form translations directly from the Greek. These two versions, and especially that of the *Nova Ethica*, open up a new and striking view of the scholar's literary activity. When Aquinas moved Pope Urban to order a new translation of Aristotle from the original, William of Moerbeka and those others who presently

[1] See *ante*, p. 125.
[2] Colophon to cod. lxxix. 18 of the Laurentian Library.
[3] See *ante*, p. 59.

entered upon this work were tilling no virgin soil, but a familiar field in which the plough of Scot at least had left deep furrows. Even the renowned Grostête, Bishop of Lincoln, who executed a version of the *Ethica* from the Greek about 1250, was but following in the path which this earlier master had opened up. Michael Scot here takes rank with Boëthius and Jacobus de Venetiis, who were among the first to seek these pure and original sources of Aristotelic doctrine. He appears as one who not only completed the knowledge of his time with regard to the Arabian philosophy by translating Averroës, but who gave some help at least to lay the foundation of a more exact acquaintance with the works of Aristotle by opening a direct way to the Greek text. We may even see a sign of this remarkable position in the place of honour given, perhaps accidentally, to Scot's version of the *Nova Ethica* at the opening of the St. Omer manuscript. He stands between two ages, and lays a hand of power upon each.

It is hardly necessary to add that in this he shines all the more brightly when compared with his great detractor. Roger Bacon, secure in the consciousness of his commanding abilities, attacks with a rare self-confidence, not Michael Scot alone, but all the scholars of his time. Not four of them, he says, know Hebrew, Greek, and Arabic.[1] Those who pretend to translate from these tongues are ignorant even of Latin, not to speak of the sciences treated of in the books which they pretend to render intelligible. Busy in penning these diatribes, Bacon does not seem to have reflected that the best

[1] *Opus Tertium*, Master of the Rolls ed. p. 91.

way of reproving the imperfections of which he
complained would have been to shame these scholars
to some purpose by producing better versions on
his own account.   But the truth of the matter lies
here, that Bacon was no linguist.   This appears
plainly from the tale he tells against himself in the
Compendium Studii ; how a hard word in Aristotle
had baffled him till one day there came some outlandish students to hear him lecture, who laughed
at his perplexity, telling him it was good Spanish
for the plant called Henbane.[1]   'Hinc illae lachry-
mae' then, and a plague on Michael Scot and all
his tribe, who know Spanish so well they will not
put a plain Latin word for the puzzled professor
to understand.   No wonder that to Scot rather than
to Bacon, for all his genius, that age owed the chief
part of the first translation of Aristotle and a good
beginning of the second.   ¡

---

[1] *Compendium Studii*, p. 467.   The *De Plantis* is found at p. 83 of
MS. Fondo Vaticano 4087.

CHAPTER VII

THE return of Michael Scot from Spain to the Imperial Court was doubtless a striking moment, not only in the life of the philosopher himself, but in the history of letters. He then appeared fresh from a great enterprise, and bringing with him the proofs of its success in the form of the Latin Averroës. We cannot doubt that his reception was worthy of the occasion and of one who had served his master so faithfully.

Frederick was now returned to his dominions in the south. He had established his imperial rights in Germany at the cost of a campaign in which the pretensions of Otho were successfully overcome, and, on his return homeward in 1220, he had received the crown once more in Rome at the hands of the supreme ecclesiastical authority. His progress was indeed a continual scene of triumph. Arrived at Palermo, the court gave itself up to feasting and gaiety of every kind.

Two ancient romantic authorities[1] choose with dramatic instinct this moment, and these gay and voluptuous surroundings, as the *mise en scène* amid which they show us Scot again appearing to resume

[1] Namely the novel called *Il Paradiso degli Alberti* (Bologna, Wesseloffsky, 1867, vol. ii. pp. 180-217), and No. xx. of the *Cento Novelle Antiche* (Testo Borghiniano).

the place he had quitted more than ten years before. It is quite possible that there may be a measure of historic truth here, as well as the art which can seize or create an occasion, and which loves to contrast the triumph of arms with the more peaceful honours of literary fame. Frederick, we must remember, in a sort represented both. He was Maecenas as well as Caesar. In welcoming Michael Scot and doing him honour at these imperial banquets he was but crowning the success of an enterprise in which his own name and interest were deeply engaged.

Traces of the impression made by this highly significant incident have been preserved in the arts of poetry and painting as well as in that of prose romance. Dante, who wrote his *Divine Comedy* less than a century later than the time of Scot, has given the philosopher a place in his poem, describing him as :

'Quell' altro, che ne' fianchi è così poco,
Michele Scotto fu.'[1]

The commentators, with great reason, refer the epithet 'poco' to the manner of Scot's dress. It would seem that the Spaniards of those days differed from the other European nations in their habit. They wore a close girdle about the waist, like the *hhezum* of the East ; and indeed they had probably taken the fashion from long familiarity with their Moorish masters and neighbours.[2] Scot must have adopted such a dress while at Toledo, and thus, when he returned to Palermo, the singularity of his appearance struck the eyes of the court at once. The impression proved a remarkably enduring one, since, even in Dante's day, it still persisted, offering

[1] *Inferno*, xx. 115, 116.
[2] The *faja* still worn in Spain is a direct survival of this custom.

itself, as we have seen, to the poet as a picturesque means of presenting the famous scholar to the world, not without a hidden reference to what was certainly one of the crowning moments of his life.

We may suspect indeed that the fashion of Scot's dress was more than simply Spanish ; for the mode of Aragon at least must surely have been too familiar at Frederick's court to excite so much attention. The philosopher had lived long in close company with the Moors of Toledo and Cordova. What he wore was probably no mere fragment of Eastern fashion but the complete costume of an Arabian sage. The flowing robes, the close-girt waist, the pointed cap, were not unknown in Sicily where there was still a considerable Moorish population, yet they must have sat strangely enough upon Scot when once he declared himself for what he was : the reverend ecclesiastic, the Master of Paris, the native of the far north.

There is a fresco on the south wall[1] of the Spanish Chapel in the cloisters of Santa Maria Novella of Florence which contains a figure answering nearly to this conjecture regarding Scot's appearance. It is that of a man in the prime of life, slight and dark, with a short brown beard trimmed to a point. He wears a long close-fitting robe of a reddish colour, noticeably narrow at the waist, with a falling girdle. On his head is a tall red pointed cap from which the ringlets of his dark hair escape on each side. He stands among the converts of the Dominican preachers and bends towards the spectator with an intense expression and action as he tears the leaves out of a

---

[1] According to ecclesiastical reckoning ; the direction of the altar being taken as eastward. The frontispiece reproduces part of this fresco.

heretical book [1] that rests on his knee.   It would be too much to assert that the figure we have described was meant as a portrait of Michael Scot, yet considering the place he holds in the *Divine Comedy*, it is not impossible that such an idea may have crossed the artist's mind and left these traces in his work. Certainly no better pictorial illustration can be found, at once of Dante's lines, and of the somewhat equivocal reputation which began to haunt Scot from the time of his return to court.   There was indeed a singular fitness in the Moslem dress considered as the daily wear of one who, though a Christian and a Churchman, had just done more than any living scholar to introduce the Moorish science and philosophy in the West.   His choice of such a fashion is evidence that Michael Scot possessed a ready adaptability to his circumstances, and even a vein of aesthetic and dramatic instinct which we might not otherwise have suspected.   But it is not to be forgotten that his versions of Averroës were already condemned by the Church, and that the very manner of Scot's appearance when he brought them from Spain must have heightened the suspicions of heresy which began to attach themselves to the translator of these forbidden works.   The only hope for such a man was that he might be induced to tear his book and turn to less dangerous pursuits.   This is exactly the idea which the painter of the Spanish Chapel has expressed, and in a form which accords so remarkably with the picturesque description of Michael Scot by Dante.[2]

[1] See *infra*, chap. ix.

[2] The fact that Averroës himself is painted on the opposite wall holding in his hand the *Great Commentary* seems highly to increase the probability that the figure here described was meant for Michael Scot, the recognised interpreter of that forbidden philosophy.   Averroës occupies a similar position in Orgagna's fresco in the Campo Santo of Pisa.

If the philosopher did not actually take such extreme measures with the creatures of his brain and pen, the versions he brought to Sicily were at least suppressed in the meantime, being concealed in the imperial closet till a more suitable opportunity should occur for their publication. This done, their author devoted himself to pursuits less likely to attract unfavourable notice than those in which he had been lately engaged.

The place and duty which most naturally offered themselves to Scot were those of the Court Astrologer. We have seen him occupied in this way already, before he left Palermo for Spain, and there seems no reason to doubt the tradition which says that such was indeed the standing occupation of his life, and one which he resumed at once on his return. To this application of celestial science the opinion of the times attached no sinister interpretation, and Scot, finding himself the object of suspicion on account of his late studies and achievements, must have fallen back with a sense of security, strange as it may seem, upon the casting of horoscopes and the forming of presages founded on the flight of birds and the motion of animals.[1]

It is therefore in all likelihood to this period in his life that we are to ascribe several works on astrology and kindred subjects which bear the name of Scot. They may have come from his pen by way of supplement to the doctrine which he had expounded so many years before in the *Liber*

---

[1] Scot reckoned twelve signs in augury answering to the twelve celestial houses. Six came from the right hand : Fernova, fervetus, confert, amponenth, scimasarnova, scimasarvetus ; and six from the left: Confernova, confervetus, viaram, harenan, scassarnova, scassarvetus. See the *Physionomia*, chap. lvi.

Introductorius.[1] Such are the *Astrologia* of the Munich Library,[2] and a curious volume preserved in the Hof-Bibliothek of Vienna with the following title : ' Michaelis Scoti Capitulum de iis quae generaliter significantur in partibus duodecim Caeli, sive Domibus.'[3] The *De Presagiis Stellarum et Elementaribus*, and the *Notitia convinctionis Mundi terrestris cum Coelesti*, cited by the writer on Scot in the *Encyclopedia Britannica*, belong apparently to the same class.

We shall probably commit no error in assuming that the astrological views of Scot at this period were substantially the same as those embodied in his earlier writings on that subject.[4] In after ages they were severely censured by Pico della Miran-

[1] Unless indeed these, or some of them, should prove to be merely detached fragments of the *Liber Introductorius* itself, like those at Milan, Padua, and Rome. See *ante*, p. 27.

[2] No. 1091. It is perhaps the same as the *Astrologorum Dogmata*, which appears in the lists of Bale and Pitz.

[3] No. 3124. Incipit : ' Primum signum duodecim signorum.' Explicit : ' principio motus earum.'

[4] As a characteristic specimen, we may take the chapter of the *Liber Introductorius* on the moon as it is given in the Roman MS. (Fondo Vaticano 4087, p. 38ro.). It commences thus : ' Luna terris vicinior est omnibus planetis.' Some passages are curious, as when Scot says that the moon has her light from the sun and he again receives his ' a summo coelo in quo Trinitas residet.' The heathen, he adds, used to call the moon Diana, and the sister of the sun, whom they named Apollo. Her proper figure is that of a virgin with a torch in either hand whereof the flames are triple to signify the Trinity, that ' true light which lighteneth every man that cometh into the world' (S. John i. 9). ' Virgil saith of her " tria Virginis ora Dianae," that is heavenly, earthly, and infernal. Her power causes hunters to profit more by night than by day, and the owl and night-hawk sleep all day that they may follow their prey by night. Such creatures of the night are hated by the rest and hate them in return. The wolf hates the sheep, and birds the owl. This last is of use in fowling when they use a night-hawk. Builders, too, know that wood must be felled in the wane of the moon or it will warp.' It ends thus : ' Explicit Liber quem edidit micael scotus de signis et ymaginibus celi, qui scriptum (sic) et exemplatum fuit per me baltasaram condam (quondam) Domini Dominici in mccccxx de mense Aprilis Deo gratias Amen.'

dola, who says of Scot's doctrine concerning the stellar images: 'These invisible forms can be discerned neither by the senses nor by right reason, and there is no agreement regarding them by their inventors, who were not the Chaldeans or Indians but only the Arabs.' . . . 'Michael Scot mentions all these (images) as things most effectual, and with him agree many astrologers, both Arabian and Latin. I had heard somewhat of this doctrine, and thought at first that it was meant merely as a convenient means of mapping out the sky, and not that these figures actually existed in the heavens. . . .'
'From the Greeks astrology passed to the Arabs and was taught with ever-growing assurance. . . .'
'Aboasar, a grammarian and historical writer, took this science from the Greeks, corrupting it with countless trifling fables, and made thereof an astrology much worse than that of Ptolemy. . . .'
'In those days the study of mathematics, like that of philosophy in general, made great progress in Spain under King Alphonso, a keen student in the calculus, especially as applied to the movements of the heavenly bodies. He had also a taste for the vain arts of the Diviner, having learned no better; and to please him in this many of the most important treatises of that kind, both Greek and Arabic, have been handed down to our own day, chiefly by the labours of Johannes Hispalensis and Michael Scot, the latter of whom was an author of no weight and full of superstition. Albertus Magnus at first was somewhat carried away with this doctrine, for it came with the power of novelty to his inexperienced youth, but I rather think that his opinions suffered change in later

life.'[1]   Mirandola belonged to another age than that of Scot, when purer conceptions of astronomical science were already beginning to prevail, but the very opinions he condemned held a real relation to that progress.   They encouraged in early times, as may be seen in the case of Alphonso himself, a study of the heavenly motions without which no true advance could have been made.

A story told by the chronicler Salimbene may, if rightly understood, show us that Michael Scot too, for all his astrological dreams, was a clever calculator and thus stood well in the line on which true advance in astronomy was even then proceeding.   The Emperor asked him one day to determine the distance of the *coelum*, which probably means the height of the roof, in a certain hall of the palace where they happened to be standing together. The calculation having been made and the result given, Frederick took occasion to send Scot on a distant journey, and, while he was away, the proportions of the room were slightly but sufficiently altered.   On his return the Emperor led him where they had been before and asked that he should repeat his solution of the problem.   Scot unhesitatingly affirmed that a change had taken place; either the floor was higher or the *coelum* lower than before : an answer which made all men marvel at his skill.[2]   Greek science had taught the art of measuring inacessible distances by means of angular observations, and this art was well understood by

---

[1] *Opera Omnia*, Bale, 1527. *In Astrologiam*, lib. viii. chap. vi. and lib. xii. chap. vii.

[2] In No. 1 of the *Cento Novelle Antiche* Frederick answers the ambassadors of Prester John by saying that the best thing in the world ' sì è misura.' This may possibly refer to his passion for mathematics.

the Arabs. The *Optica* of Ptolemy were already translated into Latin from an Arabic version by Eugenio, admiral to King Robert of Sicily during the twelfth century,[1] and mathematical instruments were known in that kingdom whereby angles could be taken and measured with some nicety. Scot must have possessed such an *astrolabe* and the skill to use it with great delicacy, if we have rightly read the terms of the problem he solved so unhesitatingly. There is no cause for wonder then in the fact that, where pure and legitimate astronomy was concerned, this philosopher, who had won fame in his student days as the mathematician of Paris, who was now widely known as the translator of Alpetrongi, and who as a keen observer and ready calculator was well qualified for original research, should have taken a high place in these studies on his own account, and should have come to be acknowledged as a master in them. Even Bacon, who blamed Michael Scot so bitterly when language or philosophy were in question, speaks in a different way here, calling him a 'notable inquirer into matter, motion, and the course of the constellations.'

This well-earned celebrity may have been owing in no small degree to a mathematical and astronomical work produced by the philosopher after his return to court. Sacrobosco, the famous English astronomer, had just risen into notice by his treatise on the *Sphere*. This book was not indeed very remarkable in itself, but it obtained an extraordinary currency during the Middle Ages, and after

[1] MSS. of this work are in Paris, Ancien Fonds, 7310; Milan, Ambrosiana, T. 100; Florence, Bibl. Naz. xi. D. 64, II. ii. 35, and Rome, Fondo Vaticano, 2975.

K

the invention of printing as well as before it :[1] a
popularity chiefly due, we may believe, to its
suggestiveness, which caused many of the learned
to enrich the *Sphere* of Sacrobosco with their own
notes and observations. One of the first to do so
was Michael Scot. His commentary on the work
of Holywood contains several subtle inquiries and
determinations regarding the source of heat, the
sphericity of the heavenly bodies, and other matters,
which have been repeated by Libri with the remark
that their author must have been far in advance of
his times.[2]

We may notice here a curious legend of Naples
to which Sir Walter Scott has drawn attention in
the account he gives of his great namesake.[3] It
would seem to suggest that this age, perhaps by
means of Michael Scot, was acquainted with philosophical instruments rarer if not more useful than
the astrolabe. The romance of *Vergilius* tells how
that hero founded ' in the middes of the see a fayer
towne, with great landes belongynge to it ; . . . and
called it Napells. And the fandacyon of it was of
egges, and in that towne of Napells he made a tower
with iiii corners, and in the toppe he set an apell
upon an yron yarde, and no man culd pull away
that apell without he brake it ; and thoroughe that
yren set he a bolte, and in that bolte set he a egge.
And he henge the apell by the stauke upon a cheyne,
and so hangeth it still. And when the egge styrreth,
so shoulde the towne of Napells quake; and when the
egge brake, then shulde the towne sinke.' The
reference here is of course to the *Castel del Ovo* at

----

[1] See *Narducci's Catalogue* of the Boncompagni MSS., Rome, 1862.

[2] *Histoire des Sciences Mathématiques.*

[3] *Lay of the Last Minstrel*, Author's Edition, Note 3 I.

Naples, a fortress which we know to have been built, or at least strengthened, by Frederick II. What if the rest of the legend embalm, like a fly in amber, the tradition, strangely altered, of some instrument set up there to measure the force of the earthquakes so prevalent in that part of Italy ?

Such a notion is not the pure matter of conjecture it may at first sight seem to be. Frederick was in relation with those who might well have put him in possession of this among other secrets. When the Tartars stormed the *Vulture's Nest*, as it was called, in the Syrian castle of Alamout, they found an observatory well supplied with instruments of precision, and that of all kinds.[1] Now this place was the last refuge of the Assassins, that strange sect who owned obedience to the Old Man of the Mountain. Frederick II. when in the East paid these people a visit,[2] and again at Melfi, in his own dominions, he received their ambassadors and entertained them at a great banquet.[3] Considering then the Emperor's well-known curiosity in all matters of physical science, we may feel sure he would profit by any improvements or discoveries the observers at Alamout could communicate. If the contrivance set up at Naples was really a *seismometer*, this would furnish a curious comment on Bacon's statement that Michael Scot excelled in investigating the movements of matter.[4]

Passing to what rests on more certain evidence, we find Scot's fame in those days attested by one

---

[1] Lenormant, *Quest. Hist.* vol. ii. pp. 144, 145.

[2] *Cento Novelle Antiche*, No. C.

[3] 22 July 1232. See 'Ann. Colon. Max.' in Pertz, *Scriptores Rei Germanicae*, xvii. 843.

[4] 'Physicorum motuum.' The passage will be found in the *De Utilitate Linguarum*.

of his most distinguished contemporaries, and that in a way which makes him appear as an honoured master in the science of algebra, then lately intro- duced from the Moorish schools. This improvement and testimony were both of them due to a certain Leonardo of the Bonacci family of Pisa, who was, perhaps, the first to bring the new method of cal- culation to the knowledge of his countrymen. His father had been overseer of the customs at Bougie, in Barbary,[1] on behalf of the Pisan merchants who traded thither. Observing the superior way of reckoning used by the Moors in that country, he sent home for his son that the boy might be trained in this admirable way of counting. Leonardo per- fected his art in after years by travel and study in Egypt, Syria, and Greece, as well as in Sicily and Provence. The ripe fruit of this knowledge saw the light in 1222, when he published for the first time his famous *Liber Abbaci*. It consisted of fifteen chapters, in which the author declared the secret of the Indian numerals as well as the funda- mental processes of algebra.[2]

This brief account of one who must ever hold an honourable place in the history of mathematical science may enable us to value at its true worth the praise which Leonardo bestowed on Michael Scot. It seems that the first edition of the *Liber Abbaci* was not entirely satisfactory. Scot wrote a letter to the author which possibly contained

[1] This city was founded in 1067-68 by En-Nacer ben Alennas ibn Hammad, who made it his capital.

[2] MSS. of the *Liber Abbaci* are to be found in Florence, Bibl. Naz. i. 2616, iii. 25, and xi. 21. The first of these has been exactly reprinted by Boncompagni at Rome, 1857. Other MSS. are in the Boncompagni library, see *Narducci's Catalogue*, Nos. 176 and 255. The most im- portant work on the whole subject is 'Della Vita e delle Opere di Leonardo Pisano,' by Boncompagni, Rome, 1852.

strictures on the work, and asked that a copy of the emended edition should be sent him. Pisano replied by dedicating the book to his correspondent. It appeared in 1228, and contained a prefatory letter, in which the author addresses Scot in the highest terms of respect, calling him by that title of *Supreme Master* which he had won at Paris, and submitting the *Liber Abbaci*, even in this its final form, to his further emendation. This *laudari a laudato* must have been most grateful to the philosopher, and it enables us to see the standing he had among the mathematicians of his time. One would almost be disposed to infer, from the respect Pisano paid him, that Scot himself had composed or translated some lost work on algebra. In another connection we shall find reason to think that this conjecture may be well founded.[1]

Besides the practice of astrology and his deeper researches in astronomy and mathematics, Michael Scot devoted himself to another profession, that of medicine. This was then a science very imperfectly understood, yet here too, in the years that followed his return to court, Scot made a name for himself as a physician, and contributed something to the advancement of human knowledge in one of its most important branches. The healing art in Europe had only just begun to emerge from that primitive state in which savage peoples still possess it ; overlaid by charms and incantations ; the peculiar department of the wise woman, the sorcerer, and the priest. Among the Latin races the lady of the castle and the *bella donna* of the village still cared for rich and poor in their various accidents and sicknesses,

---

[1] See *infra*, chap. ix.

as indeed they continued to do for several ages more. Only crowned heads, the wealthiest of the nobility, or the rich merchants of the cities, began to require and employ the services of regular physicians. These were generally Jews, sometimes Moors ;[1] and thus fashion and experience alike began to make popular among our ancestors the superior claims of science in medicine. Such science had undoubtedly survived from the days and in the works of Hippocrates, Galen, and Celsus, and was now preserved in the theory and practice of the Arabian schools.

This point once reached, a further advance soon became inevitable. Attention had been called to a deeper source of medical knowledge than that generally possessed in the West. Learned men, whose tastes led them this way, naturally sought to inform their minds by procuring translations of the Arabic works on medicine. The just fame of Salerno, a medical school which had been founded in the closing years of the eleventh century by Robert Guiscard, depended on the intelligent zeal with which this plan of research was then pursued.[2] The kingdom of Sicily indeed occupies as important a place in the progress of the healing art as Spain itself does with regard to the history of philosophy and of science in general.

Frederick II., as might have been expected, did much to encourage and regulate these useful studies.

[1] The University Library of Genoa has an interesting MS. (F. vii. 10), written in Arabic by an African hand. It belonged, A. H. 483, to Judah ben Jaygh ben Israel, servant of Abu Abdallah Algani Billah, a Moor of Malaga. It contains medical works by Johannes ben Mesue, Rases, Alkindi, Geber, and others.

[2] For an account of the school of Salerno, see Sprengel, *Versuch einer pragmatischen Geschichte der Artzneykunde*; Carmoly, *Histoire des Médecins Juifs*, Bruxelles, 1844 ; and De Renai, *Collectio Salernitana*, Naples, 1852.

We have already noticed the bent of his mind towards comparative physiology, and the daring experiments he carried out, *in corpore vili et vivo.*
One of the first literary and scientific works which
he commanded, or at least accepted when it was
dedicated to him, was a compilation from three
ancient authors upon a medical subject.[1] He was
then but eighteen years of age. As time went on
his interest in this science continued, and became
the motive to a liberal and enlightened policy. He
regarded medicine as a matter of national importance, and strove by wise laws to make the practice
of that profession as intelligent and useful as possible. He protected the faculty at Salerno and
created that of Naples. None might lecture elsewhere in the Sicilies, and every physician in the
kingdom must hold testimonials from one or other
of these schools, as well as a government licence
to practise. The course preliminary to qualifica-
tion consisted of three years in arts and five in
medicine and surgery. As a guide to the professors,
the doctrine of Hippocrates and Galen was declared
normal in the schools; yet, lest this should become
merely formal and traditional, directions were given
that the students should have practice in anatomy.
Regarding the related trade of the apothecary, the
laws denounced the adulteration of drugs. Physicians
might not claim a greater fee than half a *tarcn* of
gold per diem, which gave the patient a right to
be visited thrice in the day. The poor were to be
attended free of charge. We have thought it right
to be particular in these details, as they throw
light on the times, and on Scot's own practice as

[1] The *De Urinis.* See *ante*, p. 20.

a physician. Considering indeed the place he held about the Emperor's person, and the high estimation in which his master held him, it seems not at all improbable that his may have been the hand which drew these wise enactments, or his at least the suggestion which commended them to Frederick. They must in any case have been the rules under which he carried on his work as a doctor of medicine.

This branch of Michael Scot's activity relates itself easily and naturally to what we already know of his acquirements and familiarity with the Arabian authors. It was from the *De Medicina* of Rases that he borrowed so much material for his *Physionomia*. The *Abbreviatio Avicennae* too, which he translated for Frederick in 1210, was in no small part a treatise on comparative anatomy and physiology, nor is it likely that he can have missed reading the famous *canon* of the same author, in which Avicenna expounds a complete body of practical medicine. We need not wonder then to find that, on Scot's return to court, his work on Averroës done, he added the practice of physic to his duties as Imperial Astrologer. This new profession must have offered itself to him as another means of securing a general forgetfulness of the questionable direction in which his philosophical studies had lately carried him.

He seems in fact to have won almost as much fame in medicine as he had made for himself in the study of mathematics. Lesley says ' he gained much praise as a philosopher, astronomer, and physician.' Dempster speaks of his ' singular skill,' calling him ' one of the first physicians for learning'

---

[1] *Historia Ecclesiastica*, xii. 495. Dempster professed at Pisa and Bologna between the years 1616 and 1625.

and adding that Camperius[1] had the highest opinion of him. An anonymous writer, *De claris Doctrina Scotis,* is even more precise, telling us that Scot was noted for the cures he effected in difficult cases, and that he excelled in the treatment of leprosy, gout, and dropsy.[2]

Some slight remains of this skill are to be found in the libraries of Europe; for Michael Scot was a writer on the science of his art as well as a practising physician. The chief of these relics is a considerable work on the urine. This subject had been widely, if not deeply, studied by the more ancient medical authorities, whose investigations appear in the *Ketab Albaul* of Al Kairouani,[3] and in a book to which we have already more than once referred: the *De Urinis* compiled for Frederick in 1212.[4] The same title belongs to one of the treatises by Avicenna, which has been reprinted in the present century.[5]

The *De Urinis* of Michael Scot seems now extant in the form of an Italian translation alone. The exact title is as follows: ' Della notitia e prognosticatione dell'orine, secondo Michele Scoto, cosi de' sani, come delli infermi,' or, more briefly, ' El trattato de le urine secondo Michaele Scoto.'[6] The

---

[1] This was Symphorien Champier, physician to Henry II. of France.

[2] See the Sibbald Collections, Advocates' Library, Edinburgh.

[3] See D'Herbelot. This author was a Jew.

[4] See *ante,* pp. 20, 151. Further investigation might show that it was Michael Scot himself who undertook this work for the Emperor. In that case it would probably be the original from which the two Italian versions mentioned above were made. Nor is it unlikely he should have devoted himself to medicine as early as 1212 considering the nature of the work by Avicenna on which we know he was engaged in 1210.

[5] In Ideler's *Physici et Medici Graeci Minores,* Berlin, 1842, vol. ii.

[6] Florence, Bibl. Naz. xv. 27, cod. chart. saec. xv. ; Naples, Bibl. Naz. cod. chart. saec. xv. from the Minieri Riccio collection.

author enumerates no less than nineteen divisions of his subject, which he seems to have studied very exactly. This work long remained an authority in the medical schools, as appears, not only from the two translations we have noticed, but also in the fact that large use was made of it in a later collection which commences thus: 'In the name of the Lord, Amen. These are certain recipes taken from the book of Master Michael Scot, Physician to the Emperor Frederick, and from the works of other Doctors.'[1]

There has also come down to us a prescription called *Pillulae Magistri Michaelis Scoti.*[2] It enumerates about a dozen ingredients and the scribe has added

[1] Vatican, Fondo della Regina di Svezia, 1159, p. 149. This treatise closes thus : 'et istud sufficit tempore presenti facto urinarum. Finis urinarum Magistri Michaelis Scocti. Incipit Practica Magistri R. de Parma Medecinarum.'

[2] British Museum, add. mss. 24,068. This is a volume in 8vo containing a medical collection. It belonged in 1422 to Heinrich Zenner and afterwards to Magister Wenceslaus Brock. No. 22, at fol. 97vo, is as follows : 'Pillulae Magistri Michaelis Scoti, quae fore competunt omnibus egritudinibus, et non possit scribi earum bonitas, unde nolo eas amplius laudare etc. Recipe Aloe epatice optimum, uncias iii., brionie, mirobolonorum indorum, reb. belliricorum, emblicorum, citrinorum, masticiis, dyagridii, azari, rosarum, Reubarbari an unciam i. Confice cum succo caulium vel absynthii. Dosis sit vii. vel v. Et iste competunt convenienti et ydonea dieta observata. Et valent iste pillulae contra omnem dolorem capitis, ex quacumque causa, vel ex quocumque humore procedat, purgant mire omnes humores, Leticiam generant, mentem acuunt, visum reddunt et reparant, auditum restituunt, Juventutem conservant, Scotomiam et vertiginem reparant, canes (? canities) retardant, memoriam conservant, Emigraneam depellunt, oculos illuminant, aciem reparant, et in puerilem etatem reducunt. Et si aliquis humorum est impedimenti in gingivis et dentibus, medifica[n]t et in soliditatem conservant, arterias de flemate purgant, Epiglotum et uvam (?uvulam) cum voce clarificant, appetivam virtutem confortant, Stomachum epar et splenem coadjuvant. Sonitum aurium et surditatem tollunt, causas febrium omnino extingunt et auferunt, ascarides vermes necant, omnibus etatibus et temporibus tam masculino quam feminino sexui conveniunt.' In the Laurentian Library, xii. 27. p. 48, I find a similar prescription which may have been given either by Michael Scot or Master Volmar who succeeded him as court physician. It is as follows : 'Pulvis Domini Fred. Imperatoris, valens contra omnium humorum exceptionem et precipue contra fleumaticum et melanconicum, ex quibus diuturnae infirmitates capitis et stomachi habent [?] provenire. Valet quippe contra defectum visus et stomachi

an extravagant commendation of its healing powers. Mineral medicines were evidently not in fashion in those days; for the recipe speaks only of simples derived from herbs of different kinds. It is to be observed that this agrees exactly with the practice of Salerno, as the Materia Medica of that school was chiefly drawn from the botany of Dioscorides afterwards expounded by Ibn Beithar of Malaga, the great Moorish authority on the healing virtues of plants. There is no reason then to doubt the truth of the title which ascribes the prescription for these pills to Michael Scot. It is in any case a curious relic of early medical practice.

It is possible that the great plague which fell

debilitatem cibaria sumpta digeri et membris incorporari facit, valet contra stomachi ventositatem Scotomiam ante oculos inducentem, restaurat memoriam quocumque humore perditum, verum(?) dolorem ex frigiditate provenientem mitigat. Recipe : Carium, petrosillini anisi, marati, sexmontani, Bethonice, Cymini, calamite, pulegii, ysopi, spicenardi, piperis, sal gemme, rute, centrumgalli, herbae regiae, heufragie, olibani, mastici, croci, mirabolanorum, omnium, et plus de citrinis, an. ꝫ l. et utaris omni tempore indifferenter. Addenda sunt ista ; Cynamomi, Schināti, maiorane, folii balsamite, mzimi, (?) cardamomi, galenge, regulitie, an. ꝫ l. pulverizza, et utaris indifferenter.' The MS. is in a hand of the thirteenth century. The Myrobalans, long discarded from the Pharmacopœia, were the dried fruits of various species of Phyllanthus and Terminalia which grow in India. They are still used in native practice, especially in the preparation of the *Bit laban*, a remedy in rheumatic gout prepared by calcining these seeds with the fossil muriate of soda. See *Asiatic Researches*, xi. pp. 174, 181, 192. The bellirica and emblica are other species of the same plant, the Terminalia. See Bauhin's *Historia Plantarum*, 1613. The Dyagridium or Dacridium is an alternative name for scammony. Azarum, the same as asarum, the Aristolochia. Maratum or Marathrum an old name for fennel. Reb. is probably the Robes of the early chemical authors=a vinegar, here impregnated with the active principle of the fruits prescribed. Cyminum =cumin. Calamita=mint. Pulegium=pennyroyal, another of the mints. Salgemma=rock-salt. We shall become familiar with this term in perusing the *Liber Luminis* of Michael Scot. Centrumgallus, according to Du Cange, the common garden cockscomb. Herbia regia, the Ocymum citrinum or citron basil. Olibanum, frankincense. Galengha, the root of a species of Alpinia. Regulitia, liquorice. I have been greatly helped in identifying several of these forgotten simples by the kindness of Mr. J. M. Shaw, sub-librarian to the Royal College of Physicians, Edinburgh.

upon Palermo at the time of Frederick's marriage
may have been, in part at least, the occasion of
that interest which both the Emperor and his
astrologer took in the healing art. These epidemics,
which in several of their most fatal forms are now
only known by tradition, were the dreaded scourge
of the Middle Ages ; their prevalence being no doubt
due to the rude and insanitary habits of life which
were then universal. We read of another infectious
sickness which attacked Frederick and his crusaders
when they were on the point of sailing from Brindisi
in 1227. The season was one of terrible heat, so
great indeed that one chronicle says the rays of the
sun melted solid metal ! Lying in the confinement
of their galleys on an unhealthy coast the troops
suffered severely. At last rain fell, but immediately poisonous damps arose from the steaming soil,
and the plague began to show itself. Two bishops
and the Landgrave of Thuringia were among the
victims of the pestilence, and very many of the
crusaders died. Frederick himself ran considerable
risk of his life. Against the advice of his physician
he had exposed himself to the sun in the course of
his journey to Brindisi. After three days with the
fleet he was obliged to return on account of the
state of his health, when he at once went to the
waters at Pozzuoli, which proved a successful cure.
Michael Scot must have entered into these affairs
with a large concern and responsibility for his
master's health, and we shall think much of the
importance and consequence he enjoyed at this time
when we remember that the chief object of his care
as a physician was the life of one on whom interests
that were more than European then depended.

CHAPTER VIII

THE various occupations in which Michael Scot engaged upon his return to court were not without their due and, as we believe, designed effect. The part he had taken in producing the Latin Averroës was soon forgotten when it appeared that no immediate publication of these proscribed works was intended by the Emperor. Scot now stood boldly before the world in no suspicious character; distinguished only by his great learning and the fidelity with which he discharged his offices of astrologer and physician about the Imperial person.

This rehabilitation of his fame opened the way to further honours and emoluments which Frederick soon began to seek on his servant's behalf. Scot had never quite lost character as a churchman, and the member of a great religious Order, though his studies had carried him far from the somewhat narrow and beaten track of an ordinary ecclesiastical education. Like Philip of Tripoli, he was probably in holy orders, and even held a benefice, while, as we see from the dedication of his *De Coelo et Mundo* to Stephen of Provins, he was careful, even in the wildest heats of his work on Averroës, to keep in touch with those who held high positions in the Church. Soon after his return from Spain a resolute and repeated attempt was made to secure for him some ecclesiastical preferment.

Honorius III. then sat in the Chair of St. Peter. In 1223 a dispensation was granted by the Curia allowing Michael Scot to hold a plurality. At the same time the Pope wrote to Stephen Langton the Primate of England, desiring that Scot should be preferred to the first suitable place which might fall vacant in that country.[1] Honorius was then at peace with the Emperor, and we may believe that it was in consequence of some strong representation made by Frederick that he took such an interest in the fortunes of this Imperial *protégé.*

The application to Canterbury was entirely in accordance with the habits of the time ; for England was then the constant resource of the Popes when they wished to confer a favour on any of their clergy. Many and deep were the complaints which this practice awakened among the priesthood of the north. A like abuse of influence appeared in Scotland as well. Theiner reports the case of a clerk named Peter, the son of Count George of Cabaliaca, on whose behalf the Pope wrote in 1259 to the Canons of St. Andrews, desiring that he might be reinstated in his benefice of China-chim (Kennoway in Fife) which he had forfeited as an adherent of the Empire.[2] It is only fair, however, to notice that there were instances of the contrary practice. In 1218, for example, one Matthew, a Scot, was recommended by Honorius to the University of Paris for the degree of

---

[1] Year viii. of his Pontificate, namely Jan. 16, 1223. See the interesting article by Milman in the *Miscellany of the Philobiblon Society,* vol. i. 1854. He refers to the papers of Mr. W. R. Hamilton in the British Museum, and especially to vol. ii. pp. 214, 228, 246.

[2] *Monumenta, sub anno* 1259, Feb. 12.

Doctor, that he might teach there in the faculty of Divinity.

It may seem remarkable that the Pope did not address his application in Scot's favour to St. Andrews rather than to Canterbury. We are to recollect, however, that in 1223, the relations between Scotland and the See of Rome were still somewhat strained. The North had not yet forgotten what took place in 1217, when Gualo came thither as Legate to lay the Interdict upon Scotland. Churches were closed by this severe sentence; the sacraments forbidden; even that of extreme unction denied to the people; the dead were buried without service, and all marriages were celebrated in the churchyards. When the interdict was removed in the following year, the duty of proclaiming that remission was intrusted to the Prior of Durham and the Dean of York, who made a solemn progress in the Kingdom to announce the Pope's clemency. We may feel sure that these events were not forgotten in five years by a proud and independent nation like the people of Scotland, and Honorius must be thought to have judged rightly in supposing his application on Scot's account had a better chance of being effected by the English than by the Scottish Primate. Nothing indeed was overlooked that might give force to the recommendation. The Pope accompanied his request with a generous testimony to the scholar's ability, saying that he was distinguished, even among learned men, for his remarkable gifts and knowledge.[1] Thus everything seemed to promise

---

[1] 'Quod inter literatos vigeat dono scientiae singulari.'

that Michael Scot would soon enjoy a rich English living; the *El dorado* of the foreign clergy in those easy days of sinecures secured by dispensations of plurality and non-residence.

Meanwhile, however, a much more favourable occasion offered itself to the Pope for securing the interests of Frederick's *protégé*, and one which dispensed with any concurrence of the English Primate in the matter. In the same year which witnessed his application to Stephen Langton a vacancy occurred in the Archbishopric of Cashel. The chapter of that see proposed a candidate of their own to Honorius, probably the Bishop of Cork, but the Pope saw his opportunity and named Michael Scot for the vacant benefice. The obedient Chapter at once proceeded to elect him. The consequence being to their apprehension a foregone conclusion, the Curia issued another dispensation permitting this favourite of fortune to hold the Archbishopric along with all his other benefices.[1] So nearly did Scot come to the possession of a high place in the Church, and an office which would surely have altered his fame in the ages that were to come.

But those who thus took into their hands the shaping of the future for Michael Scot were soon to learn that the man they had to deal with was of another nature than their own; a very Scot in his scruples and the conscientiousness with which he gave effect to them. Incredible as it must then have seemed, remarkable as it would be even in our own day, Michael Scot refused Cashel,[2] and

---

[1] Theiner, *Monumenta*, p. 23, *ad annum* viii. Hon. III. *i.e.* 1223.
[2] Declinature noted June 20, 1223.

this for a reason which showed how high was the
conception he had formed of the pastoral office.
His *nolo episcopari* proceeded on the ground that
he was ignorant of the Irish language. He would
not, it seems, be a chief pastor without the power
to teach and feed the flock committed to his
care. He would not consent to be intruded upon a
people to whom he must have proved unacceptable,
nor would he, in the too common fashion of the
day, commit his duties in Ireland to a suffragan,
while enjoying ample revenues and a lordly title
in Italy.

It is somewhat startling to find a principle
not unheard of in the Scotland of our own century
so clearly grasped and so conscientiously followed
by this *non-intrusionist* countryman of ours six
hundred years ago. Yet Michael Scot did not
stand alone in his sacrifice even in these slack
times, as may be seen by the case of his namesake, John Scot, who was Bishop of Dunkeld during
the pontificate of Clement III.[1] This earlier Pre-
late ruled a vast diocese which included the country
of Argyll as well as the more eastern parts of
central Scotland. His conscience became uneasy
under the responsibility, and, unwilling to continue
the spiritual overseer of those whom from his
ignorance of their language he could not edify,
he wrote to the Pope, desiring that Argyll might
be disjoined from Dunkeld, and that Ewaldus his
chaplain, who knew Erse, might have charge of
the new diocese as its Bishop. This was actually
done in 1200, and the good Bishop died in great
peace two years later. 'How can I give a com-

---

[1] Milman's *Church History*, vol. iv. p. 17.

fortable account to the Judge of the world at
the last day,' so he had written to Clement, 'if
I pretend to teach those who cannot understand
me? The revenues suffice for two Bishops, if
we are content with a competency, and are
not prodigal of the patrimony of Christ. It is
better to lessen the charge and increase the
number of labourers in the Lord's Vineyard.' In
some such terms must Michael Scot too have
declined Cashel. His case, as well as that of
Dunkeld, is enough to show that ecclesiastical
corruption, though widespread, was not, even in
those days, universal. May no Cervantes of the
Church ever arise in Scotland to laugh such
sacred chivalry away!

The disappointment he nevertheless felt on this
occasion may probably have encouraged Scot in
his attachment to the court and to his new duties
there as astrologer and physician, in which, as we
have seen, he rose to such acknowledged eminence.
Frederick did not, however, lose sight of his purpose to procure him preferment. The first application to Canterbury having met with no re-
sponse it was renewed four years later in 1227, by
Gregory IX., who in that year succeeded Honorius
in the Chair of St. Peter. This new Pontiff was
destined to become the Emperor's most bitter and
relentless foe, but as yet he remained on good
terms with Frederick and inclined to show him
favour. He seems to have made no difficulty in
taking up the case of Michael Scot, and even
added on his own account a eulogy meant to
forward the scholar's claim; representing him as
a distinguished student, not only in Latin letters,

but also of the Hebrew and Arabic languages.[1]
So far as can be seen, however, the attempt of
1227 shared the fate of that which had been
made in 1223. Canterbury gave no signs of acqui-
escence, and Michael Scot, for all his distinction,
remained without the preferment which his friends
so constantly sought to obtain for him.

There is reason to think that from this time a
change took place in the spirit of the philosopher.
The natural chagrin he must have felt as it became
plain that no position he could accept would be
offered to him in the Church affected deeply his
fine and sensitive nature. He soon passed into
a brooding and despondent mood, which remained
unaffected by all the praise and fame paid by the
learned world as a tribute to his remarkable talents
and achievements. It is in this change of temper
to a morbid depression that we are to find the
occasion and inspiring spirit of those strange prophetical verses which bear his name and which
differ so widely from all the other productions of
his pen.

Such compositions were indeed far from being
uncommon in Italy. The reputed prophecies of
the Erythræan Sibyl were extant in the form of
an epistle supposed to be addressed to the Greeks
under the walls of Troy. This curious composition
is said to have been rendered into the Greek
language from the Syriac by a certain Doxopatros.
His version was one of those volumes which had
reached Sicily from the library of Manuel Com-

---

[1] 'Nec contentus littera tantum erudire Latina, ut in ea melius
formaretur, Hebraice et Arabice insudavit laudabiliter et profecit, et sic
doctus in singulis grata diversorum varietate nitescit,'—Hamilton MSS.
in British Museum, vol. iii. p. 57,

nenus Emperor of Constantinople, and was then translated into Latin during the twelfth century by Eugenio, admiral to King Roger. A series of poets from Giovacchino di Fiora[1] to Jacopone da Todi[2] then chose the prophetic lyre and made it resound with dark sayings and predictions of misfortune and ruin. Especially worthy of study in this connection are the verses ascribed to *Merlin*, which declare the fate of many Italian cities.[3] That Michael Scot gave his talents to this kind of composition rests on evidence as convincing as any which establishes the other events of his life. Pipini the chronicler says that 'he was reputed to have the gift of prophecy, for he published verses in which he foretold the ruin of certain Italian cities as well as other circumstances.'[4] An earlier, indeed a contemporary, authority, Henry Abrincensis, in a poem presented to Frederick II. in 1235 or the early months of the following year, speaks of Michael Scot as 'another Apollo,' 'a prophet of truth' possessed of 'hidden secrets' and the author of 'certain predictions regarding thee, O Caesar.'[5]

Quotations from the prophecies of Scot were made by Villani.[6] The lines referring to Florence may still be read in a manuscript of the Riccardian

---

[1] He was a Calabrian abbot, who died in 1202.

[2] This author died in 1306.

[3] See Muratori 'Rerum Italicarum Scriptores,' viii. (1726) ad calcem *Mem. Potest. Reg.*

[4] Muratori, *Op. cit.* ix. 669 B.

[5] 'Quaedam de Te presagia, Cesar,
A Michaele Scoto me percepisse recordor.
Qui fuit astrorum scrutator, qui fuit Augur,
Qui fuit Ariolus, et qui fuit alter Apollo.'
Poem of Henri d'Avranches in 'Forschungen zur Deutschen Geschichte,' xviii. (1878), p. 486.

[6] Vol. x. p. 105. See also the same vol., pp. 101 and 148.

Library in that city,[1] and in another, preserved in Padua,[2] we find the following title : 'Here begin certain prophecies of Michael Scot, the most illustrious astrologer of Lord Frederick the Emperor, which declare somewhat of the future, to wit, of certain Italian cities.' This shows that verses, bearing to have been composed by Scot, were current at an early date, though the scribe of the Paduan manuscript has forgotten to fulfil the promise he makes in his title, for that which follows it is not the poetry of Scot but only a dull treatise on Latin prosody.

It is to Salimbene that we owe the preservation of these verses in their most complete form. He must have taken much interest in them, as he is careful to give, not only the original Latin, but an Italian translation as well. From his pages then we shall borrow the text of these curious lines.[3] According to Salimbene they are these :

'Regis vexilla timens, fugiet velamina Brixa,
Et suos non poterit filios, propriosque, tueri.
Brixia stans fortis secundi certamine Regis,
Post Mediolani sternentur moenia gryphi.
Mediolanum territum cruore fervido necis,
Resuscitabit viso cruore mortis.
In numeris errantes erunt atque silvestres.
Deinde Vercellus veniunt Novaria Laudum.
Affuerit dies, quod aegra Papia erit,
Vastata curabitur moesta dolore flendo.
Munera quae meruit diu parata vicinis,
Pavida mandatis parebit Placentia Regis.
Oppressa resiliet, passa damnosa strage,
Cum fuerit unita in firmitate manebit.
Placentia patebit grave pondus sanguine mixtum.
Parma parens viret, totisque frondibus uret

---

[1] L. ii. xvii. 338, p. 183vo.
[2] Bibl. Univ. No. 1557, p. 43. This MS. is of the fifteenth century.
[3] 'Chronica F. Salimbene,' Parma 1857, pp. 176-177.

Serpens in obliquo tumido, exitque draconi.
Parma, Regi parens, tumida percutiet illum
Vipera Draconem, Florumque virescet amoenum.
Tu ipsa Cremona patieris flammae dolorem
In fine praedito,conscia tanti mali,
Et Regis partes insimul mala verba tenebunt.
Paduae magnatum plorabunt filii necem
Duram et horrendam, datam catuloque Veronae.
Marchia succumbet, gravi servitute coacta
Ob viam Antenoris quamque secuti erunt.
Languida resurget, catulo moriente, Verona.
Mantua, vae tibi, tanto dolore plena,
Cur ne vacillas nam tui pars ruet?
Ferraria fallax, fides falsa nil tibi prodiat,
Subire te cunctis cum tua facta ruent
Peregre missura quos tua mala parant
Faventia iniet tecum, videns tentoria pacem
Corruet in festem ducto velamine pacis.
Bononia renuens ipsam vastabitur agmine circa
Sed dabit immensum, purgato agmine, censum.
Mutina fremescet sibi certando sub lima
Quae dico tepescet tandem trahetur ad ima.
Pergami deorsum excelsa moenia cadent
Rursus, et amoris ascendet stimulus arcem.
Trivisii duae partes offerent non signa salutis
Gaudia fugantes vexilla praebenda ruinae.
Roma diu titubans, longis terroribus acta
Corruet, et mundi desinet esse caput.
Fata monent, stellaeque docent, aviumque volatus,
Quod Fridericus malleus orbis erit.
Vivet Draco magnus cum immenso turbine mundi.
Fata silent, stellaeque tacent, aviumque volatus
Quod Petri navis desinet esse caput.
Reviviscet Mater : malleabit caput Draconis.
Non diu stolida florebit Florentia florum.
Corruet in feudum dissimulando vivet.
Venecia aperiet venas, percutiet undique Regem.
Infra millenos ducenos sexque decennos
Erunt sedata immensa turbina mundi
Morietur Gripho, aufugient undique pennae.'

It would be difficult to determine how much of
the original composition of Scot these verses preserve, and how much they owe to later hands. We
cannot be mistaken, however, in remarking their

uniform tone of melancholy and apprehension, with the burden of its constantly recurring ' corruet,' or in taking this as a true index to the state of the author's mind.

Pipini records two other prophecies of Michael Scot which serve to confirm this observation in a high degree.[1] The astrologer, he says, forecast the manner of the Emperor's death, which was to take place *ad portas ferreas*, at certain gates of iron, in a town named after Flora. This prediction was generally understood of Florence ; the rather perhaps that the church of Santo Stefano there was called *ad portam ferream* ; and Frederick accordingly avoided coming to that city.[2] During his last campaign in 1250, however, he fell sick at the town of Fiorentino or Firenzola in Apulia, and lay in a chamber of the castle. His bed stood against a wall recently built to fill up the ancient gateway of the tower, while within the wall there still remained the iron staples on which the gate had been hung. Uneasy at the progress of his disease, and hearing something of these particulars, the Emperor fell into deep thought and then exclaimed, ' This is the place where I shall make an end, as it was told me. The will of God be done ; for here I shall die,' and soon afterwards he breathed his last.

The other prediction which the chronicler attributes to Scot relates to the occasion of his own death. This, he said, would take place by the blow of a

---

[1] Muratori, *Op. cit.* ix. 660 B.

[2] Similar deceitful prophecies are not uncommon in mediæval story Walter Map in the *De Nugis Curialium* tells how Silvester II. was assured by his familiar spirit that he would not die till he had said Mass at Jerusalem. The prediction was fulfilled, however, when the Pope did so at the altar called ' in Gerusalemme' in one of the Roman Churches, and soon thereafter expired.

stone falling on his head. His calculations were
so exact as even to furnish him with the precise
weight of this instrument of fate. Being in church
one day, with head uncovered at the sacring of the
Mass, a stone, agreeing in all particulars with his
prediction, was shaken from the tower by the
motion of the bellrope and wounded Scot to death.

There is much in these tales which lies apart
from the course of a sober biography; belonging
rather to that legendary and mystic fame of the
philosopher which we shall immediately proceed to
consider. Something, however, in which all these
prophecies agree deserves our attention here, and
that is their sombre and menacing character. 'Rui-
nam predixit,' says Pipini, referring to Scot's verses
on the Italian cities, and his thoughts, whether
engaged with Frederick's fate or his own, seem at
this time to have followed the same dark and
ominous course. Death and destruction now filled
all his mind, much as if he had been a Highlander
gifted with the fatal power of the *Taisch* : a seer to
whom all things looked darkly, and all men wore a
shroud, longer or shorter, to mark the time and the
manner of their end.

With Michael Scot's account of his own fate
Pipini joins another curious matter, that of the *cervi-*
lerium.[1] This was a plate or cap of steel meant to
be worn under the ordinary covering of the head as
an additional defence, and the chronicle says that
Scot invented and wore it that he might be safe
from the danger he foresaw. Taking this together

---

[1] Muratori, *Op. cit.* ix. pp. 128 B, 670 ; and xiv. p. 1095. Other
forms of this word are *cerebrerium, celeberium* or *cerobotarium.* It is
of course derived from *cerebrum,* and the English equivalent would be
brainpiece.

with the prophecies, both general and personal, we can find no better explanation than that which bids us see in the whole what indicates a case of ecstatic melancholy such as would seem to be the sad heritage of not a few finer natures sprung of the stock from which Michael Scot descended. We hear the same sad note in the strange jingle he wove so long before in the preface of his *Physionomia* : ' Nos ibimus ibitis, ibunt. Omnia pereunt, praeter amare Deum,' and one would fain hope that in his frequent fits of depression Scot may have indeed found rest in what he thus declares to be the only abiding portion of the soul. The wild account of his illness at Cordova, and of the dreams which then visited him is not to be neglected in this connection. Perhaps the cloud then first fell which in after-years returned upon him with such redoubled gloom. Thus the traits of Scot's youth fit well the picture we are now constrained to form, and the whole gives promise that here at last we may have touched upon the man himself as he was, physically, mentally, and spiritually. A slight worn body spent with arduous study, like a sheath which the sword has almost broken through ; a soul possessed with the sense of Divine things, yet sad, and subject to strange illusions ; a conscience morbidly awake and painfully scrupulous ; a mind to which almost every branch of knowledge was familiar, and not incapable of striking out here and there in a path of its own : if these be not Michael Scot, scholar in the court and courtier in the schools, then it may safely be said that no indications exist which can ever reveal to us this striking personality as he lived and moved in the world.

We seem to see in him a Pascal of the thirteenth
century; and this all the more that Michael Scot
resembled that great genius not only in the mystical
and superstitious side of his nature but in his devotion to mathematical science.   How piquant is the
contrast between this mighty and gifted child of the
mist and the northern hills and those sunny southern
lands of grape and fig, of white cliff, marble column
and laughing summer sea, where most of his life was
spent.   No wonder that those among whom Michael
Scot lived found him somewhat of a mystery at all
times, and, especially in these later days of his
burdened spirit, took him for a Mage, weaving his
dark sayings into regular prophecies.   The Latin
races have never been famous for their power to com-
prehend the northern character.   How much less
was it likely they should in the case of one who
seems to have presented every feature of that racial
type in its extremest form?   In our own day this
incapacity takes the way of accusing as madness all
that it cannot fathom of Celtic or Teutonic ways.
In the times of Scot the same impatience found a
more modest expression.   He was incomprehensible,
therefore he must be inspired; gifted with the prophet's divine and incommunicable fire.

We may take it for granted that much of Michael
Scot's dissatisfaction and depression upon his disappointment in seeking ecclesiastical preferment
arose from the feeling that he had made a great
sacrifice in vain.   The best years of his life, and the
most strenuous labours of his mind, had been given
to his version of Averroës not without the hope that
he was here laying the foundation of a great literary
and philosophic fame.   Moved by a prudence, which

was not altogether selfish since it concerned the Emperor's reputation and policy quite as much as his own, he had submitted to necessity, and saw his translation suppressed for the sake of avoiding offence. The sacrifice was great and doubtless keenly felt, and when in spite of this policy he found himself still without the position he had confidently hoped for, with what bitterness must the reawakening of his literary ambition have been attended. Near ten years had been lost since his return from Spain, and still Scot's Averroës slept, unknown to the schools, in the honourable but unprofitable seclusion of the Imperial closet. With the death of these hopes of preferment, however, all reason for this unfortunate reserve came to an end so far as Scot was concerned. As soon as he had once made up his mind to think no more of a great ecclesiastical career he was free to urge his master with all insistence to carry out their long-cherished plan, and secure undying fame for both by publishing the new Aristotle in the Universities of Europe.

Nor was there anything in the policy of the time which made Frederick unwilling to further a project which he had all along designed. From the moment of his elevation to the See of Rome Gregory IX. had displayed a firm and unbending temper towards the Emperor. Frederick felt the first instances of his harshness in 1227, when, returning sick and feeble from the baths of Pozzuoli, he found himself excommunicated because he had not sailed to Palestine with the Crusade. This severe sentence was renewed in 1228. Frederick reached the Holy Land that year, but only to meet a mutinous spirit, encouraged among the Crusaders there by the Pope's orders. On his return in 1229 the sharp edge of discipline was again drawn against him, and we need not wonder if such repeated severity at last convinced the Emperor that there was no hope of living at peace with Rome, nor any reason to study further accommodations with one who seemed determined to be his enemy. The moment had now come when restraints, long submitted to for the sake of policy, being removed, Frederick might well bethink him of his former plans so long held in reserve, and take measures to carry out his purpose of enriching the learned world with the prohibited books of Averroës.

This plan not only promised to fulfil a long cherished desire and mortify an implacable foe, it must also have presented itself in the light of a welcome concession made to a deserving servant of the Crown. Michael Scot had laboured long to form the works in question. His interest, as well as every other reason, now demanded that they should lie no longer concealed. The fame he was certain to gain by this publication would be the best consolation, perhaps the only one now possible, for his disappointments in the ecclesiastical career. To employ him actively in the matter may well have appeared not only just, considering his previous interest in it, but the best cure for a spirit sadly disordered and depressed. We need not wonder that Frederick at last fully formed his resolution, or that he chose Michael Scot as the means of carrying out a publication that was now definitely determined on.

An imperial circular announced to the learned

the nature and origin of these new versions.[1] This letter was designed to secure for them such general interest and attention as was due to works of the first importance. Opening with the avowal of his devotion to the cause of letters, a confession which he supported by quoting from the *Metaphysica*, Frederick touched upon the manifold cares of state which the conduct of his affairs in the Empire involved. He added that he had never allowed these to occupy his whole attention, but had still devoted part of his time to the pursuits of learning. His mind, he said, had been particularly attracted to the works of Aristotle with the commentaries of the Arabian philosophers, especially those concerning mathematics, and the books called *Sermoniales*. Finding that they were inaccessible to Latin scholars, owing to their obscurity and the foreign tongues in which they were written, he had commissioned learned men to translate these works, desiring them to preserve in their versions the exact style as well as sense of the original. The treasures thus procured he would not keep in obscurity, but designed to publish them for the general good. He addressed himself to the most famous schools of Christendom as the proper means of obtaining the diffusion of this wisdom among those who were able to profit by it.

Which then were the universities intended by the Emperor? That of Naples certainly in the first place, for it was his own creation.[2] Bologna, also, we may believe, judging by the estimation in which we know him to have held that still more ancient

---

[1] See the *Epistolarium* of Petrus de Vineis. Jourdain reprints thi letter with a French translation in his *Recherches*, pp. 156-162.

[2] In 1224.

seat of learning.[1]   Copies of Frederick's letter are
indeed extant, which actually bear the address, ' To
the Masters and Scholars of Bologna.'   Nor can
we think that he forgot Paris, the great centre of
European culture.   At least one text has preserved
this the most natural of all directions :—' To the
Doctors of the Quadrivium at Paris.'[2]   Thus far
then the course of Scot's journey on this important
business is plain.   In it he but reversed the progress he had made in early years, revisiting in the
contrary order the scenes of his former studies.   His
own remarkable fame, the widespread curiosity concerning the books he brought, and his official character as Frederick's Ambassador of Letters, must
have secured him everywhere a cordial and distinguished reception.

There is reason to think that his travels did
not end when he had reached Paris.   Tradition says
he crossed the Channel and visited both England
and Scotland, where his medical skill was highly
appreciated.   It is indeed to an English author that
we owe the knowledge of this journey performed
by Michael Scot.   The words of Roger Bacon are
of capital importance here, not only telling us of
Scot's travels, but showing the nature of the work
he carried with him in that progress, and the en-
thusiasm with which these books were received.
' In the days of Michael Scot,' he says, ' who, about
the year 1230, made his appearance with certain
books of Aristotle and commentaries of learned men
concerning physics and mathematics, the Aristo-
telian philosophy became celebrated in the Latin

---

[1] Frederick sought at Bologna for scholars to fill the chairs in Naples.
[2] Martenne, ' Vett. scriptt. et Monumenta,' ii. 1220.

Schools'[1] At the time of which he speaks, Bacon, born in 1214, may probably have been at Oxford pursuing his studies. It is not necessary to dwell upon the support which this brings to the tradition of Scot's visit to England. We may take it as almost certain that Oxford was one of the universities where he appeared and was made welcome.

The tradition that he thereafter pursued his journey to Scotland rests rather upon arguments derived from the probability ofthe case than from direct evidence. Scot had been a lifetime absent from his native land, and, finding himself so near it, a strong impulse must have urged him to revisit the scenes of his boyhood. Nor is it easy to account for the fact that his fame, though he spent so much of his time abroad, attained, and yet retains, such a currency in the North, except upon the supposition that he did actually yield to this attraction and thus once more made himself a familiar figure in the land of his birth.

One matter of great interest is at least certain. Scot's death occurred just at this time, when he was in the very height of his fame and influence, and probably while he was still in the North. The account, so often repeated and reprinted, which makes him live almost to the close of the century need not occupy our attention more than a moment. Already incredible from the time when Jourdain discovered that Scot's version of Alpetrongi had been produced in 1217, such a notion becomes more than ever impossible since we have been able to

---

[1] *Opus Majus*, pp. 36, 37, ed. Jebbi. 'Tempore Michaelis Scoti, qui, annis 1230 transactis, apparuit, deferens librorum Aristotelis partes aliquas de naturalibus et mathematicis, cum expositoribus sapientibus, magnificata est Aristotelis philosophia apud Latinos.'

carry the time of his mature literary activity back to the year 1210. Vincent of Beauvais, writing about 1245, talks of 'old Michael Scot' in such a way as to suggest that he had by that time been long in his grave. But the convincing evidence, though hitherto little noticed, is to be found in the poem of Henry d'Avranches, from which we have already quoted some lines in another connection. This author remarks regarding Michael Scot:

'Thus he who questioned fate, to fate himself submitted,'

which shows that the time of his death must have been earlier than 1235, the date when Abrincensis composed his poem.[1]

The question is thus reduced to the narrow limit of five years; since Bacon says Scot was alive and busy in his great mission in 1230. Within this period he must have passed away, and probably his death happened nearer the earlier than the later date; considering the tone in which Henry d'Avranches speaks of the departed sage. He may well therefore have died while on the borders of Scotland. This idea agrees curiously with the fact that Italy has no tradition of his burial-place, while on the other hand northern story points to his tomb in Melrose Abbey, Glenluce, Holme Coltrame, or some other of the great Cistercian foundations of that country. Satchells, who visited Burgh-under-Bowness in 1629, found a guide named Lancelot Scot, who took him to the parish church, where he saw the great scholar's tomb, and found it still the

---

[1] 'Veridicus Vates Michael, haec pauca locutus,
Plura locuturus obmutuit, et, sua mundo
Non paciens archana plebescere, jussit
Eius ut in tenues prodiret hanelitus auras.
Sic acusator fatorum fata subivit.' *Op. cit.* verse 80 *et seq.*

object of mysterious awe to the people there.[1] The resting-place of Michael Scot will never now be accurately known, but there is every reason to suppose that it lies not far from that of his birth, in the sweet Borderland, amid the green hills and flowing streams of immemorial story.

Here then we leave the life that has been the subject of our study, and not without the tribute of a certain envy paid to so happy a fate as that of Michael Scot. Like another and far greater man, whose sepulchre also was not known among his people, Scot died in the fulness of his powers and fame, while yet his sight was not dim, nor his natural force abated. He was denied indeed the entry to those broad kingdoms of knowledge which later times enjoy, but we may truly think of him as one who stood in his own day upon a height from which something of that fair land of promise could at least be divined, and manfully did his part in leading the progress of the human mind onward to those more perfect attainments now within the reach of every patient scholar.

We may recollect in closing this inquiry that the *Abbreviatio Avicennae* was published in 1232 at Melfi. This treatise, though it came in the Latin version from the hand of Scot, did not fall within the scope of the publication made so widely in 1230; since the Emperor's object at that time was to acquaint the world with the commentaries of Averroës. The manner in which the *Abbreviatio* saw the light was somewhat remarkable. Henry of Colonia was the scholar selected by Frederick for

---

[1] 'History of the Rt. Hon. Name of Scot,' in *Lay of the Last Minstrel*, Note W.

the work of transcribing it from the imperial copy.
A regular diploma passed the seals authorising him
to do this work, and from that writ we find that he
completed it at Melfi, on the vigil of St. Laurence
in the house of Master Volmar the imperial physician.[1] We may surely see in these facts a further
likelihood that by this time Scot was already dead.
Another holds his place as court-physician, another
wields his pen, or at least furnishes the copy from
which the world at large first came to know one
of his most important and characteristic works.
May we not take it then, that in ordering this
diploma to be drawn, Frederick desired to show
his concern at hearing he had lost so faithful and
able a servant, and his anxiety that no time should
elapse before the publication of his remaining works?
Thus regarded, the *Abbreviatio* was a wreath laid on
the grave; a tribute to the translator's memory,
while in itself it was a seal set to the fame of Michael
Scot as in his day the chief exponent of the mighty
Aristotle, and one who by these labours succeeded
in directing for many ages the course of study in
the European Schools.

[1] The diploma is dated at Melfi on the 9th of August 1232. The
colophon to the copy then made of the *Abbreviatio Avicennae* is as
follows : 'Completus est liber Avicenne de animalibus, scriptus per
Magistrum Henricum Coloniensem, ad exemplar magnifici Imperatoris
nostri Domini Frederici, apud Meffiam civitatem Apulie, ubi Dominus
Imperator eidem Magistro hunc librum premissum commodavit, anno
Domini MCCXXXII, in Vigilia Beati Laurentii, in domo Magistri Volmari
medici Imperatoris.' See Huillard-Bréholles, *Hist. Diplom. Frid.* II.,
vol. iv. part i. pp. 381-2.

CHAPTER IX

HITHERTO we have taken little notice of the fame by which Michael Scot is most widely known in literature; preferring to speak first of the authentic facts and real employments of his life, so far as these can now be ascertained. It would be improper, however, to close our investigation without taking some account of that darker reputation which has so long represented him to the world as a magician and dealer in forbidden lore. If we have deferred so long the consideration of this matter, the reason may be found in the fact that there seems to be no truth in such stories. They live only in legend, and in the literature of romance, and must therefore be held apart by a firm line from the domain of sober historical inquiry.

This conclusion, be it observed, is not based upon the prevailing opinion of the present day that such arts are impossible, nor has it thence been reached by way of the inference that because magic is impossible, therefore Michael Scot cannot have meddled in it. Such was not at all the view held in the thirteenth century. Then scholars as well as the unlearned, and clergy as well as laity, believed firmly in the possibility, nay, the reality, of what they regarded as an unwarrantable interference with the order of nature. This belief makes it a fair subject of discussion in regard to any one of that age whether or not he may have practised forbidden arts. The question in Scot's case is a highly curious one, and, without further apology, we now proceed to examine it in detail.

The most famous schools of magic in those days were fixed by popular tradition in the Spanish cities of Toledo and Salamanca, especially the former. Magic, indeed, was generally spoken of as the *scientia Toletana*. The *Morgante Maggiore* of Pulci may furnish us with a fair example of the common belief : [1]

> 'Per quel ch'io udì gia dir, sendo in Tolleta
> Dove ogni negromante si racozza.'

and again :

> 'Questa città di Tolleta solea
> Tenere studio di Nigromanzia.
> Quivi di magica arte si legea
> Pubblicamente, e di Piromancia
> E molti Geomanti sempre avea
> E esperimenti assai di Idromanzia.'

Caesar Von Heisterbach, the anecdote-monger of the century, relates more than one diverting tale of necromantic prodigies, the scene of which he lays at Toledo. The most remarkable of these stories tells how some Germans came thither to learn magic.[2] Their teacher in this art called up certain spirits, who appeared first as armed men, and then in the form of lovely maids. One of the students was thereby allured and carried off. The others

---

[1] See this poem, canto xxv. oct. 42 and 259. Consult also Soldan, *Magia Antica*, and *Storia dei Processi di Stregheria*, and *Conrad de Marburg*.

[2] *Illustrium Miraculorum*, v. 4. See also i. 33 for another tale of the same kind.

drew their swords and threatened the master with death, until, overcome by fear, he used his power to secure their companion's return.

From the favourite locality of these legends we may infer that the magic then in vogue was that of the Arabs, which, especially in Spain, had now begun to supplant the ancient and primitive European superstitions. This magic was not a mere ritual of spells, such as that of the Chaldean monuments, but rather a complete theurgy, like the magic of Egypt; the corruption of an ancient and elaborate religious system.[1] The Arabian mage pretended to bow the superior powers which other men could only worship, and boldly bade them do his will. It is hardly necessary to say that such a system did not originally belong to the Arabs, who had been, until the days of Mohammed, a rude and savage people. They learned it in Syria and Egypt, where the theories of Porphyry and Iamblichus still held sway.[2] In their hands this magic became enriched with many new conceits, such as the nimble fancy of these children of the East knew well how to interweave with all that they touched. The stars, they held, were the centres of supreme influence, but had certain correspondences with earthly things; with herbs, with stones, and even with sounds. These were in a sort the offspring of heaven, for plants of power were precious things put forth by the sun and moon; the minerals were condensed and congealed by the same heavenly agency in a planetary hour, and earthly voices, even the cries of dumb animals,

[1] See Lenormant, La Magie Chaldéenne.
[2] See Wright's Cat. of the Syriac MSS. in the British Museum. Iamblicus occurs in cod. dccxxix.

were but the far echo of the music heard in heaven, the music of the spheres.

So far, indeed, this was but common doctrine, shared by all the science of the time, and eminently expounded in every astrological system. The magic founded upon it began with the notion that this close correspondence between heaven and earth might carry an influence able to react in an upward, contrary, and unnatural direction. Plants and precious stones, rightly employed, might prove able to bind the stellar powers on which all depended. Names and forms of conjuration might control the superior spirits which the stars represented. Hence arose a whole system of magical practice, in which, from the circle of the sorcerer—a symbol representing on earth the motion of the upper spheres—the vapour of mingled herbs and minerals rose to heaven above the glowing brazier, accompanied by recited spells. It is curious to notice that when, after several ages, this essentially Eastern and theurgic necromancy [1] gave place to the witchcraft of the North, with its dark demonolatry, the essential idea of the Arabian magicians still survived. Its influence may be traced in the importance always attached in popular belief to the *reversal* of natural practice, as a means of securing supernatural power and effect. Hence the bizarre details which crowd the witch trials of the sixteenth and seventeenth centuries : how hags walked backwards, or *withershins*, that is, against the course of the sun, or changed a prayer into a spell by muttering it in a contrary sense.

---

[1] I use this word in the general sense then given to it, which seems to indicate how little the Greek language was understood in those days.

The Arabian magic as understood in Spain during the thirteenth century is very fully expounded in a curious work called *Picatrix*.[1] This book explains that the fundamental idea of the art was reaction leading up to transformation or magical change, adding that this reaction may be seen in three different regions of being; first among the elemental spirits themselves, next between these and matter, and, last, the reaction of one kind of matter upon another, as in alchemy. The second of these kinds of reaction admits the influence of earthly things upon the heavenly spirits, and is the foundation of that kind of magic which the *Picatrix* proceeds to expound, in details which are often much more curious than edifying. This book has special value as showing the intimate relation between magic and the ordinary studies of those times. Aristotle is often quoted in it,[2] and the position of necromancy with regard to other branches of science is clearly defined. It is not hard to see that, when thus understood, this art must have allied itself closely with astronomy and astrology on the one hand, and with alchemy on the other. In the account given by Bacon of Avicenna's philosophy, he says that the third great division of that author's works, and one which had never appeared in Latin, was that devoted to the most hidden parts

---

[1] Said to be written by Norbar the Arab, who compiled it from many sources in the twelfth century. It consists of four books : I. De Coelo, II. De figuris Coeli, III. De proprietatibus Planetarum, IV. De proprietatibus Spirituum; and was translated into Latin by command of Alfonso X. (1252-84). Two MSS. of this version exist in the Bib. Naz. of Florence, XX. 20 and 21. Arpenius gives some account of it in his 'De prodigiosis Naturae,' Hamburg, 1717, p. 106. It is to be hoped it may never be translated into any modern language.

[2] As the author of the *De Coelo et Mundo*, the treatise most nearly bordering on this magical doctrine.

of natural philosophy.[1]   The science of those days left an acknowledged place for the occult and the mysterious among its doctrines.   This place was filled by magic, a study forbidden indeed by the Church, but generally recognised as occupying a real though secret department among the other sciences and arts.   The tradition we so often meet with that masters of necromancy actually taught the art of magic in Toledo, Salamanca, and perhaps Padua, seems but a reflection in later times of what was then the genuine belief of European scholars.

There is thus no reason why Michael Scot should not have devoted himself to what was the subject of actual and serious study during the times in which he lived, and especially so in the country where his chief literary labours were carried on. Were we to follow the mere likelihood of the case, his interest in astronomy and alchemy would lead us to think it very possible he might have studied an art that was so closely connected with these. But to change such a possibility into a certainty, or even a probability, something more convincing than any *a priori* argument must be found.   If no actual proof of Scot's magical practice be forthcoming we must be content to leave the matter where we found it ; in the realm of dim and unsubstantial tradition.[2]

[1] 'In quo exposuit secretiora Naturae.'—*Opus Majus*, p. 37.

[2] That the Arabian magic was familiar to Scot, there can, however, be no manner of doubt.   Take, for instance, the following passage from the *Liber Introductorius* (ms. Bodl. 266, p. 113) : 'Puteus, qui alio nomine sacrarius, navigantibus per contrarium eo quod sequitur caudam scorpionis inter astra, et dicitur poetice quod Dii prius fecerunt in eo con[junctio] nem et sacrificium, cum esset locus secretus intrinsecus, et locus plenus spiritibus multe sapientie, a quorum astuciis pauci evadunt, et ipsi sunt fortiores ceteris ad opera conjuratorum de omni dum con[junctio] ne removentur obedientes vate (?) et[iam] ante pyromancie.   Illos libentius convocant contra ceteros, et sibi reperiunt in agendo valentiores, set ipsi

The true criterion here must doubtless be sought in the evidence furnished by contemporaries regarding the fact alleged. In the case of Michael Scot such evidence is forthcoming, but we may say at once that it proves upon examination to yield a distinctly negative result. His fame in those days was such that he is mentioned by several important writers of his own age, such as Bacon, Albertus Magnus, and Vincent of Beauvais. None of these has a word to say of Scot's reputation as a necromancer. Some may urge that an argument from silence is unsatisfactory ; but does it not gain great force from the consideration that two of these witnesses are decidedly hostile to Scot? Bacon, especially, seems to have lost no opportunity of blackening his character. To these men Michael Scot was a sciolist, a mere pretender to knowledge, ignorant even of Latin ; the very charlatan of the schools. He was a plagiarist too ; one who passed off the work of another man as his own ; nay, darker than all, he was a heretic, or so Albert would make him ; a philosopher who interpreted and exceeded the forbidden doctrines of Averroës. Is it not certain that, if Scot had really practised magic in spite of the prohibitions of the Church, we should

sunt multis penis ignis afflicti, et ex hac de causa nigromantici requirunt studiose Puteum intueri, sive stellas Sacrarii, ut eorum auxilio plenius operentur optata. Et dicitur a multis quod de illo exeunt lapides et sagipte tonitruale, opere spirituum inferorum. Cum non sit ymago celi, habet stellas pervisibiles quatuor, dispositio quarum sic certificatur : in superfitie flammarum exeuntium sunt duo, et duo parum sub ore puthealis, et hec est forma in celo aspectus sui.' Over against this we find the application, as follows : Natus in hoc signo erit gratiosus habere experimenta et scire incantationes, constringere spiritus et mirabilia facere, et mulieres convincere artis ingeniosus erit, quietus, sagax, et plus pauper quam dives, et uti metallis, et alchemesta, et nigromanticus et erit homo quietus, ingeniosus, sagax, secretus, debilis, pauidus, timidus, etc.' The superstition of which Mirandola accuses Scot is very evident here, but it is no less plain that the author's purpose was astrological and not magical.

have heard of this charge from these active and
bitter detractors? Our conclusion from their silence
is therefore neither far to seek nor hard to defend.
These tales, we must hold, were not current in the
lifetime of Michael Scot, nor for many years after.
They had no foundation in fact, but were the fancies
of the following generation, and thus passed into
the settled tradition which has ever since per-
sistently associated itself with the philosopher's
name.

But this conclusion raises another question.
How did such a tradition arise, and what were the
points of attachment to which these stories clung?
The ground for the legend of Michael Scot would
seem to have been prepared by the close connection
between him and his master the Emperor Frederick
II. Every student of those times knows well the
storm of invective and the weight of calumny which
fell upon that great monarch as the consequence of
his feuds with the See of Rome. He was officially
declared to be no Christian but the mystic Beast
of the Apocalypse, vomiting blasphemies. He was
accused of having produced the apocryphal work
De Tribus Impostoribus. His private life became
the subject of grave scandal and repeated censure.
Men were taught to believe that he revelled in a
harem of Saracen beauties, and was addicted to
infamous immorality, as well as to forbidden arts.
These accusations were current, not only in
Frederick's own lifetime, but long afterwards. They
may be studied at large in the Papal Epistolaries,[1]
and a striking example of their current popular
form is found in the following barbarous lines which

[1] See especially the circular letter of Gregory IX., anno 1239.

we borrow from an obscure author[1] who used his pen in the service of the Guelfs :

> 'Amisit Astrologos, et Magos, et Vates,
> Beelzebub et Ashtaroth proprios Penates,
> Tenebrarum consulens per suos Potestates
> Spreverat Ecclesiam, et mundi Magnates.'

When we remember that Michael Scot was the man whom Frederick loved to consult and employ, we understand what effect this depreciation of the master's fame must have had on that of his servant. If the Emperor made Beelzebub and Ashtaroth his gods, Scot must soon have been recognised as the go-between in this infernal business.

Such an impression would naturally be heightened by the recollection of the years which had been spent by Michael Scot at Toledo and Cordova. We have already noticed the dark reputation which attached to the former of these places. It is only needful here to add that Scot's ecclesiastical character would by no means hinder the unfavourable inference that must have been drawn from his lengthened residence in the chief seat of magical study. St. Giles before his conversion, and Gerbert, afterwards Pope Sylvester II., were commonly reported to have learned the black art at Toledo. As to Cordova, the *Picatrix* mentions the discovery of a magic book in the Church there,[2] which shows that the supernatural fame of Toledo attached itself also to this city.

It is far from improbable that the nature of Scot's studies in these places may have inclined men to believe in the stories told of him as a

---

[1] Albert Beham, *Regist. Epistol.* p. 128.
[2] Book iv. chap. ix. 'De imaginibus quae virtutes faciunt mirabiles, et fuerunt inventae in libro qui fuit inventus in Ecclesia de Cordib.'

necromancer. He spent his time upon Arabic
texts, and, with the fanatical clergy, not to speak
of the common people whom they taught, the Moors
and all their works were accursed. No one could
meddle much with them save at the cost of such
accusations of diabolic dealing. Nor was it merely
the language but also the very subject of Scot's
studies that was suspicious. Since the days of the
Alexandrian school there had grown up round the
name of Aristotle a strange legend which represented
him as a magician ; none other than the great
sorcerer Nectanebus of Egypt, the true father, by
an infamous sleight, of Alexander of Macedon.[1]

Nectanebus, so the tale ran, was King of Egypt,
and learned in all the magic arts of that mysterious
land. When war threatened he would fill a vessel
with water and float upon it enchanted ships of
clay. Thus could he divine the success or failure
of his country's arms. One day, however, as he
was busy in this spell, the old gods appeared to
guide the craft he had designed as models of the
hostile fleet. Nectanebus gave up all for lost,
shaved his head, and in the disguise of a philosopher, fled to Pella in Macedonia, where he lived
by practising the arts of an astrologer and prophet.
Olympias consulted him to know whether she might
hope to give an heir to her husband Philip, then
absent from his capital. Nectanebus bade her

---

[1] Nectanebus, sometimes spelt Neptanebus, is perhaps the 'Naptium'
of the *Picatrix* (iii. 8). See also on this curious subject the *Pancrates*
of Lucian, the verses of Adalberone or Ascelin (A.D. 1006) in the *Recueil
des Hist. des Gaules* (Bouquet x. 67), the English romance of *Alisaundre*
(Early English Text Soc. 1867) and the *Alexander* of Juan Lorenzo
Segura de Astorga. In this last poem, which belongs to the thirteenth
century, the hero's arms are said to have been forged by the fairies.
There is an article on 'Nectanebo' by D. G. Hogarth in the *Eng. Hist.
Review*, Jan. 1896. The same mystic fame attached itself to Pythagoras.

expect the honour of a visit from Jupiter Ammon himself, and, dressing in the horns and hieratic robe proper to the character he assumed, became, by her whom he seduced, the father of Alexander the Great. The child was born amid thunder and lightning, and was soon committed to the care of Nectanebus who became his tutor : a clear point of connection with Aristotle, who really filled that office. One day tutor and pupil walked on the edge of a cliff, when the philosopher uttered a prophecy to the effect that Alexander was fated to kill his own father. The boy, who fancied that Philip was meant, took the words so ill that he flung his tutor over the rock, and thus instantly fulfilled the prediction. This tale can be traced from its appearance in the Pseudo-Callisthenes through the series of Byzantine chroniclers— Syncellus, Glycas, John Malala, and the author of the *Chronicon Pascale*—to the later romances where it is repeated and amplified. The whole Middle Age believed it. Not till the fourteenth century did a doubt of its truth appear,[1] and that it was current in the west of Europe at the time of which we write appears plainly in the preface to the *Secreta Secretorum*, which has the following significant remark, 'which Alexander is said to have had two horns.'[2] The real meaning of the legend probably lay in a patriotic desire to vindicate for Egypt, though subdued by Alexander, the honour of having originated the Greek philosophy.[3]

[1] In the poem of Albéric de Besançon.

[2] St. Chrysostom (A.D. 398) speaks of the custom of using brass coins of Alexander as amulets.

[3] It is a curious fact that under the historic Nekhtneb (362-45 B.C.) the Greek philosophers Eudoxus and Chrysippus spent eleven years in Egypt to learn the astronomical secrets of the priests.

The thirteenth century, however, knew nothing of such explanations; cherishing the tale rather on account of the wild mystery which it breathes. No wonder then if the labours of Michael Scot as an exponent of Aristotle gave some force to the popular idea that he dealt in forbidden arts.

Need we point out that the same may be said of his fame as a Master in astrology and alchemy? We have seen how close was the relation in which these sciences stood to the magic of the day. As to mathematics, for which Scot was so renowned, it is to be observed that the kind of divination called *Geomancy*, which was performed by casting figures in a box filled with sand, was remarkably like the method of working sums which is still practised among the Moors.[1] We may add that the facility with which difficult problems could be solved by the new methods of calculation borrowed from that people must have seemed little less than supernatural to those as yet unacquainted with the secrets of algebra.

It seems probable indeed that at least one starting-point of Michael Scot's legendary and romantic fame may be looked for in the very quarter to which we have just begun to direct our attention. There is in the author's possession a manuscript which promises to throw some light on the obscurity of this matter.[2] It consists of sixteen quarto pages

---

[1] A *Geomancy*, said to be the work of Scot, is preserved in the Munich Library, No. 489 in 4to, saec. xvi. See the *Thousand Nights* for instances of the prevalence of this art.

[2] This MS. reached me from Germany. It is unbound and contained in an envelope made from the leaf of an old choir-book covered with manuscript music. This cover is secured by three large seals bearing the arms of Dunkelsphuhl, to which family it seems to have belonged. The preface is dated at Prague. It is possible the MS. may have had something to do with the magical studies of Dr. John Dee, who spent some time in Prague at the beginning of the seventeenth century. See Appendix IV.

written on parchment in a hand of the seventeenth century, and contains a short preface, followed by two distinct works. One of these professes to be an Arabic original, and the other a version of the same in Latin, said to come from the pen of Michael Scot. The title of the work deserves special attention. It is as follows: 'Almuchabola Absegalim Alkakib Albaon; *i.e.* Compendium Magia Innaturalis Nigrae.' Now, although the so-called *Arabic* of the manuscript quite defies the best efforts of scholarship to decipher it, this word almuchabola is perfectly authentic, familiar even, being the common term in that language for what we call algebra.[1]

This then seems to afford an actual example of the way in which the Moorish science of numbers might be mistaken for something magical. When we examine the manuscript more closely the suggestion which its title affords becomes still stronger. Here and there, amid the strange characters of an unknown tongue,[2] are designs of a curious kind; parallelograms enclosed in bounding lines of red, and containing erratic figures also in red, that show luridly against the black background with which the outlines are filled. The Latin version explains that these are the signs of the demons whom the accompanying spells have power

---

[1] Leonardo Pisano uses this word in the *Liber Abbaci.* See p. 187vo of the Florence MS. Bibl. Naz. i. 2616, where the following passage occurs: 'Secundum modum algebrae et almuchabalae, scilicet ad proportionem et restaurationem.' In an ancient list of works by Gerard of Cremona (? the younger) found in the Vatican (No. 2392) we have this title: 'Liber alcoarismi de iebra et almucabula tractatus.' See Boncompagni's *Life of Gerard,* Rome 1851. Works on almuchabola are found also under the names of Al Deinouri, Al Sarakhsi, Al Khouaresmi, Khamel Schagia ben Aslam, and Al Thoussi. See D'Herbelot.

[2] They show a distinct likeness to the Magreb or West African writing.

to summon or dismiss. No one, however, who compares them with the graphic statements of mathematical problems in the margin of the *Liber Abbaci* can fail to be struck with the resemblance.[1] The one book seems, in regard of these figures, but a degenerate copy of the other, made by some scribe who did not understand the matter he had in hand, and who darkened the ground of his designs to heighten the fancied terrors of the subject.

It would not be easy to miss the meaning of this mistake. Michael Scot had probably written or translated a treatise on algebra. We may remember how well such a conjecture agrees with the tone of Pisano's dedicatory letter to him, in which he submitted the *Liber Abbaci* to Scot's revision, and acknowledged him as a supreme master in this branch of science. It is difficult to account for this fame save by supposing the existence of an unknown work by Michael Scot on the veritable Almuchabola, of which this pretended treatise on magic is all that now survives. The mistake that gave it so corrupted a form could hardly have been made as late as the seventeenth century, when such things were well understood. The manuscript, though dating from that time, is probably only a copy of one much older. The preface, indeed, mentions the year 1255 as the epoch of translation, and, although Michael Scot had then lain more than twenty years in his grave, this date would suit well as the birth-hour of a legend which, though certainly later than Scot's

---

[1] This resemblance should be studied in the remarkably beautiful MS. of the *Liber Abbaci*, numbered xi. 21 in the Bibl. Naz. Florence.

own day, had yet made considerable progress in the popular mind before the close of the century. This explanation of the matter receives some indirect support from a remark of Bacon's. 'It is to be noticed,' he says, 'that many books are taken for magical works which are in reality nothing of the kind, but contain true and worthy wisdom.'[1] He adds that there are several ways of concealing one's doctrine from the vulgar, such as the use of Hebrew, Syriac, and Arabic characters, and the *Ars Notoria* or shorthand. There is much reason to think it was in this very way that Michael Scot had suffered. A mistake like that indicated by Bacon was probably the real origin of his mysterious reputation as a magician.

As soon as the mistake had once been made, and the notion of Scot's magical powers had fairly taken possession of the popular mind, it was greatly reinforced by the association of his name and memory with the still living and adaptable Arthurian legend. Alain de l'Isle, who lived as late as 1202, says that the tales proper to this romantic cycle were so heartily believed in Brittany that any one casting doubt upon Arthur's return would have been stoned by the people.[2] From the Trouvères the legend passed to the Troubadours of the south of France. When the Normans established themselves in Sicily, these latter poets, represented, it is said, by Pietro Vidal, and Rambaldo di Vaqueiras, carried to this new home of their race the *materia poetica* which had so long engaged the best talents of France. The religious war which desolated Provence in the beginning of the thirteenth century

[1] *Epistola de Secretis*, ed. Master of the Rolls, Longmans, 1859, pp. 531, 544. [2] *Explanatio in Prophetias Merlini*, iii. 26.

completed the dispersion of the Troubadours. Many found a refuge in Italy and Sicily. They communicated an emotional impulse which led to the formation of the Italian language as a means of literary expression. Through them the inheritance of the Arthurian tales was secured to the people of the South, who soon began to localise the chief incidents of this romantic cycle in the island of Sicily.[1]

Gervase of Tilbury tells us that near the town of Catania lies the burning mountain of Etna, called by the people *Mongibello,* and famed among them as the abode of King Arthur, who, they said, had lately been seen there. The matter fell out thus. The Bishop of Catania's palfrey escaped one day from his groom, and was lost. The man sought his charge everywhere, and at last ventured to enter an opening he perceived in the hollow part of the hill. Here he found a narrow winding path which led to a pleasant land within Etna, and to a palace, the home of Arthur. He entered the palace and found the King lying on a royal couch. Arthur bade him welcome, listened to his story, and called for the steed to be brought that the Bishop might have his own again. He further told his visitor that, having been wounded in battle with Modred and Childeric king of Saxony, he had come to this retreat that he might heal him of his mortal sickness. Gervase adds that Arthur, not content with restoring the horse, paid tithe to the Bishop as one of the dwellers in his diocese, 'which was a wonder to all that heard it.'[2]

---

[1] See the interesting work by Graf, *Miti, Leggendi e Superstizioni del Medio Evo,* Torino, Loescher, 1893.

[2] 'Otia Imperialia' in Leibnitz *Scriptores Rerum Brunsvicensium,* i. 921.

Caesar von Heisterbach has the same tale in his collection, but repeats it with some variations. In his pages the pleasant land of Avalon, with its peaceful palace, becomes a dark abode of fire, answering more nearly to the actual phenomena of the mountain. Arthur hence issues a dread summons to the owner of the palfrey, who in this tale is a Canon of Palermo, bidding him appear in that infernal region within a fortnight. The churchman obeys by dying at the time appointed.[1] The terror which enters into this form of the story is even heightened by Stephen of Bourbon when he comes to repeat it.[2] On the other hand the easy, pleasant, semi-pagan tone observed in Gervase of Tilbury lives again in the French romance of *Florian and Florete*.[3] Here we see the kingdom within Etna before Arthur came thither, and find it a land of faery, where the King's sister Morgana holds her flowery court. The *Fata Morgana*, as she is called, is still remembered on these southern coasts. When the mirage appears in the Straits of Messina, and houses and castles are seen hanging in thin air, the people call them by the name of that mysterious princess. They think that the sides of Etna have become transparent, and that what they

---

[1] *Illustrium Miraculorum*, xii. 12. The next tale, in chap. xiii., relates how some men, wandering by chance on Etna, heard a voice cry from under the hill 'Prepare the fires.' This was heard by them a second time, and then the cry was 'Prepare a great fire,' upon which other voices asked for whom this should be done, and the answer came back that it was for the Duke of Thuringia, a friend and trusty servant of these lower powers. This the hearers made faith of in a writing given to the Emperor Frederick, and it presently appeared that Bertolph of Thuringia, a noted tyrant, heretic and persecutor of the Church, had died at the very day and hour when these voices were heard on Etna.

[2] See *Anecdotes Historiques*, by Lecoy de la Marche, Paris, 1877, p. 32.

[3] This romance was published by the Roxburghe Club, London, 1873.

behold is the realm of faery with the Fata Morgana's palace in the midst.

These legends show that Avalon, first dreamed of in the far North, had by this time been carried southward to find a new locality under Etna, and that already the mystic king, who dwelt with his court in the land of shadows till he should again return to earth, had taken a firm hold of the southern fancy. It was but a step more then, and one very easily taken, when men began to see in the Princes of the Hohenstaufen, and the chief figures of their court, the heirs of this legend in some of its most important features. Frederick Barbarossa, for example, was commonly said to pass the ages between death and life in a hollow hill. The Germans identified this abode with the Kyffhauser, and expected the Emperor's return in the spirit of the tales told of Wodan, Frau Holda, and Frau Venus, in their national mythology.[1] It was even reported that a bold shepherd armed with the mysterious *key-flower* had forced the secret, entering these recesses of the hill and beholding Barbarossa as in life, with his red beard growing through the marble table at which he sat asleep. The romantic heritage next fell upon Barbarossa's grandson Frederick II. It was long before the adherents of the Empire who had staked so much upon their great champion's bold defiance of the Papacy could bring themselves to believe that he was really dead. In 1250 his corpse was carried in solemn procession from Fiorentino, where he died, to Palermo, the place appointed for his burial. There he soon lay in the ancient sarcophagus brought from Cefalù;

---

[1] See Grimm's *Deutsche Mythologie.*

his robe embroidered about the hem with Cufic characters, and the sceptre and apple of empire in his powerless hands ;[1] but still the Ghibellines could not give up the hope that one day he would wake again, and lead them to the victory they looked for.

This expectation was much strengthened by a prophecy then current under the name of the Abbot Joachim. 'There cometh an Eagle, at whose appearing the Lion shall be destroyed : yea a young Eagle who shall make his nest in the den of the Lion. Of the race of the Eagle shall arise another Eagle called Frederick. He shall reign indeed, and shall stretch his wings till they touch the ends of the earth. In his days shall the chief Pontiff and his clergy be despoiled and dispersed.'[2] On the other side a Guelf poet, whose name we do not know, associated Frederick II. with Arthur in the following lines :

'Cominatur impius, dolens de jacturis
Cum suo Britonibus Arturo venturis.[3]

The collection called the *Cento Novelle Antiche* reflects this myth very plainly ; for, in the strange tales then told of Frederick and his court, we seem to see these personages already transported to a kind of fairyland, where the laws of earthly life no longer hold good. The scene is unmistakably laid in the Avalon of Arthur and amid his shadowy court.

[1] The sarcophagus was opened in 1781 and all was found as described above. The body of the great Emperor was in good preservation and with it were remains of Peter II. of Aragon, and Duke William, son of Frederick II. of Aragon.

[2] German prophecies of the same kind are given by Grimm, *op. cit.*

[3] See Pertz *Scriptores Rerum Germanicarum*, xviii. 796.

One of the most striking incidents which marked the long funeral procession of Frederick II. through the southern provinces of Italy was furnished by the grief of a faithful band of Saracens, who, with dishevelled hair and cries of sorrow, accompanied the body of their great benefactor to its last resting-place. It is probable indeed that these people, of whom Frederick had not a few both in Sicily and in various colonies on the mainland, may have joined very heartily with their Christian neighbours in giving currency to the latest application of the Arthurian legend. In all essential features it must already have been familiar to them as a form of myth long known in the East. Even the romance of Nectanebus already noticed had a certain historical basis. In the fourth century before Christ a king called Nekhtneb reigned in Egypt. He was defeated by the Persians, and fled into a distant province of Ethiopia. Thus the ancient national dynasty of the Pharaohs came to an end, but the people long refused to believe that their king was dead. They consulted an oracle, which told them he would return, as a young man, to conquer the enemies of his country. This prophecy was engraved on the base of the royal statue and served long to sustain the national hope. The same dreams appeared in connection with the much more recent Mohammedan power. The *Shi'ah* and *Sunnee* sects of Islam held firmly to the idea that the twelfth Imam was not really dead, but would return to earth. This mysterious person was *El Mohdy*, the last incarnation of the Deity, as they supposed. He was said to dwell in a cave near Bagdad, whence he would one day reappear to oppose *Ed Dejal*, the

Moslem Antichrist, in a time of great trouble, when he would overthrow him and his ally the *earth-beast* in final conflict near Aleppo. Mohammed himself was said to have retreated with Abu Bekr to a cave, where they lay concealed behind a spider's web, as the Scottish tale says Bruce did before his decisive appearance and victory. The influence of these myths may be seen even during the lifetime of Frederick II., when the extravagant hopes of his followers led them to use language regarding the Emperor which was applicable only to the Deity. We may see in this an anticipation by hyperbole of the apotheosis granted him by the Ghibellines after his death.[1]

As for Michael Scot himself, it was a very natural progress of the popular imagination which made him play Merlin to the Emperor's Arthur. That this place in the growing legend was actually his, seems probable from the fact that, in the romance of *Maugis* (or Merlin) *and Vivien*,[2] the hero is made to study his art in Toledo, where Scot had notoriously been. Mysterious caves, the refuge of slumbering heroes, were spoken of as existing both near that city and Salamanca. It may be that we here touch on the origin of Scot's legendary connection with the Eildon Hills in his own border-land. That the Scottish Avalon lay beneath these there can be little doubt. Sir Walter Scott repeats a traditional tale which reminds us unmistakably of those given by Gervase of Tilbury and Caesar von Heisterbach. A countryman of Roxburghshire had sold a horse to an old man of the hills. Pay-

---

[1] For example, he is called : Dei 'coöperator, et Vicarius constitutus in terris' ; 'the cornerstone of the Church,' etc. See Huillard-Bréholles *Vie et correspondance de Pierre de la Vigne*, Paris, Plon, 1864.

[2] See also another romance called *L'Histoire de Maugis d'Aygremont*.

ment was appointed to be made at midnight, on Eildon, at a place called the *Lucken Howe.* When the coin, which was of ancient and forgotten mintage, had been duly handed over, the old man invited the other to view his dwelling. They passed within the hill, where the stranger was surprised to see ranks of steeds ready caparisoned : a silent cavalier in armour standing by the side of each. 'These will wake for Shirramuir,' said his guide. In the cave hung a sword and a horn. 'The sound of this horn,' the old man told him, 'will break the spell of their slumber.' The countryman caught it to his lips and blew a blast. The horses neighed, pawed the ground, and shook their trappings, while the knights stirred, and the place rang again with the sound of their arms. He dropped the horn in fear, and heard a voice which said : 'Woe to him who does not unsheathe the sword ere he has blown the horn.' He was then carried back again to the hillside, and could never more discover the entrance to that subterranean realm.[1]

An English form of the same tale has been preserved, and is worth notice as containing what may possibly be a reference to Michael Scot's prediction regarding Frederick's death 'at the iron gates.' The story says that 'in the neighbourhood of Macclesfield, on Monk's Heath, is a small inn known by the designation of 'The Iron Gates,' the sign representing a pair of ponderous gates of that metal opening at the bidding of a figure enveloped in a cowl, before whom kneels another, more resembling a modern yeoman than one of the

---

[1] See also Leyden's *Scenes of Infancy,* pt. ii.

twelfth or thirteenth century, to which period this legend is attributed. Behind this person is a white horse rearing, and in the background a view of Alderley Edge. The story is thus told of the tradition to which the sign relates :

' A farmer from Mobberly was riding on a white horse over the heath which skirts Alderley Edge. Of the good qualities of his steed he was justly proud, and while stooping down to adjust its mane previously to his offering it for sale at Macclesfield, he was surprised by the sudden starting of the animal. On looking up he perceived a figure of more than common height, enveloped in a cowl, and extending a staff of black wood across his path. The figure addressed him in a commanding voice : told him that he would seek in vain to dispose of his steed for whom a nobler destiny was in store, and bade him meet him when the sun was set, with his horse, at the same place. The farmer, resolving to put the truth of this prediction to the test, hastened on to Macclesfield fair, but no purchaser could be obtained for his horse. In vain he reduced his price to half; many admired, but no one was willing to be the possessor of so promising a steed. Summoning, therefore, all his courage, he determined to brave the worst, and at sunset reached the appointed place. The monk was punctual to his appointment. "Follow me," said he, and led the way by the *Golden Stone, Stormy Point* to *Saddle Bole.* On their arrival at this last-named spot, the neigh of horses seemed to arise from beneath their feet. The stranger waved his wand, the earth opened and disclosed a pair of ponderous iron gates. Terrified at this, the horse plunged and threw his rider, who, kneeling at the feet of his fearful companion, prayed earnestly for mercy. The monk bade him fear nothing, but enter the cavern, on each side of which were horses resembling his own in size and colour. Near these lay soldiers accoutred in ancient armour, and in the chasms of the rock were arms and piles of gold and silver. From one of these the enchanter took the price of the horse in ancient coin, and on the farmer asking the meaning of these subterranean armies, exclaimed : " These are caverned warriors preserved by the good genius of England, until that eventful day when, distracted by intestine broils, England shall be thrice won and lost between sunrise and sunset. Then we, awakening from our sleep, shall rise to turn the fate of Britain. This shall be when George, the son of George, shall reign. When the forests of Delamare shall wave their arms over the slaughtered sons of Albion. Then shall the eagle drink the blood of princes from the headless cross (query, corse ?). Now haste thee home, for it is not in thy time these things shall be. A Cestrian shall speak it and be believed." The farmer left the cavern, the iron gates closed, and though often sought for, the place has never again been found."[1]

Arthur, the King of Faery, has dropped out of these legends in the course of their transmission to modern times, but in another story, told of the Eildon Hills, his sister, the Fata Morgana, still lives and reigns ; for she is no doubt the *Faery Queen* with whom Thomas Rhymer spent so many years underground ere he returned with the gift of pro-

---

[1] Timbs's *Abbeys, Castles, and Ancient Halls of England and Wales:* London, Warne, vol. iii. p. 126.

phetic truth.   In the Scottish legend, which makes
Michael Scot have much to do in forming these
hills to their present shape, we seem to see him
occupying his natural place in the myth as that
Merlin whose art composed and maintained the
magic kingdom of Avalon, where Arthur sleeps
with Morgana till the hour of his return.

The fertile fancy of these ages ran to the formation of other points of likeness.   Merlin had his
Vivien, who betrayed him to his loss of life and
power by a spell of his own composing.   So Michael
was said to have loved a beautiful woman, who,
Delilah-like, left him no peace till he told her the
poison which alone had power over his charmed
life : the broth of a breme sow, of which accordingly
he died, taking it confidently from his false leman's
hand.[1]   Michael too, like Merlin, had his *Book of
Might*; for the same fancy which materialised
Frederick's heretical tendencies, and made them
objective in the supposed work *De Tribus Impostoribus*, soon did the like by those diabolical arts
in which Scot was said to have excelled.   It is
possible that some reference to this may have been
intended in the book which is held by the magician
in the S. Maria Novella fresco.   The plan of these
paintings in the Spanish chapel at Florence was
drawn out with great care by Fra Jacopo Passavanti, a learned monk of that convent.   He has
left a series of Lenten sermons, collected and en-
larged by himself, and published under the title of
Lo Specchio di vera Penitenza.[2]   The last two
chapters of this work are devoted to the reproof of

---

[1] *Lay of the Last Minstrel*, Note Y.
[2] I quote from the edition of Florence, 1580.

magical arts ; a subject which the author would
seem to have studied closely. He may have been
influenced in this direction by S. Augustine's
De Civitate Dei, which he translated into Italian.
More than one passage of the *Specchio* may be
cited as illustrating the frescoes of the Spanish
Chapel. He tells us, for example, that the devil
is said to be able to teach science to his
disciples in an incredibly short space of time, however rude and ignorant they may be. For this
purpose he has given them a book called the *Ars
Notoria*,[1] the same which is so severely condemned
by Aquinas. Now, as Aquinas, with open book of
heavenly doctrine, is figured in the chief position
on the opposite (north) wall of the chapel, it is no
unreasonable conjecture which finds in the magician's book on the south wall a pictorial representation of the *Ars Notoria* as it was conceived by
Passavanti. Elsewhere in the volume he again
returns to the subject of magical works.[2] Zoroaster,
he says, first learned the art from demons, and caused
it to be written on two columns, one of marble to
survive the floods, and one of terra-cotta to resist
the fire. This diabolic teaching, thus preserved,
flourished among the Egyptians, Chaldeans,
Persians, Indians, and other Oriental nations who
remained its chief exponents, 'though perchance,'
adds Passavanti, 'it may be more studied among
ourselves than we are ready to believe.'[3] This

---

[1] P. 343.   See *ante*, pp. 140, 192, and Renan's *Averroës*, p. 314.
[2] P. 375.
[3] I cannot leave this interesting though obscure author without
noticing the undoubted reference he makes in his *Specchio* to the Gipsies.
'Certain people,' he says (p. 351), 'have a superstition regarding
lucky and unlucky days, which have been pointed out to them by those
who call themselves Egyptians.' We have hitherto supposed that 1422

passage may serve to show why the artist of the
Spanish Chapel was directed to draw his Magus in
the fashion of the East, and helps us to understand
the prejudice which Michael Scot's outlandish costume must have raised against him. It is in any case
certain that the stories of his supernatural power
became both memorable in substance and rich in
details by association with the tales of Arthur.

was the time when Gipsies first appeared in the West. That year is
cited by Muratori in his *Dissertazioni* as the date of a document which
speaks of the coming of Andrew, who called himself Duke of Egypt, and
all his tribe. Passavanti, however, wrote about 1350, so that the epoch
of migration must be carried back at least a century.

CHAPTER X

THE attachment of Michael Scot to his master, the Emperor Frederick II., may be conceived as acting in a double sense to procure him his mysterious fame. With the Guelfs, who bitterly opposed that great monarch and his followers, it of course became a reason for believing him to have practised the blackest of arts. With the Ghibellines, on the other hand, who formed the imperial party, and saw a very Arthur in their famous leader, it served to confirm his character as a Mage and man of mysterious might.

Commencing then with one of the first, and certainly the most famous of the authors who have spoken of Scot in this romantic and legendary style, the observation just made will enable us to understand without much difficulty the sense of Dante's reference to the magician. The poet represents himself as reaching the fourth division of the eighth infernal circle, when Virgil draws his attention to one of those who suffer there, and says :

> ' Michele Scotto, fù, che veramente
> Delle magiche frode seppe il giuoco.' [1]

Dante was a Ghibelline, and must therefore be supposed to have known well the tradition of com-

---

[1] *Inferno*, xx. 116, 117.

manding supernatural power woven by his party about the name of Scot. There is, however, a strong element of contempt and reproof in his lines, and this must be explained by a point of view which was peculiar to himself. The *Commedia*, and especially the *Inferno*, where this passage occurs, is nothing if not a retrospect of the past. In it Dante calls up the mighty dead and subjects them to review; his principle of judgment being largely, but by no means solely, drawn from political considerations. Even more decidedly was it moral, and thus, while in not a few instances he displays the working of party-spirit, in others he permits himself to part altogether with the current Ghibelline views.

His reference to Michael Scot, then, is undoubtedly a case of the latter kind. As a seer whose attention was fixed on the past he was naturally impatient of those who pretended to unfold the future. Scot, as the author of prophetical verses, seemed to Dante a fair object for censure, as one who had degraded the sacred art of the bard to serve the purpose of a charlatan. He placed him with Amphiareus, with Teiresias and the other diviners, who, because they sought to pry into the future, appeared to the poet with their heads turned backward in punishment of their presumption. An additional proof that this was in fact the reason for Dante's harsh dealing with Scot may be seen in the *Dittamondo* of Fazio degli Uberti. This poem, composed towards the end of the fourteenth century, was modelled on the *Divine Comedy*, and expressly formed to expound it. Here are the lines which correspond in the

Dittamondo to those of Dante relating to Michael Scot :

'In questo tempo che m'odi contare
Michele Scotto fù, che per sua arte
Sapeva Simon Mago contraffare,
E se tu leggerai nelle sue carte
Le profezie ch'ei fece, troverai
Vere venire dove sono sparte.'

Here the reader will observe that the prophetical writings of Scot are distinctly mentioned, and we are not left, as by Dante, to infer, merely from the company in which we find him, the view that was taken by the poet of his character and fame.

It was to reinforce this unfavourable judgment based on other grounds that Dante adopted the legend already popular regarding Scot's magical studies. In doing so he gave the matter a turn which widely separated his version of the tale from the prevailing Ghibelline stories, told no doubt with bated breath, but told on the whole to Scot's credit. In thus dealing with the legend Dante made use of a distinction well known to the Arabs, and now becoming familiar also in the West : that, namely, which divided the art of magic into the real and the illusory ; called by Eastern magicians *Er Roóhhánee* and *Es Seémiya*.[1] The former was noble magic, and acted in power upon high spirits, subduing them to the magician's will; being either white or black according to the purpose that was sought by their aid. The latter, on the other hand, produced no real effects whatever on material things, but moved altogether in the sphere of mind. At its highest it gave a mastery, which was perhaps

[1] Lane's *Modern Egyptians*, 1837, vol. i. p. 360. For a tract on *Es Seemiya*, by the Shaik Ali Al Tarabulsio (of Tripoli), who composed it in 1219, see Asseman, Cat. Bibl. Pal. Med. p. 362.

hypnotic, over the senses of those whom the magician sought to delude. At its lowest it was the art of the juggler and his apes, cheating eye and ear by tricks like those which have survived to form our modern conjuring entertainments.[1] Here the apparatus of the higher magic was still used, but so as to be degraded and distorted from its original purpose. The circle now served to secure the mage, not from the assaults of supernatural beings, but from the indiscreet approach of too curious spectators. The brazier with its cloud of dense and stupifying smoke served to affect the senses of the subject; the strange sound of recited spells to impress his imagination; the magic mirror to fix his attention, till he became the wizard's captive and obedient to his every suggestion. This was the art of *glamour*, as it used to be called, which, in one sphere, seemed to change a ruinous and cobweb-hung hall into a bower of delight; in another, made visions of distant places and future times appear in mirrors or crystals; in yet another, provided the philtres which provoked love, the ligatures which restrained it, and even dealt in that accursed spell of *envoutement* which promised to procure for jealousy and hatred all their wicked will.

Such then were the *magiche frode* of which Dante accuses Scot, and it is easy to see that the sting of the verse lies just here; in the unreality it attributes to this magician's art, much as if the poet had called him in plain prose, 'no mage, but a common juggler.' Resenting Scot's pose as a

---

[1] See the *De Secretis* of Bacon for a curious account of these tricks as practised in his day.

prophet, and persuaded of the futility of such dreams in comparison with the splendid and enduring certainties of his own art, Dante used that gift with cruel force to convey a similar accusation regarding the romantic fame of the philosopher, holding him up to the world as no mighty master of mysterious power, but, in this too, a mere impostor.

The anonymous Florentine, in his comment on the *Divine Comedy*, softens the matter a little, and at the same time imports into it a confusion of thought very difficult to unravel, when he says : 'This art of magic may be employed in two ways; for either magicians compose by cunning certain bodies, all compact of air, which yet appear substantial; or else they show things having the appearance of reality but not in truth real, and in both these ways of working was Michael a great master.' There is an attempt here to vindicate for Scot a higher place than that of the mere charlatan, but the commentator's distinction is one not readily or clearly to be apprehended, and we may greatly doubt if it ever entered his author's mind.

The hint thus given was speedily acted upon. For to it, no doubt, we owe the numerous tales regarding Michael Scot of which Benvenuto da Imola and the anonymous Florentine speak. Landino gives a specimen, as follows. During the philosopher's residence in Bologna he used to invite his friends to dinner, but without making any preparation for their entertainment. When the hour struck, and the guests were seated at table, they found it nevertheless covered with the choicest viands. Their host would then explain that one dish came from the royal kitchen at Paris, another from that of the English king, and so on with the rest. Jacopo della Lana repeats the same story, but with certain variations.[1] According to this commentator, Michael Scot always kept the best company, living in all respects as a gentleman and cavalier. In his tricks of the table he did not spare even his own master, but, while choosing his boiled meat from Paris, and his roasts from London, would always procure his *entrées* from the King of Sicily's provision. The anonymous Florentine adds another tale to the same purpose, saying that his guests once asked Scot to show them a new marvel. The month was January, yet, in spite of the season, he caused vines with fresh shoots and ripe clusters of grapes to appear on the table. The company were bidden each of them to choose a bunch, but their host warned them not to put forth their hands till he should give the sign. At the word 'cut,' lo, the grapes disappeared, and the guests found themselves each with a knife in one hand, and in the other his neighbour's sleeve. Francesco da Buti adds the significant note, 'all this was nothing but a cheat; for they only seemed to feast, and either did not really do so, or else took the dishes for something quite other than they really were.' This is enough to show that the sense we have given to Dante's words is one which found favour in early times.

Boccaccio, commencing his lectures on Dante in the Church of San Stefano at Florence in October 1373, proceeded in them no further, unfortunately, than the seventeenth canto of the *Inferno*, so that

---

[1] *Inferno di Dante col Comento di Jacopo della Lana*, Bologna, 1866, vol. i. p. 351.

we are deprived of his notes on the passage which
refers to Michael Scot. In the *Decamerone*, however, he treats the subject in a passing way ; making
a citizen of Bologna speak of the magician's residence in that town.[1] Scot, he said, had performed
many prodigies there, to the delight of sundry
gentlemen his friends, and at their request had,
on his departure, left behind him two scholars, who
kept up fairly the traditions of his art. This seems
to indicate that Boccaccio had in mind the stories
told by the other commentators on Dante, and the
tone of his novel supports the conjecture that he
agreed with the great poet and with Da Buti, in
regarding these prodigies as pertaining to the department of fictitious magic.

More interesting, perhaps, are the tales which
involve Michael the magician with the fates of his
great master, Frederick II. In the *Paradiso degli
Alberti*,[2] for example, we read how, at the feast
given by the Emperor to celebrate his coronation at
Rome, which had taken place on November 22, 1220,
the company were entertained by a strange event.
They were just in the act of washing their hands
before sitting down to table in the great hall at
Palermo. The pages were still on foot with ewers
and basins of perfumed water and embroidered
towels, when suddenly Michael Scot appeared with
a companion, both of them dressed in Eastern robes,
and offered to show the guests a marvel. The
weather was oppressively warm, so Frederick asked
him to procure them a shower of rain which might
bring coolness. This the magicians accordingly did,

[1] In the ninth novel of the eighth day.
[2] *Wesseloffsky*, Bologna, 1867, vol. ii. pp. 180-217.

raising a great storm, which as suddenly vanished again at their pleasure. Being required by the Emperor to name his reward, Scot asked leave to choose one of the company to be the champion of himself and his friend against certain enemies of theirs. This being freely granted, their choice fell on Ulfo, a German baron. As it seemed to Ulfo, they set off at once on their expedition, leaving the coasts of Sicily in two great galleys, and with a mighty following of armed men. They sailed through the Gulf of Lyons, and passed by the Pillars of Hercules, into the unknown and western sea. Here they found smiling coasts, received a welcome from the strange people, and joined themselves to the army of the place ; Ulfo taking the supreme command. Two pitched battles and a successful siege formed the incidents of the campaign. Ulfo killed the hostile king, married his lovely daughter, and reigned in his stead ; Michael and his companion having left to seek other adventures. Of this marriage sons and daughters were begotten, and twenty years passed like a dream ere the magicians returned, and invited their champion to revisit the Sicilian court. Ulfo went back with them, but what was his amazement, on entering the palace at Palermo, to find everything just as it had been at the moment of their departure so long before ; even the pages were still going the rounds with water for the hands of the Emperor's guests. This prodigy performed, Michael and the other withdrew and were seen no more, but Ulfo, it is said, remained ever inconsolable for the lost land of loveliness and the joys of wedded life he had left behind for ever in a dream not to be repeated.

This tale appears also in the *Cento Novelle Antiche*,[1] but in that collection the place of Michael Scot and his companion is taken by 'three masters of necromancy.'

In the *Pseudo Boccaccio*[2] we find another tale, referring to the later and less happy period of the imperial fortunes. The scene is laid in Vittoria, the armed camp which Frederick pitched so long before the walls of rebellious Parma. The Parmigiani had made a successful sally, forced the defences of Vittoria, and were plundering the place. A poor shoemaker of Parma, who made one of this expedition, was lucky enough to come upon the imperial tent itself. Entering, he found a small barrel, which he caught up and carried back to his home. On trial it proved to contain excellent wine, which the shoemaker and his wife drank from day to day, till at last it occurred to them to wonder why the supply never came to an end. They opened the barrel to see, and found within it a small silver figure of an angel with his foot planted on a grape, also of silver, from which flowed constantly the delicious wine they had so long enjoyed. 'Now, this was made by magic art,' continues the commentator, 'and by necromancy, and it was Thales, otherwise called Michael Scot, who contrived it by his skill and power.' Needless to add that, by this indiscreet curiosity, the charm was broken, and the generous wine flowed no longer to gladden the hearts of the shoemaker and his wife.

We have thus traced the development of the

---

[1] No. xx.
[2] *Chiose sopra Dante*, published by Lord Vernon ; Florence, 1846, pp. 162 163.

legend as far as the close of the fourteenth century. During the next hundred years no notable addition seems to have been made to it, nor does it appear to have attained any further expression of a remarkable kind in the region of pure literature. But the fifteenth century had by no means forgotten Michael Scot, nor the tales that embodied his mysterious fame. This, in fact, seems to have been the period when most of the magical works attributed to the philosopher's pen were composed, and commended to the world under the reputation attaching to so great a name. Such are the spell, which exists in writing of this age, in the Laurentian Library of Florence,[1] the *Geomantia* of the Munich Library,[2] and, perhaps, the *Cheiromantia*. As, however, a tract on at least one of these latter subjects is attributed to Gerard of Cremona in the Vatican list,[3] it is possible there may here have been only some not unnatural confusion between two authors who were closely associated in much of the literary work they accomplished in Spain.

To the sixteenth century belongs the mock-heroic poem entitled *De Gestis Baldi*, composed by the famous macaronic writer Teofilo Folengo, who wrote under the assumed name of Merlin Coccajo. A considerable passage in this curious production is devoted to Michael Scot, of whom the poet speaks in the following terms :

'Ecce Michaelis de incantu regula Scoti,
Qua, post sex formas, cerae fabricatur imago
Demonii Sathan Saturni facta plumbo
Cui suffimigio per serica rubra cremato

---

[1] Pl. lxxxix. sup. cod. 38.   [2] No. 489.
[3] Fondo Vaticano 2392, p. 97vo. and 98ro. See Boncompagni, *Della vita e delle opere de Gherardo Cremonese* ; Roma, 1851, p. 7.

Hac, licet obsistant, coguntur amore puellae.
Ecce idem Scotus qui stando sub arboris umbra
Ante characteribus designet millibus orbem.
Quatuor inde vocat magna cum voce diablos.
Unus ab occasu properat, venit alter ab ortu,
Meridies terzum mandat, septentrio quartum.
Consecrare facit freno conforme per ipsos
Cum quo vincit equum nigrum, nulloque vedutum,
Quem, quo vult, tanquam Turchesca sagitta, cavalcat,
Sacrificatque comas eiusdem saepe cavalli.
En quoque dipingit Magus idem in littore navem
Quae vogat totum octo remis ducta per orbem.
Humanae spinae suffimigat inde medullam.
En docet ut magicis cappam sacrare susurris
Quam sacrando fremunt plorantque per aera turbae
Spiritum quoniam verbis nolendo tiramur.
Hanc quicumque gerit gradiens ubicumque locorum
Aspicitur nusquam ; caveat tamen ire per altum
Solis splendorem, quia tunc sua cernitur umbra.'[1]

Here the legend is not only considerably enriched, but it has recovered much of its original tone. Michael Scot again appears rather as the mighty mage than as the adroit juggler which Dante had represented him to be. One would say Folengo had read the spell of Cordova, where a circle similar to that described by him is actually proposed. The use of magical images too, on which he insists, is the very art which the Arabian author of the *Picatrix* professes to teach.

These then, or such as these, must have been the ' old wives' tales ' spoken of by Dempster, who says that store of them passed current in his day.[2] He was, like Michael Scot himself, a Scotsman long resident in Italy, who taught in the universities of Pisa and Bologna at the commencement of the seventeenth century :[3]   an origin and situation

---

[1] *Maccheronea*, xviii.
[2] ' Innumerabiles fabulae aniles circumferuntur, et jam nunc hodie. *Hist. Eccl.* p. 494.   [3] *Obiit* 1625.

very favourable to the knowledge of these stories, both in their Italian and Scottish form. That they had at an early period become part of the romantic heritage of Scotland seems very certain. An anonymous author supplies us with the Italian view of the matter when he says that the great magician taught the Scots his art to such a degree ' that they will not take a step without some magical practice,' and adds that he introduced into Scotland the fashion of ' white hose, and gowns with the sleeves sewed together.' [1]

Perhaps the best known of these Scottish tales is that which relates how Michael Scot had a particular spirit as his familiar, and describes the difficulty he felt in discovering new tasks for his supernatural servant. Sir Walter Scott says that this story had made so deep an impression, that in his day any ancient work of unknown origin was ascribed by the country people either to Sir William Wallace, Michael Scot, or the devil himself.[2] But, as commonly told, the legend refers to certain outstanding features of the country which are natural and not artificial ; a fact which may possibly account for its persistence and survival in this form and not in the others. Michael is said to have commanded his spirit to divide Eildon Hill into three.[3] The feat was accomplished in a single night, but, the magician's instructions being very precise, and the spirit finding one of the peaks he had formed greater, and another less than the mean, accommodated the matter very

---

[1] ' Chiose anonime alla prima Cantica della *Divina Commedia* ; Torino, Salmi, 1865, p. 114.

[2] *Lay of the Last Minstrel*, Note W.   [3] *Ibid.* Note Z.

skilfully by transferring what seems like a spade-
ful of earth, still visible as a distinct prominence
on the sky-line of the hill. Next night brought
the need for another task, and Michael gave orders
that the river Tweed should be bound in its course
by a curb of stone. The remarkable basaltic dyke
which crosses the bed of the stream near Ednam
is said to have been the result of this command.
On the third night, finding his familiar still keen
for employment, Scot bade him go spin ropes of
sand at the river mouth. This task proved so
difficult as to relieve the magician from further em-
barrassment. It is said to be still in progress, and
the successive attempts and failures of the spirit
are pointed out as every tide casts up, or receding,
uncovers, the ever-shifting sands of Berwick bar.

Another Scottish story, borrowed perhaps from
the relations between Michael Scot and Frederick II., and possibly suggested by the philosopher's
journey in 1230, speaks of a high commission he
once held from the King of Scotland.[1] Some
Frenchmen, it is said, had commenced pirates,
and had plundered Scottish ships. The King
chose Michael as his ambassador, sending him to
Paris to demand justice and redress. The magician, however, made none of the ordinary prepara-
tions for so considerable a journey, but opened
his *Book of Might* and read a spell therein;
whereupon his familiar appeared in the form of
a black horse, just as Folengo describes him. In
this shape the demon carried his rider through
the air with incredible speed. When the channel
lay beneath them, he asked Michael what words

[1] *Lay of the Last Minstrel*, Note Y.

the old wives in Scotland muttered ere they went to sleep. A less adroit wizard would have simply repeated the *Paternoster*, and thus furnished the excuse sought by the demon, who would then have hurled his rider into the sea. Michael, however, contented himself by sternly replying; 'What is that to thee? Mount Diabolus, and fly;' and, the demon being thus outwitted and compelled, they presently arrived in Paris. Finding the French King unwilling to hear his representations, Scot asked him to delay giving a final refusal till he should have heard the horse stamp three times. At the first hoof-stroke, all the bells in Paris rang. At the second, three towers in the palace fell; and the horse had raised his foot to stamp once more, when the King cried, 'Hold,' and yielded him to do as his cousin of Scotland desired.

A more trivial and domestic tale is that which relates how Michael met and overcame the Witch of Falsehope.[1] He was then residing at Oakwood Tower, and, hearing much talk of this woman's craft, he set forth one day to prove her. The witch was cunning, and denied that she had any skill in the black art, but, when Scot absently laid his staff of power upon the table, she caught it to her and used it upon him with such effect that he became a hare; in which shape he was hotly coursed by his own hounds. Taking refuge in a drain, he had just time to reverse the spell and resume his own form before the hunt reached his hiding-place. Thus Michael returned to Oakwood with a high impression of his neighbour's skill and malice, and fully resolved to have his revenge at the first

[1] *Lay of the Last Minstrel*, Note Y.

opportunity. This occurred next harvest, when, under pretext of sport, he sent his servant to the witch's house to beg some bread for the hounds. Met with the refusal that was expected, the man acted upon his master's instructions by privately fixing to the door a scroll containing, amid magical characters, the following rhyme :

> 'Maister Michael Scot's man
> Socht breid and gat nane.'

Meanwhile the witch-wife had returned to her work; which was that of boiling porridge for the shearers. As soon, however, as Scot's man had left the door, she began to run round the fire like one crazy, repeating as she ran the words of the spell. In a little the harvesters returned from the field to their dinner, but, as each passed the enchanted door, the spell took him, and he joined the dance within. Meanwhile Michael and his men and dogs stood not far off on the hill, whence they could command a full view of what went on. The last to leave the field was the goodman, who, suspecting something more than common from the attention Scot was paying to his house, was too cautious to enter immediately, as the rest had done. He went to the window, and through it beheld the orgy, now become terrible, and in the midst of all his wife, half dead from compulsion and exhaustion, dragged around the house and through the fire by the bewitched servants. Suspecting how matters stood, he went to Scot, who, relenting, told him how to remove the spell by entering the house backwards, and then taking the scroll down from the door. This he did, and the unearthly dance ceased, but it was long ere those who had taken part in it forgot the power of the magician, or ventured again to provoke his resentment.

The northern tales had much to say of Michael's *Book of Might*, from which he learned his art, and of his burial-place, where it lay interred with him. Dempster tells us that, in his boyhood, it used to be said in Scotland that Scot's magical works were still extant, but might not be touched for fear of the powerful demons that waited on their opening.[1] This form of the legend belongs then to the latter part of the sixteenth century. In the beginning of the next age, and precisely in the year 1629, occurred the traditional visit of Satchells to Burgh-under-Bowness.[2] This author declares that one named Lancelot Scot showed him in that place something taken from the works of the mighty magician :

> ' He said the book which he gave me
> Was of Sir Michael Scot's Historie ;
> Which Historie was never yet read through,
> Nor never will, for no man dare it do.
> Young scholars have pick'd out some thing
> From the contents, that dare not read within.
> He carried me along the castle then,
> And shew'd his written Book hanging on an iron pin.
> His writing pen did seem to me to be
> Of harden'd metal, like steel or accumie,
> The volume of it did seem so large to me
> As the Book of Martyrs and Turks Historie.
> Then in the church he let me see
> A stone where Mr. Michael Scot did lie.
> I ask'd at him how that could appear :
> Mr. Michael had been dead above five hundred year ?
> He shew'd me none durst bury under that stone
> More than he had been dead a few years agone,
> For Mr. Michael's name does terrifie each one.'

---

[1] 'Et, ut puto, in Scotia libri ipsius dicebantur, me puero, extare, sed sine horrore quodam non posse attingi ob malorum daemonum praestigias quae, illis apertis, fiebant.'—*Hist. Eccl.* p. 495.
[2] *Lay of the Last Minstrel*, Note W.

It will be observed that Satchells hesitates here
between the title of knighthood which had been
bestowed on Scot for a century past on the authority
of Hector Boëce, and the more authentic dignity of
Master which was really his. He also antedates
the philosopher's lifetime by more than a hundred
years; so that plainly what we have in these verses
is legend and tradition rather than history.

This is probably the latest appearance in
literature of the old stories concerning Michael Scot
told in the old way. Naudè[1] and Schmutzer[2]
presently came on the scene, in the late seventeenth
and early eighteenth century, with their critical
defences of Scot, all too imperfectly informed regarding his real reputation. In our own age the
poems of Sir Walter Scott and Rossetti, while
serving to show that so great a name has not been
forgotten, breathe, it is plain, an entirely different
spirit. They are but the romantic and sentimental
revival of tales that the poets and their world had
already ceased to believe.

Changed habits of thought, reaching and affect-
ing every class of society, make it useless now to
seek in Scotland for any new developments of the
legend of Michael Scot. This is not so certainly
true, however, of the South of Europe; of Italy,
Sicily, and Spain, where he was once a familiar
figure. There the slow progress of education has
left the common people still in possession of much
legendary lore, and even of the living faculty by
which in past ages such tales have been formed.
To ascertain what an Italian story-teller in the

---

[1] *Apologie des Grands Hommes accusez de Magie*, Paris, 1669.
[2] *De Michaele Scoto, Veneficii injuste damnato*, 1739.

present year of grace would make of the name and fame of Michael Scot were clearly a curious and interesting inquiry. It is one which, on actual trial, has yielded two tales differing considerably from any hitherto published.[1] As these are certainly the very latest additions to the legend, they deserve a place here at the close of our collection. Freely rendered into English they run as follows:

'Mengot was a notable astrologer and magician. Mengot was his true name,[2] but he had many surnames besides; among which was that of Scotto. This name of Scotto was given him by a princess. One night the Prince, her husband, happened to be in a company where the talk turned on the virtue of women, and the Prince said he would put his hand in the fire if his wife were not faithful to him; so sure was he of her virtue. Then spoke up another of the company, who made light of the caresses and compliments with which women use to deceive, and told a tale for the Prince's warning. "There was once a man," said he, "who thought as you do, dear Prince; for he took his wife for a pattern of virtue, and would have pledged, not his hand only, but his very life that she was so. It

---

[1] My readers owe these tales to the kindness of Mr. C. G. Leland, who procured them for me from an old Florentine woman. She is familiar to Mr. Leland's friends as 'Maddalena,' and is the depository of that traditional lore on which he has so happily drawn in his *Legends of Florence*. Her stories are interesting if only as an example of folk-lore up to date, and of the way in which an Italian mind deals with the legend of Michael Scot, while some points they offer are certainly original and highly curious.

[2] This may be a variant of 'Maugis' or Merlin. In the romance of *Maugis d'Aygremont* we find the following passage: 'Il n'y avoit meilleur maistre que lui . . . et l'appelloit-on Maistre Maugis.' On the other hand Mengot is a genuine early Teutonic name. 'Et hic liber finitus est per manus Mengoti Itelbrot, Anno domini m°ccc°lxxxv.' is the colophon to a manuscript of the *Almagest* of Ptolemy in the Vatican, Fondo Palatino, 1365, p. 206ro.

happened, however, that he had a friend who knew
of the wizard whom they call Mengot, dwelling
without the Croce Gate of Florence, and having his
house below the ground, closed by a flat stone of
the field so as to be secret.   Those who would
inquire of him must pass to the place and cry
'Mengot! Master Mengot! I seek a favour of thee,
and, if thou tell me true, I shall not stint thy
reward;' whereupon he doth straightway appear.
This then was what the friend of the too confident
husband did, for he summoned Mengot, and, in
presence of all, said to him : 'Tell me the truth,
and whether the wife of this gentleman deserves his
confidence or not.'   After some thought, the wizard
replied, 'Do you wish a true answer, or one made to
please ?   I should be sorry to hurt the husband's
feelings.'   When all desired to have the truth,
Mengot told them that the lady in question had
gone to a place in the Via Calzaiuoli where
disguises were arranged, and that she would be
found next day dressed as a servant in the course
of carrying on a vulgar intrigue in the Ghetto.
Now all this was verified ; for the wizard told them
even the very house in the Via delle Ceste where she
would be found with her lover, and it proved to be
exactly as he had said."   When this tale was done,
all who heard it cried that Mengot should be
summoned again, to see whether the Princess were
faithful or not.   So they called him, as had been
done in the other case, but with the same result ;
for here also the Prince's confidence had been
misplaced, and that in a high degree.   Then said
the Princess, between rage and shame, " Hast thou
scotched me this time ; but next time I will scotch

thee."[1] She straightway sought a witch, said to be more powerful than Mengot himself, and, telling what had happened, promised her gold by handfuls if she would revenge her on the wizard. The woman told her to be easy, for she would arrange the matter. She paid Mengot a visit as if to take his advice, and, stealing his magic rod, struck the ground three times, whereupon Mengot was turned into a hare, and fled from his habitation. Having foreseen, however, by his art that such danger might arise, Mengot had prepared a pool of enchanted water at his door. Into this he now leaped, and by its virtue was able to resume his proper form. The first thing he did was to seek the magic rod, and, finding it still in his house, he struck the witch on the head. She became a skinless[2] cat, and in that form haunted the guilty Princess for her sins; while Mengot was ever afterwards distinguished by the name of Scot.'

The second tale is to this effect:

' Michael Scotti the wizard was a mighty master of witchcraft. There came to him one day a young lady, richly dressed, and wearing a thick veil. She told him that she wished to become a witch that she might cast a spell upon the child of a man who had forsaken her for another woman, now his wife; for she said that to bewitch this child would be the best revenge she could have. Michael was willing to content her; but we must here remark that wizards and witches gain their power, either at

---

[1] ' M'hai *scottato* me, ma ora *scotto* te.' This play on words is the turning-point of the tale.

[2] ' Scorticata.' It may be that a play on words is intended here also.

birth or as a legacy from some dying person who has the gift. In either of these cases, when the wizard or witch takes the form of an animal, both body and soul are present wherever the form may appear. If, on the other hand, any one becomes a witch of her own desire, as in the case before us, her spirit may move and act under such a form, but her body lies all the while where she left it. But to our tale.'

'Michael accordingly took his Magic Book, and the skin of a cat, and kindling some hempen fibre[1] in an earthen pot, he commenced to read his spells, which had such effect that the spirit of the young lady entered into the skin of the cat. In the form of that animal she then went about her business, while her body remained still in the chair where she was sitting. At her return the wizard read again in his book, whereupon the spirit of the new-made witch returned to her body as before. Michael gave her a book of this kind, and the skin he had used, and every night she turned herself into a witch, and became so wicked as to cast ill upon many children, and even on an infant brother of her own.

'Thus the sorceress was hardly entered on her power ere she brought about the death of her rival's child, and killed many others, but an end was presently put to these ill-doings. Her brother, whom she had bewitched out of jealousy, wasted away, and the parents were in despair, as none of the physicians whom they consulted could understand the case. One morning the child told them

---

[1] This is no doubt the *benj* or *bhang* of the Arabs and Indians which still furnishes them with a potent narcotic.

he had suffered much during the night from a cat,
which leaped upon his bed, howled, and played
the most frightful antics. They then began to
suspect witchcraft, and resolved that the household
should watch during the next night. On the
stroke of twelve a cat was seen coming out of
their daughter's room. One of the servants gave
chase, and another went into the room, fearing that
the young lady had also been bewitched, and saw
her lying on the bed as cold as marble. The cry
arose that she was killed. The parents, mad with
grief, made after the cat to destroy it, but with
leaps and bounds, it kept them busy all night as if
they had been huntsmen chasing a hare, and all in
vain. As the bells began to sound for matins the
cat ran into the young lady's room, and the mother,
beating her brow, exclaimed : "she who has bewitched my son is none other than his sister."
Rushing into the room they found her, no longer
like a dead body, but all panting from the night-
long chase. Her mother searched all the corners,
and finding the book and earthen pot, bade throw
them into the Arno. They then besought their
daughter to undo the mischief she had wrought
upon her brother, and so many more, and to promise
she would never do the like again ; but to nothing
of this would she consent. Then they threw her out
of window in fear and to the breaking of her bones.
The servants came and took her up ; laying her on
her bed again ; telling her to heal her brother. Not
even in the last moments of life, however, would
she repent. She could not die till Mengot had
read for her a spell of loosing, and on him therefore
she still lay crying. The servants told this to

her parents, who bade put horses to the carriage
and fetch the wizard, who was presently with
them. First he commanded her to cure her
brother, and then he read for her in his Magic
Book that she might be loosed, and so she died.
But when the skin and earthen pot were cast
away, they sank straight underground. Thus the
witch, who still came back every night to get the
skin, and take the form of a cat, found all her
magic art in vain; for Michael Scotti had taken
her power away.'

'Desinit in piscem mulier formosa superne!' To
such vain and trivial conclusions has a reputation,
justly renowned in its own day, been reduced in
ours. Michael Scot, now become a *troglodyte*, lifts
his head timidly and occasionally from a den in the
Florence fields; he who, while alive, filled Europe
with his fame, and, by his *Averroës*, ruled the
schools of Padua as late as the seventeenth century.
If a remedy is still to be had for this, the fruit of
Guelphic rancour, it must be found in the direction
we have sought to keep throughout these pages :
that of a serious and impartial study of Scot's life,
and of those labours of his in philosophy and science
which are so really, though remotely, connected
with the intellectual attainments of our own times.

APPENDIX

APPENDIX I

✠ Experimentum Michaelis Scoti nigromantici.[1]

Si volueris per daemones haberi scientem, qui in forma magistri ad te veniet cum tibi placuerit, expedit tibi primo habere quandam cameram fulgentem et nitidam, in qua nunquam mulier non conversetur, nec vir ante inchoationem triginta diebus, computato itaque tempore taliter quod xxxj die fit luna crescens[2] –o– eius hora, castus per septimanam, rasus totus, ac etiam lotus, necnon vestimentis albis indutus. Solus in ortu solis, in quo, et ipsa hora habeas quoddam vas in quo sit lignum aloes camphora et cipressum cum igne, ex quibus fiat fumus, et primo te totum suffumiga, scilicet primo faciem, deinde alia, postea etiam totam cameram. Quo facto, habeas oleum bacharum et totum te unge a capite usque ad pedes, hoc facto, volve te primo versus ortum, et sic dic, flexis genibus : O admirabilis et ineffabilis et incomprehensibilis, Qui omnia ex nihilo formasti, apud quem nihil impossibile est, te deprecor cum humilitate vehementi ut mihi, famulo tuo tali, tribuas gratiam cognoscendi potentiam tuam, Qui vivis et regnas cum Deo Patre per omnia saecula saeculorum, Amen. Praesta quaesumus mihi tutellam angeli tui, qui me custodiat, protegat, atque defendat, et adjuvet ad huius operis consummationem, et faciat me potentem contra omnes spiritus ut vincam etiam dominer eis, et ipsi adversus me terrendi vel laedendi nullam habeant potestatem, Amen. [here follow verses 25-28 of Psalm 119.] Similiter versus occasum, meridiem, et septentrionem, et debes scire quod, quando vertis te, debes te totum expoliare nudum, deinde dicere has orationes : quo facto, debes te induere dicendo hunc psalmum, [Psalm 76 : 1- .] usque *quomodo cogitatio hominis,* etc. quo dicto, et inducto, dic tu haec verba [Psalm 37 : 30.] Quibus dictis habeas unum frustrum panni albi de lana, quae nunquam fuerit in usu, et habeas quandam columbam albam totam vel –o– cuiuscumque coloris sit, et trunca eius collum, et collige eius sanguinem in vase vitreo, et de dicta columba sive _–o– sanguinando dictum cor in 1°. o. Fac cum dicto corde cruentato, in dicto panno, circulum, ut apparet in-

---

[1] Laurentian Library, P. lxxxix, sup. cod. 38, p. 409 (old number 256) verso.
[2] Here and elsewhere in this text are astrological signs which cannot be reproduced in print.

ferius, quo facto, intra circulum cum ense in manu: qui ensis
debet esse lucidissimus, cum quo ense avis caput debet truncari
ut dictum est, et ipsum tenendo per cuspidem, aspiciendo versus
orientem, dic sic: O misericordissime Deus, Creator omnium,
et omnium scientiarum Largitor, Qui vis magis peccatorem
vivere, ut ad penitentiam valeat pervenire, quam ipsum mori
sordidum in peccatis, Te deprecor toto mentis affectu ut cogas et
liges istos tres demones, videlicet Appolyin, Maraloch, Berich,
ut debeant per virtutem et potentiam tuam mihi obedire, servire,
et parere, sine aliquo fraude, malignatione vel furore, in omnibus
quae praecipio: Qui vivis et regnas in unitate Spiritus Sancti,
Amen. Debet haec enim oratio dici novies versus orientem,
deinde debes dicere, Appolyin, Maraloch, Berich, Ego talis vos
exorcizo et conjuro ex parte Dei Omnipotentis Qui vos vestra ela-
tione jussit antra subire profundi, ut debeatis mittere quendam
spiritum peritum dogmate omnium scientiarum, qui mihi sit
benivolus, fidelis, et placidus ad docendum omnem scientiam
quam voluero, veniens in formam magistri ut nullam formidinem
percipere valeam, fiat fiat, fiat. Item conjuro vos per Patrem et
Filium et Spiritum Sanctum ut per haec sancta nomina quorum
virtute ligamen, scilicet Dober, Uriel, Sabaoth, Semonyi
Adonayi, Tetragramaton, Albumayzi, Loch, Morech, Sadabyin,
Rodeber, Donnel, Parabyiel, Alatuel, Nominam, et Ysober,
quatenus vos tres reges maximi et mihi socii, mihi petenti, unum
de subditis vestris mittere laboretis, qui sit magister omnium
scientiarum et artium, veniens in forma humana, placibilis
aplaudens mihi et erudens me cum amore ita et taliter quod in
termino xxxta dierum talem scientiam valeam adipisci, pro-
mittens post sumptionem scientiae dare libi licentiam recedendi,
ut hoc etiam totiens dici debet. Hac oratione vero dicta, ensem
depone et involve in dicto panno, et facto vasiculo, cuba super
ipso ut aliquantulum dormias. Post sompnum vero surge et
induas te: quia facto vasiculo homo se spoliat et intrat cubiculum
ponendo dictum vasiculum super capite. Est autem sciendum
quod dictis his conjurationibus somnus acculit virtute divina, in
somno autem apparebunt tibi tres maximi reges, cum famulis
innumeris militibus peditibus, inter quos est etiam quidam magister apparens, cui ipsi tres reges jubent ad te ipsum venire
paratam. Videbis enim tres reges fulgentes mira pulcritudine,
qui tibi in dicto sompno viva voce loquentur dicentes, Ecce tibi
Domini quod multotiens postulasti, et dicent illi magistro, Sit
iste tuus discipulus quem docere tibi jubemus omnem scientiam

sive artem quam audire voluerit. Doce illum taliter et erudi
ut in termino xxx dierum in qualem scientiam voluerit, ut
summus inter alios habeatur : [1] et ipsum audies et videbis eum
respondere, dictum mei libentissime faciam quicquid vultis. His
dictis reges abibunt et magister solus remanebit, qui tibi dicet,
Surge, ecce tuus magister. His vero dictis, excitaberis statim et
aperies occulos et videbis quendam magistrum optime indutum,
qui tibi dicet, Da mihi ensem quem sub capite tenes. Tu vero
dices Ecce discipulus vester paratus est facere quicquid vultis ;
tamen debes habere pugillarem et scribere omnia quae tibi dicet.
Primo debes quaerere, O magister, quod est nomen vestrum : ipse
dicet, et tu scribes ; secundo, de quo ordine, et similiter scribe :
his scriptis, dabis ensem, quo habito, ipse recedet dicens,
Expecta me donec veniam : tu nihil dices. Magister vero recedet
et secum portabit ensem, post cuius recessu tu solves pannum,
ut apparet inferius,[2] etiam scribes in dicto circulo nomen eius
scriptum per te, et scribi debet etiam cum supradicto, O, quo
scripto involve dictum pannum et bene reconde : his factis debes
prandere solo pane et pura aqua, et illa die non egredi cameram
et cum pransus fueris accipe pannum et intra circulum versus
Appolyim et dic sic, O rex Appolyim magne potens et venerabilis
ego famulus tuus in te credens, et omnino confidens, quia tu es
fortior, et valens per incomprehensibilem majestatem tuam, ut
famulus et subditus tuus talis, magister meus, debeat ad me venire
quam citius fieri potest, per virtutem et potentiam tuam quae est
magna et maxima in saecula saeculorum, Amen. et similiter dicere
versus Maraloth, mutando nomen, et versus Berith similiter, his
dictis accipe de dicto sanguine et scribe in circulo nomen tuum
cum supradicto corde ut hic apparet inferius. Deinde scribe
cum dicto corde in angulis panni illa nomina ut hic apparent.
Si autem sanguis unius avis non tibi sufficeret, potes interficere
quot tibi placent : quibus omnibus factis, sedebis per totum
diem in circulo aspiciens ipsum, nihil loquendo ; cum vero
sero fuerit, plica dictum pannum spoliato, et intra cubiculum
ponendo ipsum sub capite tuo, et cum posueris dici sit plana
voce, O Appolyin, Maraloch, Berich, Sathan, Belyal, Belzebuch,
Lucifer, supplico vobis ut precipiatis magistro meo, nominando
eius nomen, ut ipse debeat venire solus ante cras ad me, et docere

---

[1] *Cf.* with the expression in the colophon ' qui summus inter alios nominatur
magister.'

[2] The manuscript shows a drawing of a magic circle here. It has the names
of demons alternately with those of the cardinal points.

me talem scientiam sine aliqua alia fallacia, per Illum Qui venturus est judicare vivos et mortuos et saeculum per ignem, Amen. Cave igitur et praecave ne signum ✠ facias, propter magnum periculum. In sompno scies quia videbis magistrum tota nocte loqui tecum, interrogans a te qualem scientiam vis adiscere, et tu dices, talem. Itaque ut dictus est tota nocte cum eo loqueris. Cum itaque excitatus fueris in ipsa nocte, surge et accende candelam, et accipe dictum pannum et dissolve, et sede in eo, scilicet in circulo, ubi nomen tuum scriptum est, ad tuum commodum, et voca nomen magistri tui, sic dicens, O talis de talis (sic) ordine, in magistrum meum datum per majores reges tuos, te deprecor ut venies in forma benigna ad docendum me in tali scientia, quia sim probīor omnibus mortalibus docens ipsam cum magno gaudio, sine aliquo labore, ac omni tedio derelicto. Veni igitur ex tuorum parte majoris qui regnat per infinita saecula saeculorum, Amen, fiat, fiat, fiat. His itaque dictis, ter aspicias versus occidentem, videbis magistrum venire cum multis discipulis, quem rogabis ut omnes abire jubeat, et statim recedent: quo facto, ipse magister dicet quam scientiam audire desideras; tu dices talem, et tunc incipies, memento enim quia tantum adiscens memoriae commodabis et omnem scientiam quam habere volueris adisces in termino xxx dierum. Et quando ipsum de camera abire volueris, plica pannum et reconde, et statim recedet: et quando ipsum venire volueris, aperi pannum, et subito ibidem apparebit continuando lectiones. Post vero terminum xxx dierum, doctus optime in illa scientia evades, et fac tibi dare ensem tuum, et dic ut vadat, et cum pace recedat. Debes iterum dicere cum pro alia ipsum invocabis habenda scientia, quod tibi dicet ad tuum libitum esse paratum. Finis capituli scientiae. Explicit nicromantiae experimentum illustrissimi doctoris Domini Magistri Michaelis Scoti, qui summus inter alios nominatur Magister, qui fuit Scotus, et servus praeclarissimo Domino suo Domino Philipo Regis Ceciliae coronato; quod destinavit sibi dum esset aegrotus in civitate Cordubae, etc. Finis

APPENDIX II

Fondo Vaticano 4428, ms. perg. in fol. saec. xiii. cum min.

p. 1 recto.   'Incipit Logica Avicennae. Studiosam animam
meam ad appetitum translationis lib. avicennae quem
asschiphe i. sufficientiam nuncupavit invitare cupiens,
et quaedam capitula. . . . in latinum eloquium ex
arabico transmutare.' Then follows a column and a half
commencing: 'Dixit abunbeidi filius ab,' (? avicennae)
which seems to give an account of the manner in
which he was wont to compose.   At the middle of
col. 2 begins a new paragraph :—'Dixit princeps
abualy alhysenni filius abdillei filius sciue' noted in
the margin as: 'Vita avicennae.' This closes at the
middle of the first col. of p. 1, verso.

p. 8 recto.   A footnote says 'translatus ab auendbuch de
libro avicennae de logico.'

p. 9 recto.   'Incipit collectio secundi libri sufficientiae a
principiis ph'ici prologus. Dixit princeps Avicenna.
Postquam expedivimus nos auxilio dei.' A short
prologue follows extending to three-quarters of a col.
Then follows the treatise: 'Iam nosti ex tractatu.'
It closes on p. 20 *recto* with the words 'per se notae
sunt. Explicit liber phisicorum avicennae Amen.'

p. 20 verso.   'Incipit liber Avicennae de celo et mundo, seu
collectiones expositionum ab antiquis graecis in librum
Aristotelis. Expositiones autem istae in quatuordecim
continentur capitulis. Per unum quod corpus per-
ficiens.' This tract closes on

p. 27 recto. with the words 'completum xv capitulum, et ideo
completione completus est liber totus, et laus sit
creatori nostro et largitori. . . . et sic pax et salus
omni animae modestae et benignae. Amen.

p. 27 verso.   'Incipit particula prima Metha^{ce} avicennae
cap. 1. de inquisitione . . . ad hoc ut ostendatur ipsam
esse de numero scientiarum liberalium. Avicenna de

philosophia prima, sive scientia prima divina. Postquam
autem auxilio Dei explevimus tractatum scientiarum
logicalium et naturalium et doctrinalium, convenientius
est accedere ad cogitationem intentionum spiritualium.'

p. 78 recto. The Metaphysica end here with the words :—'quia
ipse est rex terreni mundi, et vicarius dei in illo.
Completus est liber. Laudetur deus super omnia
. . . quem transtulit diaconus gundissalui archidyaco'
tholeti de arabico in latinum.'

p. 78 verso. 'Incipit liber primus Avicennae de anima et
dicitur sextus de naturalibus. Reverentissimo thole-
tanae sedis archiepiscopo et yspaniarum primati Johannes Avendaut israelita philosophus gratiam et vitae
futuris obsequium.' . . . 'Incipiunt capitula totius libri.
Liber iste dividitur in partes.' . . . 'Ordinatio librorum
Avicennae. Iam explevimus in primo libro.' . . .

p. 79 recto. 'Capitulum 1. Dicemus ergo . . .' The De
Anima closes on

p. 114 verso. with these words : 'sicut postea scies cum
loquitur de animalibus. Explicit sextus naturalium
Avicennae. Deo gratias et nunc et semper Amen. Qui
scripsit hunc librum Dominus benedicat illum. Ffinito
libro sit laus et gloria Christo. Incipit sermo de
generatione lapidum Avicennae. Terra pura non fit
lapis quia continuationem non facit.' The second
chapter is : 'De generatione montium' and the third
'De generatione corporum mineralium.' In the latter
chapter occurs the curious passage : 'Sciant autem
artifices alkimiae . . . et salem amoniacum' which we
have translated on p. 74.

p. 115 recto. The short tract on minerals closes at the foot of
this page with the words : 'exhibere res quaedam
extraneae. Explicit vere.'

p. 115 verso. is blank.

p. 116 recto. 'De animalibus Avicennae. Frederice, roma-
norum imperator, domine mundi, suscipe devote hunc
librum michaelis scoti ut sit gratia capiti tuo et torques
collo tuo. Incipit abbreviatio avicennae super librum
animalium aristotelis. Et animalia quaedam communi-
cant in membris, sicut equus et homo.' The treatise
closes on ·

p. 158 recto, in the usual way : 'sed de dentium utilitatibus

jam scis ex alio loco. Completus est liber avicennae
de animalibus scriptus per magistrum henricum coloniensem ad exemplar magnifici imperatoris domini
frederici apud meffiam civitatem Apuliae ubi dominus
imperator eidem magistro hunc librum permissum
comodavit anno domini m° cc° xxxij° in vigilio beati
laurentii in domo magistri volmari medici imperialis
liber iste inceptus est et expletus cum adiutorio iesu
christi qui vivit. . . .
Frenata penna, finito nunc avicenna
Libro Caesario gloria summa Deo
Dextera scriptoris careat gravitate doloris.'

In the second col. of this page commences the arabo-
latin glossary (*see* facsimile) :—
'Ex libro animalium aristotelis domini imperatoris in
margine.'
'Passer dicitur pscipsci,'
'Rumbus. sciathi.'
'Delfinis, delfinus.'

. . . .
'Fehed. leopardus.'

. . . . . .
'Ex libro secundo.'

. . . . .
'Ex tertio libro.'

. . . . . .
'Glosa magistri al.' 'Explicit anno domini m° cc° x.'

. . . . . .
Fondo Vaticano 2089 ms. in fol. perg. finiss. saec. xiii. The
first 265 pages of this volume contain the *De Causis* (pp. 1-5)
and the following commentaries by Averroës : *De coelo et mundo*
(pp. 6-195) ; *De generatione et corruptione* (pp. 195-254) ; on the
fourth book of the *Meteora* (pp. 254-260) ; *De substantia orbis*,
(pp. 260-265). Then follow the commentaries by Avicenna in
this order :—
p. 266 recto. 'Titulus, Collectio secunda libri sufficientiae
avicennae principis philosophi. Prologus. Dixit
princeps, Postquam expedivimus nos auxilio dei ab eo
quod opus fuit.' . . . 'Liber primus de quaestionibus
et principiis naturalium Capitulum de affligenda via
qua pervenitur ad scientiam naturalium per principia
eorum. Iam scisti ex tractatu.'

p. 282 verso. ' et consummate certo fine cessabit interrogatione.
Completus est primus tractatus de naturalibus cum
auxilio Dei et gratia. Incipit tractatus secundus de
motu et de quiete et de consimilibus. Capitulum de
motu. Postquam perfecimus librum de principiis.'

p. 306 verso. ' cuius tempus non habet (?) esse initium. Completa est pars secunda de collectione naturalium. Et
ei qui dedit intelligere gratiae sint infinitae. Pars
tertia de hiis quae habent naturalia ex hoc quod habent
quantitatem. Prologus de qualitate tractandi precipue
in hoc libro. Naturalia sunt corpora.'

p. 307 recto. ' et haec propositiones per se notae sunt. Explicit
liber sufficientiae avicennae. Prologus in sextum
naturalium Avicennae. Reverentissimo toletanae sedis
archiepiscopo et yspanorum primati auendeueth israelita
philosophus gratiam et vitae futuris obsequium. . . . .
Quapropter, domine, jussum vestrum de transferendo
librum avicenae (cod. 4428 p. 78 verso reads *aristotelis*)
philosophi de anima effectui mancipare curavi ut vestro
munere et meo (4428 *nostro*) labore latinis fieret certum
quod hactenus extitit incognitum scilicet an sit anima,
et quid et qualis sit, secundum essentiam rationibus
verissimis comprobatum. Haberis (4428 *habes*) ergo
librum vobis precipiente (4428 *percipientibus*) et me
(4428 omits *me*) singula verba vulgariter proferente et
dominico archidiacono singula in latinum convertente
ex arabico translatum quo quidquid aristotelis dixit
in libro suo de anima et de sensu et sensato et de
intellecto et intellectu ab auctore libri scias esse col-
lectum. Unde postquam deo volente hunc habes. In
hoc illos tres plenissime vos habere non dubiteris.'

p. 307 verso. ' Incipit sextus de naturalibus auicenae translatus
a magistro Girardo cremonensi de arabico in latinum
in toleto. Iam explevimus in primo libro.' . . .
' Capitulum in quo affirmatur esse anima et diffinitur
secundum quod est anima. Dicemus igitur quia quod
primum.'

p. 315 verso. ' Expleta est pars prima sexti libri de collectione
naturalium. Incipit pars secunda eius. Capitulum de
certificando virtutes quae sunt propriae animae vege-
tabilis. Incipiemus nunc notificare sigillatim.'

p. 322 recto. ' Completa est pars secunda sexti libri de collec-

tione naturalium. Deo sit gratia. Incipit pars eius
tertia de visu. Debemus loqui de visu.'

p. 335 recto. 'non habet sensum communem ullo modo. Completa est pars tertia sexti libri de naturalibus, Deo sint
gratiae. Incipit iiij vj libri de naturalibus. Capitulum
in quo est verbum commune de sensibilibus interioribus
quos habent animalia. Sensus autem qui est communis.'

p. 344 verso. 'et hic est finis eius quod transtulit Auohaueth
ex capitulis illius libri ad hunc locum huius libri de
anima. Completa est quarta pars sexti libri de naturalibus auxilio Dei. Incipit pars quinta libri eiusdem.
Capitulum de proprietatibus actionum et passionum
hominis, et de assignatione contemplationis et actionis.
Quoniam jam explevimus tractatum de virtutibus sensibilibus.'

p. 356 verso. 'quorum quaedam attrahunt materiam et quaedam expellunt sicut postea scies cum loquitur de
animalibus. Completus est liber de anima qui est
sextus liber collectionis secundae de naturalibus. Et
ei qui dedit intelligere sint gratiae infinitae. Post
hunc sequitur liber septimus de vegetabilibus et viij°
de animalibus qui et finis scientiae naturalis. Post
ipsum autem sequitur collectio tercia de disciplinalibus
in quatuor libris, seu arismetica, geometria, musica,
astrologia, et post hunc sequitur liber de causa cau-
sarum.' Then follows an index to the chapters of the
De Anima which ends the whole codex on p. 357 recto.

I have thought it well to give this complete account of these
two remarkable manuscripts not only because they show the
exact place held by the *De animalibus* in the body of commentaries written by Avicenna, but also on account of the view
they give of the translations made by the early Toledan school.
In this respect they serve in some measure to correct and extend
the conclusions of Jourdain. It is evident, for instance, that
Avendeath did not finish translating the *De Anima*, but only
proceeded in it as far as the end of the fourth part.

APPENDIX III

Riccardian Library, Florence, L. III. 13, 119, p. 35 verso, middle of 2nd col.

Incipit liber luminis luminum translatus a magistro michahele scotto philosopho.

Cum rimarer et inquirerem secreta nature ex libris antiquorum philosophorum qui tractaverunt de natura salium alluminum et omnium corporum et spirituum minere pertinentium nullum inveni qui completam dixisset doctrinam. Quedam tamen utilia extraxi et ea secretis nature adiunxi procedo (?) quidem brevitati et addendo quae utilia sunt in hac arte que alkimia nuncupatur. In quo talia continentur Invencio (? Intencio) causa intentionis et utilitas. Invencio (? Intencio) eius est tractare de transformatione metallorum secundum quod hermes dixit parum enim desint marti quod non fiat luna non desint aliud nisi quod non fiat tanta decoctio in eo sicut luna. Et notum est quod sicut 7 sunt metalla ita 7 sunt planete et quodlibet metallum habet suum planetam. Dixerunt ergo philosophi quod aurum est filius solis Argentum filius lune Aes filius veneris Argentum vivum filius mercurii stagnum filius jovis Plumbum filius Saturni Ferrum filius martis. Causa intentionis est ut ex tali mutatione nobiliora fient metalla. Utilitas quod habita notitia huius libri qui lumen luminum appellatur transfigurari possit mars in lunam et venus in solem et constringere omnes spiritus volantes. Quorum quaedam sunt subtilia et quaedam volativa. Volant enim sicut sulphur et arsenicum et ex illis est etiam argentum vivum. Sed primo de salibus loquamur 2° de alluminibus 3° de atramentis, 4° de pulveribus. Salium autem sunt diversorum specierum scilicet Masse Alcali Rubeum Armoniacum Nitrum salsum Agrum Allebrot albo et communis.

I have thought it best to print these parallel texts with as close adherence to the manuscript as is consistent with intelligibility, and they therefore appear in these pages with all the mistakes of the copyist.

APPENDIX III

Riccardian Library, Florence, L. III. 13, 119, p. 195 verso and p. 196, recto.

[I have re-arranged the paragraphs of this treatise so as to fall opposite the corresponding parts of the Liber Luminis, but have numbered them according to their original order so that by following the numbers the book can be read in its own proper form.]

1. De natura salium et quot sunt. Sales autem sunt diversarum specierum est enim sal commune sal masse sal gemme sal rubeum sal nitrum sal alkali sal armoniacum sal elebrot album.

Aristotle in the *De Anima* (i. 3) says that there was a legend of Daedalus which represented him as having given motion to a Venus of wood by filling it with mercury. This may have suggested the adoption of his name to the author who wrote this alchemical treatise.

Q

PRIMO DE SALE COMMUNI.

Sal autem commune convenientior est omnibus salibus scilicet marti. Dixit philosophus quod [si] quisquis ipsum prius ipsius separationem acceperit et quater per atramenta transire fecerit postea cum ana sui ydragor sublimati in aquam redire fecerit ac coagulati quod es [sic pro "aes"] cum ipso mirabiliter dealbabit et isto fit sal tostum quod tali modo fit. ℞ ex eo libram. 1. et pone in patellam ferream et combure sufficienter et iste est sal tostus.

Sal masse ponit qualiter sal in massam naturaliter redactus ut gemma Alexandrinus ungarricus Sardonicus et hermoni (?).

Sal autem alkali est nobilior omnibus salibus excepto sali alebrot facit autem coagulare alios sales. Iste autem sal fit de herba salsifera que juxta mare complicatis foliis invenitur, sive de allumine gattivo quod extrahitur de supradicta herba. Salem autem alkali prius ipsius meram separationem si quis ter per atramenta transire fecerit et eodem modo de communi masse armoniaco egerit ipsius quoque in unum redactis iterum per atramenta transire fecerit ac cum ana sui ydragor in aquam redire fecerit et coagulaverit quod convertet martem in lunam et constringet omnes spiritus volantes.

Iste autem sal inter reliquos sales retinet naturam vetetabilitatis et minere.

DE SALE RUBEO

Dictis de salibus et eorum virtutibus sequitur de sale rubeo sive Indico Dicitur autem Indicum eo quod apportatur de India est enim durissime odorifere nature rubedine quadam cum citrinitate participans. Habet autem fortem virtutem super venerem rubificandam et dando ei colorem bonum. Verum est

8. Sal gema aportatur de Hispania. Sal autem commune convenientior est omnibus creaturis. Utuntur enim ex eo in condimentis mundat enim corpora et reddit ea clara propter hoc dedit eum omnipotens Deus in cognitionem ut per eum omnia corpora conservarentur in sanitate bona. Dedit enim bestiis cognoscere eum nedum hominibus. Condiuntur enim omnia animalia cum eo et dolcañtur (? deliciantur) pecudes in eo. Et scias si sal iste accipiatur in quantitate una et ponatur in sartagine et comburatur combustione forti quod iste sal appellatur tostus. Et cum inveneris in arte ista sal tostum accipias ex isto secundum quod volueris. Verum est quod non inveni ipsum congruum in hac arte nisi raro. Eius tamen receptō est valde utilis in talem quia fingitur cum aliis salibus ad purificationem martis in lunam et est peroptimus.

7. Sal autem alkali est nobilior omnibus salibus excepto sale tabor vel alebrot. Facit enim coagulare alias sales et iste sal alcali fit de herba quadam in partibus baldrach coagulat vitrum et facit ipsum clarum atque currentem (?) mundat corpora albificat a superfluitatibus terreis ultra modum. Sal autem alkali si adjungatur cum sale masse et terantur simul et ponantur cum x partibus aque dulcis et dimittantur bulire usque ad consumptionem quarti partis et ponatur in vase virtreo ut clarificetur et cum clarificatum fuerit suaviter coletur et quod purum erit in aliquo vase mittatur et quod tenerum est abiciatur et dimittatur usque quo coagulatum fuerit et non operabis cum eo nisi tritum dissolutus quoniam operacio eius esset inutilis et si admisceris cum eo aliquantulum salis armoniaci vel boeci vel alebrot erit operacio eius fortior et convenientior omnibus operationibus. Dixit enim Abymelech quod sal alkali erit nobilior omnibus salibus et convenientior in omnibus operationibus excepto sali tabor vel alebrot. Preterea quod fit ex vegetabilibus unde retinet naturam minere et vegitabilitatis. Unde solvit vitrum et facit ipsum coagulari et clarificat ipsum clarificatione bona.

4. De sale indico rubeo. Sal autem rubeum apportatur de India et id circo vocatur sal indicum. Habet enim fortem virtutem super venere rubificando ipsum et dando ei colorem bonum. Verum est quod hoc non facit per se sed cum adjutorio videlicet cum duabus partibus istius et 3 bus salis alebrot

quod hoc non facit per se solum sed cum tercia parte sui salis alebrot rubei et virtute pulveris talparum [1] et camfore et masticis et virtutis omnia simul terantur et cum urina taxy vel gāgelis usque 7 distemperetur et cum hoc pulvere venerem tinges martemque in lunam transmutat.

DE ARMONIACO

Sal autem armoniacum est magne virtutis quoniam ex fumositate eq. ā (*sic pro* fimositate equorum) fit est autem multiplex naturale et fictitium.   Naturale aliud album aliud rubeum. Album longus est super quem lamina velociter currit.   Rubeum rotundum est et sale alebrot rubeo affiliatur velociter enim currit sine fumi emissione super laminam.   Primus in lunam secundus in solem cum ana sui pulveris talparum super omnia metalla per optime laborat.   Ficticium etiam secundum predictos modos diversificatur ad optinendam supradictam virtutem.

---

[1] The nature of this powder of moles is explained a little further on in the Liber Dedali, par. 10.

dissolvendo totum simul et addendo etiam huic terram armenie
rubeam masticem et camforam ad quantitatem 3 · 11, et salis
armoniaci 3 · 111. ista omnia simul misceantur et cum urina tapsi
distemperentur et iterum exsiccentur hoc 7 in omnibus fiat.
Pulvis iste stringit spiritus volantes albificat corpora et reddit
clara et lucida et mutat martem in lunam mutatione perfecta et
bona. Addit enim in tm̄ (? talem) rubificationem veneri quod
mutat venus in solem.

5. Aliud quod est utile mulieribus multum et maxime
dominabus. Accipe etiam de sale indico 3. 11. diligenter teratur
et distemperatur cum urina pueri virginis et sit urina libra· 1· et
ponatur in vase terreo in quo ponuntur rose et cum fit aqua rosa
et supponatur alembicho et accendatur ignis sub eo et non
multum fortis et cum videris fumum ascendere in cufa superius
tunc facias ignem levem et quod inde exierit collige et in ampulla
vitri reconde. Talis enim aqua vero ultra modum in pannis
faciei et betiginibus adalbat sēd pigines destruit omnem maculam
et si posueris in calaminas eris erit albior ad recipiendum colorem
quam scis.

14. Sal autem armoniacum est magne virtutis quoniam de
stercoribus animalium scilicet camelorum pecudum et asinorum
fit in hunc modum. In quibusdam partibus terre sarracenorum
non habentes ligna etiam ex paupertate lignorum calefaciunt
balneum cum stercoribus predictorum animalium et ille fumus
resolutus ab eis condensatur in balnea et accipitur illa talis
condensatio et teritur et bulitur cum urina puerorum tam diu
quod coagulari incipit et post modum projicitur in peraside et
colatur. Cum isto enim sale fit azurum optimum et fit in hunc
modum. Accipe de sale armoniaco et tere ipsum diligenter et
distempera cum urina pueri virginis ponendo ipsum in vase vitreo
et sepiliendo ipsum in letamine pecudum per dies 3. Post modo
habeas plagellas factas de argento et pone eas cum filo legatas ita
quod non tangas urinam et lamine sint abrase et dimittantur per
diem et noctem. Et cum autem fuerint denigrate iterum
abradantur et iterum sepiliatur et quod habebis in laminibus a
prima vice in antea erit azurum optimum et quanto plus durabunt
tanto melius erit. Verum est quod alio modo fit azurum quia
invenitur quedam vena terre juxta venam argenti illa terra
optime teritur et distemperatur cum aqua calida et ponitur
super linteum positum super aliquo vase et colatur subtiliter et
quod grassum et feculentum cadit in vase proice quando autem
fuerit purum vel juxta illud exsiccabitur et recondetur. Si

DE SALE NITRO SALSO

Sal nitrum est multiplex. Est enim nitrum qui est pulvis niger. Est etiam sal nitrum allexandrinum et Indicum sive rubeum salsum isti similiter in massa lata reducti funditur et findere facit.

Est etiam nitrum salsum de isto due sunt maneries folliatum ut talcum. Alter depillatur ut allumen de pluma in eo autem est salsedo cum punctuositate et magnus philosophus [dicit] quod si quis acceperit ex eo 3 · 1 · et tantundem pulvis talparum et exsiccaverit cum urina tassi sive gāgelis convertet martem in lunam et constringet omnes spiritus volantes. Item tolle de predicto pulvere 3 · 1 · et 5 et callaminare et trita simul et incorpora cum urina tassi vel gāgellis usque 9 cum isto pulvere super omnia metalla in solem obrigō laborare possis.

R Sossile rubificate 3 · 1 · gutte rubee 3 · 1 · et 5 pulvis talparum 3 · 1 · et parum nitri salsi ac simul trita et incorpora cum aceto et pone cum aceto et pone super m. [mercurium] et habebis solem obrigō.

autem non fuerit bene purum terantur adhuc bene et ponantur in aqua calida et accipiatur · pix · cera et masticis et dissolvatur et ducatur ita cum manu per vas ubi est azurum et depurabit eum a superfluitatibus terreis et si vena fuerit bona azurium erit bonum. Si mala azurium erit malum.

9. Sal nitri est plurium specierum. Una species est salis nitri que apportatur de Alexandria et ille est vere sal nitrum cum illo vero lavant mulieres sarracenorum pannos lineos et faciunt eos albissimos ut nix, lavant etiam facies earum et corpora sua in balneis. Destruit enim pannum faciei lentiginis et albicat optima albedine. Non extendo sermonem meum in laudes eius quia non est magne utilitatis in hoc arte nec etiam recipitur in ea quod sciatur. Alia species salis nitri que vere nitrum salsum appellatur et de eo sunt due maneries. Una quarum foliatur et altera filatur et depilatur sicut caro porcina macra et in ea est salsedo cum ponticitate. Dico enim tibi per Deum omnipotentem quod in eo est tanta virtus et utilitas quod pauci fuerunt de sapientes (sic) qui eam potuissent cognoscere quoniam in eo est secretum nature quod nullus stolidus et insipiens potest cognoscere. Sed qui sapiens est et discretus extractabit multum circa eum, Ille forte inveniet de quo cor suum gaudebit. Dixit enim hermes filius Gelbeo cum exaltatus fuerit sal nitrum salsum et acrum si in vinctum fuerit cum sale alcali erit operacio eius nobilior et magis utilis. Et dixit magnus philosophus qui multum doctus fuit in talibus quod si acceperis ex eo aliquem quantitatem et triveris eum fortiter et postea miscueris cum eo urinam tapsi et exsiccaveris ipsum et tuttueris eum fortiter usque septies et accipies tantum de pulvere cullaxe i. [e.] illius animalis que talpa vocatur quantum fuit pulvis salis nitri convertetur mars in lunam et venus in solem et constringet omnes spiritus volantes. Constringitur enim argentum vivum cum isto et non cum alio Deus scit et novit.

10. Pulvis autem culaxe debet fieri secundum hunc modum. Accipiantur enim ex eis 4 vel 6 secundum quod poteris invenire quia sub terra morantur et pones eas in testa terrea et luta ipsam luto sapientie ita quod fumus non exeat aliquo modo pone eam in furno bene calido et dimitte a mano usque ad sero vel a sero usque ad mane postea extrahe et pulveriza subtiliter et reconde et cum opus fuerit operare cum ea. et scias firmiter quod pulvis iste valet plus quam aurum et est utilis et multum conveniens multis operacionibus et habeas eum valde carum quia pauci

DE SALE AGRO

De sale agro in quo est virtus magna quam pauci sciunt et sapientes constringunt cum eo m. mundant cum eo corpora (?) et albificant ea sufficienti albedine et reddit ea clara et lucida. Et iste a quibusdam philosophis alibrot appellatur licet in veritate non sit idem et diversus quod sit frigidus et siccus quamvis videatur hoc esse contra naturam et de proprietate eius est constringere m. et omnes spiritus volantes et quanto magis studueris in eo tunc invenies eius albedinem ultra quam aliquis possit excogitare quia cum eo albificantur corpora et non cum alio deus novit. Et dixit magnus philosophus cum moriebatur filio suo O fili mi secretum tuum habeas in corde tuo nec dices alicui nec filio tuo nisi cum amplius non poteris retinere.

Desiderio desideraverunt philosophi sapientes scire veritatem huius salis. Sed pauci eam sciverunt et qui eam noverunt non dixerunt in libris suis veritatem eius secundum quod viderunt. Illinant enim martem et clarificat a superfluitatibus terreis et facit quod mars transmutatur in lunam hoc modo ℞ ex eo libra 1. gutte rubee que inveniuntur in allumine de pluma 1 · 1. pulvis talparum 1 · 1. sal armoniaci alkali arborum separatorum 3 · 6. trita omnia simul nonies et impastina et exsicca cum urina illuminata.

Postea soliatī suttus et supras es in pecia madescam pone et cola et cave ne.

fuerunt de sapientibus qui bene cognoscerent virtutem eius nisi magnus philosophus qui dixit in libris suis et est in eo id quod deest et ego temptavi et operacionem eius inveni maximam efficaciam in eo. Sed ponebam in duplo de pulvere nitri salsi.

2. Et postea est sal acrum et in eo est virtus maxima quam pauci sciunt invenitur enim in hispania et sapientes constringunt cum eo mercurium. Clarificat enim corpora munda et albificat ea albedine sufficienti. Mutat enim martem in lunam et defendit eum a superaciis et a superfluitatibus terreis et dat ei colorem bonum et clarum. Et iste a quibusdam philosophis sal alebrot vocatur et de quod scit et sint (?) generalius videatur hoc esse contra naturam et de proprietate eius est retinere omnes spiritus volantes et quanto magis studueris in eo tanto magis inveneris eius altitudinem ultra quod possit excogitari quia cum eo aluminantur (sic) vel albificantur corpora et non cum alio Deus novit. Et dixit magnus philosophus cum moriebatur O fili mi secretum tuum habeas in sinu tuo nec dicas filio tuo nisi cum eum amplius non poteris retinere quoniam in eo invenies secreta nature quam desiderio desideraverunt sapientes sed pauci intraverunt in eum et qui intraverunt operationem eius non dixerunt in suis libris secundum (? scilicet) quod viderant.

11. Aliud ad preparacionem martis. Accipe de sale alcali ƺ· x. et de sale armoniaco ƺ· 2. et tere subtiliter et distempera cum urina zazel et cum casus ad libram 1. pone in aliquo vase terreo vitreato et luta cum luto sapientie et pone in furno mediocriter calido et dimitte a mane usque ad sero vel converso. postea extrahe de vase illo si coagulatum fuerit. Si non iterum ponatur in furno super vase optime lutato et cum coagulatum fuerit teras ipsum et misce cum 3 libris aque dulcis et dimitte residere in vase vitreo et quod clarum fuerit repone ipsam aquam (?) et quod feculentum fuerit t'i eum ejice. Postea accipe laminas factas ex marte factas tot quot possunt submergi in aqua ista et dimitte ibi per ix dies. Decimo autem die pone ad ignem et dimitte bulire per magnum tempus. Et ipsis laminibus extractis et exsiccatis in igne debes accipere pannum lineum novum et balneare ipsum aliquantulum et stringe intra manus et debes ponere laminas in panno isto p'ns pulvere supradicto asperso et ponendo laminas et spargendo pulverem usque ad finem et involvendo eas in tali panno. Accipe fortiter exstringendo et pone ipsum pannum cum laminibus in vase qui dicitur alludel ponendo ipsum in fornace et super sufflando cum manticello ac bonum ignem faciendo donec sit solutum. Et caveas quod non

discooperias ante quam fundatur quoniam perderis opus tuum. Sed quum liquatum fuerit deice super ipsum parum ydragor resolutum in aqua et coagula vel parum lapidis alcotar preparati sed melius est ydragon cum parum de predicto sale balneato cum aqua et deice in aqua et habebis bonam lunam.

℞ sal atincar libra 1. gutte rubee et pulvis talparum ana l. 1. ydragor ʒ · 1 · trita simul et impastrina cum urina soliata sel' postea fac redire in aquam et coagula. De isto pulvere si posueris super m. bulliendo pulverem cum aqua dulci habebis de m. nobilem lunam.

DE SALE ALEBROT [1]

Sal allebrot album sali acro assimilatur in colore et longitudine fixionis autem et unctuositatis est fb'e locoque ipsius poni potest. Separatio autem eius ut asserant sapientes secundum hunc modum. ℞ ex eo l. i. vel gutte albe vel azuree que inveniuntur in allumine de pluma ʒ · 1 · sanguis hominis rubei ʒ · 3 · talchi mortificati ʒ · 1 · et 5 et parum sulphuris albi omnia simul trita et inpastina cum sanguine et sale et desicca ad solem. Et cum volueris operare utere eo spargendo super m. igne super accenso retinebit enim eum nec sinet volare et quantitas m. l. 5, et non plus et non moveatur ab igne usque ad magnum tempus postea in aquam proiciatur poterit enim optime malleari. Item accipe

[1] A double chloride of ammonium and mercury, represented by the formula $2NH_4Cl. H_2Cl_2, H_2O$.

discooperiatur donec bene dissolutum fuerit quia amitteres operacionem tuam. Eciam non peneteas in prolongacione ignis quoniam si ignis prolongatur aliquantulum magis ultra quam tibi videatur erit operacio tua multum melior. Sed ex abreviatione possit operacio tua destrui et in idem revertens quod prius fuerat. Stude autem inquantum potes ut videas sine discopercione magno ignis nec is quod est cruciolo albē (? albescere) videatur. Sed discooperiendo plane et si dissolutum fuerit ipsum prioce in aqua ut refrigescat. Et cum frigidum fuerit accipies in manu tua. Dico enim in veritate quod tu gaudebis de eo quia habebis lunam pretiosissimam in omni operacione.

12. Alia operacio que fit cum pulvere isto, Accipe m. et pone ipsum in luteollo in quo artifices infundunt argentum ad quantitatem quam vis et super pone de pulvere supradicto super m. cum tribus q° teis aq̄. miscendo cum digito leviter et pone ad ignem in furnello et suprapone carbones accensos in luteollo et fiat ignis mediocriter nec nimis magnus nec nimis parvus et non discooperiatur usque ad magnum tempus et postmodo proiciatur in aqua et habebis quod utile est et habebis illud bonum quod omnes sapientes desideraverunt.

13. Aliud similiter de pulvere isto adhuc expertum. Accipe 3 · 1. de supradicto pulvere et pone 3 · 5. ematicis in 3 · 5. talci merabilis et diligenter teras et accipe 3 · x. veneris et pone in panno lineo faciendo laminas de venere et spargendo pulverem super pannum et super laminas et sit pannus madefactus et stringendo totum simul et ponendo ipsum in luteollo in igne et cooperiendo ipsum carbonibus faciendo ignem nec nimis fortem nec nimis levem usque quo dissolutum fuerit et cum fuerit dissolutum proice ipsum in aquam. Habebis enim nobilem operacionem ad quam pauci devenerunt.

3. Operacio allebrot ut asserunt sapientes est secundum hunc modum. Accipe ex eo secundum quantitatem quam vis s. 3 · 5 · et tere diligenter postea habeas sanguinem alicuius hominis rubei ad quantitatem 3 · 3 · et comisce cum eo et degutta. Aut accipe 3 · 5 · de talco parum sulfuris albi et tere omnia diligenter et incorpora cum sanguine et sale et dimitte siccari in furno vel ad solem, et cum exsiccatum fuerit teratur id totum in mortario lapideo subtiliter et cum opus fuerit utere eo spargendo super m. igne super accenso et sufflando cum manticello retinebit enim eum et non sinet eum volare. Sit quantitas m. librae 5 et non plus et non removeatur ab igne usque ad magnum tempus postea in aqua proiiciatur poterit hec enim optime malleari. Accipe

v. buffones[1] et pone eos in aliquo vase unde non valeant exire
postea accipe suci affodillorum vel ermodatilorum et eleboris albi
extracti cum aceto quia aliter non poterit extrahi 1 · 2 · et pone
in vase ubi sunt buffones et dimitte eos bibere per 9 dies vel
quousque bene sint inflati tunc eos pone infra (sic) duas scutellas
ad comburendum et cave ne spitare (sic) possint ne fumus exeat
tunc pulverisa et ℞ de dicto pulvere ʒ · 1 · salis alebrot ʒ · 1 · et 5
salis armoniaci et salis alkali ana ʒ · 5 · omnia simul trita et in
pastina et deinde exsicca usque nonies cum urina tassi vel
gāgellis cum pulvere isto poteris facere mirabilia pulvis iste
constringit m. et mutat ipsum in lunam purissimam et perfectam
clarificat martem et mundificat eum a superfluitatibus terreis et
feculentis et facit quod mars transmutatur in lunam mutatione
perfecta. Si acceperis de pulvere isto ʒ · 1 · et 1 eris et miscueris
cum eo secundum quod docet in igne ubi fuerit spiritus gaudebis super operationem eius quoniam exaltavit illum super omnes
sales. Loco autem ipsius potest poni sal acrum. Item et
afronitrum. Item et salsedo muidorum (?) dummodo per
atramenta transeant. Item et salacrum dummodo per atramenta
transeat ter. Dum vero sales hēb' ad hoc separatos ad meron.
Sal alkali Semen communis. Armoniacum allm̄s jam simul fac
in aquam redire et duplum aquam quam spiritus deice et super
marmor pone et congela et ista est p'a (? pura) ceraton propter quod
vos omnes erratis credentes vos habere secundam nec primam
habetis. Postea pone inter duas scutellas vel in vase vitreo quod
melius est et claude os eius et dicoque per dimedium diem tunc
extrahe et ablue salem et invenies ipsum in speciem ceruse sed et
fixe sb'e (? sublimate) non timens ignem. Separatur enim hoc in
calcinationem ut ubicumque spiritus calcinatus intromiseris sine
dubio ex m. bonum opus habebis. Dealbat enim spiritus. Calcinat
martem ad modum mercurii nec ultra vestigia albedinis amittit
excepto sub experimento veneris. Sed si in aquam reduxeris et
postmodo teraveris sub experimento noveris. Sed si in aquam
reduxeris et postmodo teraveris sub experimento perfectissime
durabit. Incalcinatio eorum in sole unde potest fieri ut Archelaus docuit. Ac tum unde potest fieri in aqua atramenti rubi-
ficati ac per se in aqua solutiones calcinationes melius est in vase
vitreo quam in alio.

[1] The use of matters derived from the animal kingdom, carbonised toads or
moles, may be illustrated from the Liber Dyabesi (Ricc. ms. 1. iii. 13, 119, p. 4
recto) which treats of what had been 'ab omni Latinitate intemptatum' viz. the
distillation of a white land-tortoise (v. p. 7 verso). Pliny remarks that goat's
blood sharpens and hardens iron tools and polishes steel better than any file.

decem bufones tenentes venenum et fiant vive et ponantur in
aliquo vase unde non valeant exire. Postea accipe anfodillos
recentes et eleborum album in bona quantitate extrahe inde
succum cum eis quantum pones (sic), pone succum in vase illo
in quo sunt rane et dimitte eas bibere per ix dies. Tunc accipe
eas et pone in olla rudi et luta eam luto sapientie et pone ipsam
in furno ita ut animalia comburantur combustione sufficienti et
extrahe inde ea et tere diligenter et cum opus fuerit de illo pulvere accipe ʒ · 1 · de sale alebrot ʒ · 1 · de sale alcali ʒ · 5 · de sale
armoniaco tantundem et teras diligenter permiscendo cum ea
urinam tassi et iterum exsicca et tere et hoc nonies fiat et de illo
pulvere poteris facere mirabilia. Pulvis iste constringit m.
mutat jovem in lunam et albificat martem clarificat eum et dat
ei colorem bonum et clarum et mundat eum a superfluitatibus
terreis et facit quod mars transmutatur in lunam. Mirabilis
enim in suo effectu. Si vero accipies de pulvere isto ad quantitatem ʒ · 1 · et miscueris cum ere secundum quod docet et in
igne fuerit. Sapientia et sit quantitas eris ʒ · viiij. gaudebis.
Sal rubeum gummum rubeum terram armenie gerssam vel
gerussam et pulverem bufonis equaliter et operati sunt valde
in suis operibus. Habuerunt enim talem scientiam quam pauci
noverunt et benedixit eam Deus omnipotens qui causa prima
fuit omnium rerum. Dico tibi firmiter quod cum istis rebus
omnia necessaria possunt acquiri. Idcirco tacuerunt onēs et
verterunt se ad salem armoniacum nec dixerunt de eo quicquam
aperte.

Explicit prima pars et Incipit secunda de alluminibus.   Et primo de allumine Jammeno.

Allumen Jammeni triplex vocatur.   Jammenum de pluma Scagloli.   Aportatur autem de Spania.

Est autem frigide nature et sicce hoc bonitatis in se continens ut si jungatur cum re rubea facit ruborem acquirere in ea sicut alba albedine augmentare facit in ipsa.   Sicut illuminat pannos ita illuminat martem ut recipiat formam lune ut enim lana illuminatur ita et metalla illuminantur.[1]   Et quante magis mars fuerit illuminatus et depuratus a superfluitalibus a (? et) feculenciis terreis tanto efficiatur ex eo melior operatis.   Illuminatur autem sic.   Accipe urinam puerilem et per 7 dies in vase vitreo esse permitte vase obturato postea per alios 7 dies in vase transmuta distillando per filtrum semper sel' postea bulli ipsum usque ad terciam sui partem et dispuma et distilla per filtrum bis vel ter postea pondera ipsum si est libra 1, adde 3 · 11 · et 5 salis armoniaci separati ab atramento et 3 · 8 · alluminis jammeni et bulli insimul et permitte requiescere clarum solummodo accipiendo et feculentum abjiciendo et in ista urina es calefactum et intus extinctum et per alios 9 dies in ipsam stare permitte et est optime illuminatus.   Omnia etiam metalla in hac aqua taliter illuminare possis et abiliora erunt ad recipienda colorem.   Dixerunt enim vnay et melchia philosophi quod ubi mars fuerit taliter illuminatus non convertetur perfecte in lunam.   Consentiendum est eis quia philosophi fuerunt.   Oro enim quod talis illuminatio metallorum valet et utilis est omni creature Dei.

De allumine rubeo

Allumen rubeum apportatur de buzea (? Bugia) depillatur autem ut allumen de pluma.   Istud autem a quibusdam philo-

---

[1] This passage is highly significant, and furnishes a key to the title of the treatise.

16. Racio autem alluminum est secundum hunc modum. Est enim allumen salsum et alumen de rocha et alumen de bolkar et alumen jameni et alumen scaiole et alumen de pluma. Sed nota quod alumen de pluma jameni sissi idem sunt secundum quod ego credo quia inveni in libris philosophi quod eadem est virtus jameni cum virtute de pluma et sissi et est eius virtus modo albatione et retinet colorem cum conjungitur. Si vero conjungitur cum re alba facit ipsam albam et si conjungitur cum re rubea facit rubedinem acquiri in ea. Sed quidam dicunt quod sint idem in genere sed diversi in specie. Et quod alia est species aluminis jameni alia scissi et alia de pluma. Dico tamen tibi in veritate quod una et eadem est operatio etsi diversificantur in omnibus. Et scias ipsum esse frigidum et siccum tamen nec dissolvitur ab igne nisi misceretur cum rebus humidis et cum illis dissolvitur et sicut illuminat pannos ita illuminat martem ut recipiat forma lune. Et quanto magis mars fuerit illuminatus et magis depuratus a superfluitatibus terreis et feculentis tanto efficitur ex eo melior operatio. Illuminat autem secundum quod ego dixi tibi multociens faciendo laminas ex marte et accipiendo etiam alumen de pluma ad quantitatem quam vis scilicet si mars fuerit ʒ · ix · aluminis debes accipere ʒ · 2 · et tere subtiliter et misce cum ʒ · 1 · salis armoniaci triti subtiliter et debes ponere libra 1, urina (sic) pueri virginis secundum quod ego dixi tibi multocies et bulire omnia simul in vase vitreato. Postea dimitte residere et cola quod clarum est accipe et quod feculentum proice et pone laminas illas in aqua illa et dimitte ita stare per 8 dies postmodo extrahi eas et exsicca et operare cum (sic) sicut scis et habebis nobilem operacionem si bene scivisti ea que processerunt. Non habeas hoc vile quia istud est secretum maximum et non obliviscaris pannum faū et pulverem ex nitro salso acro. Aliter enim non valeat operatio tua.

6. Dixerunt cuidam (sic) philosophi quod aqua ista preparat martem ut recipiat formam lune et consentiendum est eis. Scito enimvero quod preparatio eius est optima ad recipiendum formam bonam que est utilis omni creature.

sophis allebrot rubeum appellatur eius proprietas est cum ana sui auripigmenti sublimatum rubei m. in solem transmutare. Quidam autem de philosophis scilicet Seno et Rogiel accipebant de isto allumine rubeo et ja. et gut. et de roco sal armoniaci semine amborum arsenicorum sulphuris Tartari talci Cinabrii omnium ana ponebant super m. et ex ipso extrahebunt lunam pretiosam.

DE ALLUMINE ET MAROCCO

Allumen de maroc est pulvis subrufus acetositatem parvam in se continens est autem mundificative et depurative nature.

DE ALLUMINE ZUCHARINO

Allumen zucharinum est albissime nature acetositatem mordacem in se continens locoque alluminis jameni post poni (? potest poni)

DE ROCCO

Allumen de rocco est in massa redactus acetositatem subtilem in se continens cum isto et pinguedine colcotar et melle sophisticatur borax.

17. Alumen autem de rocha non durat in igne sed siccatur et facit sicut borax de petra ex isto sophisticatur borax cum pinguedine calchatam et melle. Unde cum ponitur super ignem funditur alumen sicut et illud. De isto autem alumine nichil ad nos quoniam nullam facit utilitatem in arte ista et idcirco non curamus multum de eo loqui.

18. Aliud experimentum quod extractum fuit de libris quorundam philosophorum. Habeatur pro maximo secreto scilicet haninan camescia[1] qui summi fuerunt in arte alchimie et fuerunt de lamacha sarracenorum qui dixerunt ita nisi mars fuerit expoliatus a superfluitatibus suis non convertetur perfecte in lunam. Purgatur enim cum aqua virginum et aluminum secundum quod tu scivisti superius si tu intellexisti quod narratum est. Sed concordati sunt isti philosophi in hoc cum dixerunt. Si quis acceperit ʒ · 3· de nitro salso et adiunxeris ʒ · 2· de sale alkali et ʒ · 1· de sale armoniaco ista simul terantur et cum urina pueri virginis distemperantur ad quantitatem ʒ · viiii et de urina animalis qui tapsus dicitur ʒ · viiij. et ponatur totum in vase vitreato et sit vas lutatum luto sapientie circumcirca ita quod fumus non possit inde exire et accendatur ignis levis sub eo et dimittantur bulire valde plane a mane usque ad terciam vel a tercia usque ad nonam. Postea accipiatur et ponatur

---

[1] These are names of philosophers probably the same as the 'vnay et melchia' of the *Luminis Luminum*, the rather that the phrase 'non convertitur perfecte in lunam' occurs in both passages. I do not know how to explain the fact that two paragraphs of the *Liber Dedali* correspond so closely with one in the *Liber Luminis*.

in letamine pecudum et dimittatur ix dies. Postea accipiatur et discooperiatur. Si coagulatum fuerit bene erit sin autem non fuerit adhuc coagulatum in vase lutato reverteris adhuc in letamine pecudum et dimittatur ibi per 6 dies erit coagulatum si Deus voluerit. Tunc accipies vas et extrahes totum id de vase et teras illum diligenter trituratione bona. Postmodo accipe de pulvere isto ʒ · l· et talem camphore et ʒ · l· lapidis armenie et unam terre rubee et tantundem de alumine jameni et terantur omnia ista simul et cum opus fuerit accipe de pulvere isto. l· de laminibus sublimatis ʒ · ix· accipiendo pannum lineum grossum et balneando ipsum cum aqua parum exprimendo ipsum et supra aspergendo istam pulverem. Postea spargendo eodem modo pulverem supradictum super laminas preparatas ponendo iterum laminas et pulverem desuper usque ad complementum. Et scire debes quod in fine debes plus ponere pulverem et stringendo istas laminas in panno isto fortiter ponendo eas in luteolo et postea in igne faciendo ignem circumcirca et sufflando fortiter cum manticello donec bene dissolutum ꞌfuerit. Tempore autem dissolutionis potest esse in duabus horis si bene meditaberis et in usu habueris omnia bene habeantur usu. Et scias quod tu debes magis ponere modum in dissolutione quam in alio quia per te ipsum debes dissolvere et videre quantum tempus habes dissolutionis et secundum quod tu videris in hora secundum hoc poteris comprehendere dissolutionem eius cum pulvere et aliquantulum plus ut non decipiaris quia si aliquantulum plus fuerit in igne quam tibi videatur erit operatio tua melior. Sed si nondum esset dissolutum tu discoperiens amitteres tuam operationem.

19. Aliud secretum in quo concordati sunt omnes sapientes qui aliquid cognoverunt de arte ista.[1] Et est secundum hunc modum. Accipe libra l· sanguinis alicujus hominis rubei et sanguinem xi talparum et sex bufones ranam magnam habentem venenum et accipe libra· ll· succi anfodillorum et libra· l· succi elebori albi extracti cum aceto quia aliter extrahi non potest. Ista ponantur omnia in una olla. Postmodo habeatur alia olla in duplo maior ea vel in triplo ita quod parva possit stare in ea et distet ab alia per x digitos et plus et ponatur parva bene lutata cum rebus supradictis in olla magna et ponantur carbones inter ollam magnam et parvam et accendatur ignis circumcirca et dimittantur ita semper faciendo ignem per dies duos postea extrahe ab olla et discoperi eam et videbis pulverem nigrum.

---

[1] There is probably a reference here to the disputes which divided the different alchemical schools.

De Allumine Romano

Allumen romanum borbaci (? boraci) assimilatur acetositatem minimam in se cóntinens de minera atramenti sive alluminis Jameni extrahitur cuius proprietas est per se solvere vel cum ana sui sulphuris albificati m. ad naturam lune transformare.

Explicit secunda pars.   Incipit tertia,

De Atramentis

Ratio autem atramentorum est secundum hunc modum. Atramentorum autem sunt multe species Colcotar Calcadis vitriolum nigrum capernum viridis Cuperose.[1]

---

[1] The doctrine of the vitriols is here substantially the same as in the great work of Ibn Beithar of Malaga.

Postea accipe pellem ericii et comburatur fortiter et tere omnia trituratione forte videbis quasi argentum et miscebis talem de alio pulvere cum isto et habebis urinam tapsi et distemperabis cum ea istem pulverem ponendo ipsum ad solem per 3 dies et totidem noctes ad rorem et miscendo ipsum semper quousque desiccatum fuerit. Postea accipe de sale nitro acro quartam partem et terciam de sale alcali et tantundem de sale allap et alluminis de pluma tantundem omnia terantur simul et usui serventur. Dico enim tibi et juro quod si tu scis legere librum istum et intelligere accipere sublimare mundificare constringere ignem facere et componere res secundum quod debent componi in veritate tu habebis lunam perfectam et solem perfectum ita quod cor tuum gaudebit in ea. Sed huic arti necessarium est studium vehemens ut scias et sic forte poteris scire artem istam. Ego quidem multum studui in ea atque sudavi añquā invenirem artem istam et id quod volebam et non potui pervenire ad hoc nisi cum magno studio et labore exercitando artem usque quod inveni in ea que volui. Et ita dico tibi fili h'mē ut non sis piger in probacione huius artis quia tibi dico veritatem. Si tu probaveris artem istam invenies in ea omne bonum quod erit utile omnibus hominibus.

15. Racio alluminum et de diversis ipsorum generibus. Racio autem alluminis et atramentorum secundum hunc modum. Atramentorum vero x sunt species scilicet Colcotar Calcandis Vitriolus et viride es. Ideo enim tinguntur et denigrantur. Calcari est nobilius et magnopere valet in operatione alchimie. Purificantur enim corpora ex eo mundificantur a superfluitatibus terreis ut meliorem recipiant formam et nobiliorem. Et fit secundum hunc modum. Accipe Calcatar libra 1· et dissolve ipsa cum urina pueri virginis. Et quare dico cum urina pueri virginis quia est magis mundificata et penetrativa est et inveni quod maximus philosophus laudavit multum in suis operationibus et debet esse ad quantitatem trium librarum et facias eam bulire in vase vitreato usque ad consumationem tertie partis. Postea dimitte residere et quod clarum fuerit collige

Ex colcotar et calcadis secundum Platonem extrahuntur lapides rubei vel trahentes ad rubedinem qui loco salis indici possunt poni.

Vitriolum nigrum apportatur de Francia et idcirco dicitur terra francigena cum isto mulieres vulvam constringunt ut virgines appareant non est autem magne utilitatis in ista arte. Est autem utilis ad sublimandum ydragor cum vis facere sal naticum. Cipernum est crocei coloris mollitiem in se continens requiritur autem multum in arte ista secundum Archelaum. Viride dicitur vitriolum romanum loco etiam caperni potest poni sed nobilior est eo ut Hermes philosophus testatur in libro alluminum.[1] Atramentum nunquam pro alio ponitur. Sed cuperosum est album subazurii coloris fitque de superfluitate martis cum de minera extrahitur que quidem etiam locoalluminis romani recipiunt licet in veritate non sit idem. Explicit tertia pars.

Incipit Quarta de Spiritibus

Sunt quidam spiritus qui ad ignem in fumum convertuntur et converti faciunt alias res, Sulphur et Arsenicum et ex illis est argentum vivum. De sulphure flavo. De sulphure croceo. De sulphure rubeo. De sulphure albo. De arsenico croceo. De arsenico rubeo. Sulphuris quatuor sunt species scilicet croceum flavum rubeum et album. Croceum est magis de-

---

[1] There is a well-known tract *De aluminibus et salibus* ascribed to Rases in the Paris MS. (6514 p. 128); it also occurs in the Speciale MS.

et quod feculentum et terreum proice. In ista enim aqua apponantur lamine martis et dimittatur usque ad ix dies postea extrahe et operentur et fit cum eis luna secundum modum in igne quo modo tu pluries intellexisti. Calcandis utitur in veneris et non est eius utilitas multum in hac arte. Sed inveniuntur in eo lapides rubei qui valent multum in operatione alchimie mutando corpora planetarum. Secundum quod enim audivisti in libris cuiusdam philosophi ex calcadis vel calcatar extrahuntur lapides rubei vel tendentes ad rubedinem qui valent multum ad mutacionem metallorum naturalium transformando ea secundum quod oportet et dando ei colorem optimum. Et ego credo quod isti lapides sint de specie alluminis et si hoc esset non esset mirum si poterint perficere solem et dare ei colorem bonum. Unde sicut luna illuminatur ita metalla illuminari possunt. Verum est quod ista scientia scribi non potest nisi cum maximo studio et labore. Sed in quo tu magis debes studere est in igne et sublimationibus pulveribus et mundificare metalla secundum quod tu scivisti et intexisti superius.

Capitulum de Spiritibus Volantibus

20. Sunt autem quidam spiritus qui recedunt ab igne et in fumum convertuntur et faciunt convertere alias res sicut est sulphur arsenicum ex illis est argentum vivum. Sulphuris tres sunt species. Est enim sulphur croceum flavum et est album. Flavum autem est sicut extrahitur de vena et tunc non est purum. Purificatur enim sic quia ponitur tritum in patella ferrea et dissolvitur ab igne et cum dissolutum est tollatur et iterum ponatur in patella super ignem ut eo dissoluto ponitur in

puratum et istud dicitur cannellatum quoniam in canellis terreis ad hec factis deicitur. Rubeum aportatur de India et valet a quibusdam sal indicum dicitur licet in veritate non sit cuius proprietas est venerem cum ana sui ydragor sublimati in obrizō solem transmutare.

Album portatur de hyspania de insula quadam que belle appellatur.[1] Recipitur etiam pro nitro salso sed non equiperatur ei quoniam ille funditur et fundere facit. Istud vero fugit ab igne. Arsenici tres sunt species scilicet croceum rubeum et album. Croceum cum teritur lucens apparet ut aurum foliatum quasi ut talcum. Rubeum non ita folliatur immo est in massam reductum minorem in se ignitatem continens quam primum. Album est aliquantulum crocei subalbique coloris et minoris igneitatis est quam reliqua duo. Istud de Turciae partibus apportatur reliqua vero duo de Armenia. Explicit quarta pars.

INCIPIT QUINTA DE PREPARATIONE ALLUMINUM

In preparatione allumini sufficit ut solvatur in aqua vel in urina distillata et coletur per pannum et coaguletur.

In atramentis sufficit ut fundatur in ciato (? scyatho) super carbones et buliat quousque humiditas evaporet. Preparatio boracis est ut in testa super ignem modicum ponatur nam statim inflatur et siccatur cumque stringi ceperit tollatur nam infrigidata faciliter pulverisatur. Tunc pulverizata a massa cum modica porcine (? portione) asungia (? axungiae) donec sit sicut terra et teratur et amassetur cum ea media pars salis petrae et hoc totum sicut terra amassetur et erit tibi cerotum pretiosum corpora et spiritus terans. Sic autem boracis partem 1 · salis petrae partem 1 · ceruse partem 1 · ana de tribus addideris et

---

[1] This phrase is found in the *De aluminibus et salibus* of Rases (Paris ms. 6514 p. 128) who calls the place 'Elebla.' Vincent of Beauvais ascribes the saying to Geber.

canellis factis de ferre (sic) et istud sulfur dicitur canelatum et
est valde purum a superfluitatibus. Operatur autem aliquid de
eo in arte al- chimie sed illud est valde purum. Verum est quia
preparat artem (? martem) et dat ei colorem lune. Quidam autem
accipiunt laminas eris et ponunt eas in igne et cum sunt bene
rubee extinguunt eas in sulfure bene trito miscendo fortiter
cum aliquo ligno. Postmodo accipiunt laminas illas et ponunt
in igne et dimittunt purificari et cum volunt operari accipiunt
et componunt eas secundum quod scis et intellexisti superius.
Et quidam ponunt etiam de eo parum cum pulvere supradicto
quando apponunt martem in panno et bene accidit eis quia
sapienter agunt.

Album enim sulfur invenitur in hispania et portatur de
insula que heble appellatur. Accipitur etiam pro nitro salso
sed non equiparatur ei quoniam igne fugit sicut spiritus, ille
autem stat et non solvitur ab igne sed funditur et tu audisti
satis de eo in superioribus. Nec loquar de eo tibi amplius.
Arsenici autem due sunt species. Una est crocei coloris et alia
est rubei coloris. Croceum autem multum valet quia mulieres
utuntur eo faciendo depilatorium et preparando facies earum a
pilis. Quidam de sophistis accipiunt 3 · 1· auri limati, libra 1·
auripigmenti et terent ipsum fortiter et balneant ipsum cum
urina et ponunt totum simul in sacculo corei et stringunt ipsum
et dimittunt ita stare usque ad mensem et videtur aurum. De
rubeo arsenico fit realgar. Ista sufficiant. Et sic est finis huius
libri. Explicit liber dedali in arte alchimie.

miscueris ea fortiter cum eius oleo vel simpliciter capillorum vel
ovorum donec sit sicut massa cere et massam illam bene siccaveris.
Pro certo scias quod ceroneum istud ferrum et cristallum et
quocumque volueris lapides calces ignis huius violentia remollit
et resolvit in resolutione liquida omnia ingrediens et penetrans
et ignea virtute dissolvens.   Ceraton fit de oleis vel aquis
rectificatis · 6 · per alembich.   Fit autem spiritum ut aggerentur
utrumque partes in eis ex multis fiat unum scilicet corpus fiat
dissolubile hoc autem ex ceratione olei vel aque.   Quia spiritus
corpore vel corpus spiritibus ingredi non potest nisi oleo vel
aqua duce videlicet cum quo ceratur.   Ut enim temperatura
ferrum affirmat sic cerato spiritus in corpore nec sine ceratione
potest aliquod corpus plene rectificare.   Agnoscitur autem res
cerata hiis signis.   Res cerata sine ulla fumi emissione velociter
super laminam currit ignitam quod incerata minime agit.   Fit
autem ceracio cum oleo vel aqua rectificata hoc modo.   ℞ rem
quam cirari debet et pone in vase argenteo aureo vel stagneo et
desuper pone de oleo preparata (sic) donec fundatur ut sagimen.
Dum ita videris velociter ab igne remove et infrigidari permitte.
Eo infrigidato prova ipsum super laminam et sic resolvitur super
ipsam sicut cera ceratum est et si non reduc eam ad crucibulum
et fac sicut predixi donec sic contingat.

Quomodo medicine debent solvi

Solutio cuiuslibet rei fit super lapidem vel in viscere (?) sub
fimo seu in aqua tepida fumi resolvis melius aprobo fit ea de cā
resolutio ut spiritus vel res in lapidibus possit coagulari nam
spiritibus crudis nisi sint in lapidem constricti volueris operari
non augmentum sed decrementum volueris incurrere nisi forte
essent incalcinati vel cerati hanc scientiam (?) firmiter teneas.

℞ calcis testarum ovorum libre 5 · arsenici sublimati ʒ · 3 ·
Ag' omnia fac redire in aquam cum alembich et super marmor
productam confice quousque in similitudinem lactis redigas
laminas eris x in hac aqua extingue vel intringa et cola sic enim
ipsum durum et album in speciem meron te invenisse letaberis.
M. cum sossile et nitro salso ana in aqua resolutis ac coagulatis
es ad naturam lune reduxi.[1] ℞ vitrioli romani libra 1 · salis nitri
libra 1 · salis armoniaci ʒ · 3 · hec omnia comisce in unum terendo
et pone in curcubita cum alembico et quod distillaverit serva et
pone cum m. crudo ita quod in ʒ aque fundatur super mediam

---

[1] The use of the first person singular here agrees with the notion that in this
part of the *Liber Luminis* we have the record of the author's own experiments.
See *ante*, p. 87.

libram m. in una ampulla et pone in cineribus bene clausam et da lentum ignem per unam diem et postea invenies m. in aquam purissimam. R m. congelatum cum odore saturni partes 3 de allumine jameno partes 2 de corticibus ovorum 3 · 1 · et tere per diem 1 · et inbibe cum aceto fortissimo et ita fac 7 vicibus et solve et solvetur in aquam clarissimam et optimam pro lavandis dissolvens etiam omnia corpora calcinata in aquam. Hermes ergo alu (minis) 3 · 3 · ydragor sublimati et 3 sossile separate accipi (*sic*) et in aqua reduxi totamque in lapidem congelavi et cum isto es ad naturam lune reduxi. Ydragor et piron ana sublimatis fac redire in aquam et coagula confectio ista ex stagno lunam procreat. Pastor Saturnus dominus est yndorum et omnis voluntas populorum in illo est sicut ergo mollificatur acrem cerusam veneris et tantundem salis armoniaci et fac in viscere (?) redire aquam similiter in hac aqua Saturnum 7 · extingue et sic enim de facili colatur et purum in speciem aneron te invenisse letaberis. Recipe sulphurem vivum et ipsum cum leni igne funde et extingue in lixivio facto de calce viva et cineribus.

APPENDIX IV

Text in the author's possession.—Ms. in 4to perg. saec. xvi.
vel. xvii., red, black, and green ink.

Interpretacio et Instruccio pro Discipulis seu Amatoribus Artis
Magice pro iis scilicet ad quorum manus post obitum meum
libellus iste fortuito aliquando perventurus est.

Parvi licet Compendii libellus iste sit, magni tamen momenti
esse eundem experieris. Nam scias velim, Curiose Lector, opus
hoc in Arabica lingua conscriptum esse cuius ego per multos
quidem annos possessor virtutis in eiusdem ob linguae insciciam
ignarus semper permanseram; donec tandem auxilio Rabbi
cuiusdam extraneam hanc linguam optime callentis ad genuinum
verborum sensum, rerumque contentarum noticiam pervenissem.
Quae autem exinde expertus et adeptus sum et tu experiri
adipiscique poteris si vir constans et intrepidus sis moreve
prescripto processeris. Ast cum spiritibus astutissimis et humano
generi infensissimis tibi agendum est: Quare cum previa sane
mentis deliberacione et cautela maxima procedas necesse est.
Quod si vero rem rite tractaveris grandia et mirabilia perpetrare
poteris. Reliqua te opus ipsum satis docebit. Unum hoc ulti-
matim te enixe adhortamus ut libellum istum optime custodias,
ne in manus curiose juventutis seu ignorancium hominum
incidat. Siquidem per eius lecturam, nisi more prescripto fiat,
funestissime tragedie orirentur. Quare ipse autor in prima
pagina admonet ut in silencio legatur. Nemo igitur quiscumque
sit absque circulo clara et alto voce insertas Spirituum citaciones
legere presumat nisi miserrimum sui detrimentum et interitum
preceps ruere velit. Quapropter quicquid agis prudenter agas
et respice Finem. Vale. Michael Scotus Prage in Bohemia
pridie Id. Febr. Anno mcclv.

Sequitur interpretacio tocius operis.
Aspice Inspice pervolve alta sed
legere voce omnino cave.

Almuchabola Absegalim Alkakib Albaon *i.e.* Compendium

Magie Innaturalis Nigre, continens Citaciones et Vincula diversorum Spirituum.

Primum et maxime necessarium requisitum in experimentis Magicis Composicio Circuli est. Nam sine eo nemo a malis Spiritibus tutus foret. Quare Magister ex pelle caprina *i.e.* charta virginea faciat Circulum in latitudine novem pedum ad quem cum sanguine Columbe scribi debent nomina que videntur in figura pag. iij. (this refers to the other quire containing the Arabic original which alone has illustrations). Quodsi vero illum forcius munire cupis poteris pro lubitu addere plura ex sanctissimis Dei Nominibus Hebraicis v.g. Elohim Adonai Zebaoth Agla Jehovah, item nomina iiij Evangelistarum et iiij Archangelorum et adhuc alia que ex rituali Ecclesiastico sive aliis libris sat colligas. Secundo habeatur baculus qui abscindatur Corilo in quem inscindi et cum sanguine columbe inscribi debent verba et nomina in figura pag. iij indicata. Tereio fiat Mitra pariter ex pelle capre Alba posterior Nigra et scribantur m. ad illam cum sanguine columbe nomina que habet figura pag. iiij. Quarto Magister habeat habitum nigrum longum usque ad pedes super habitum vero Scapulare sive pentaculum factum ex ante dicta charta virginea et iterum cum sanguine columbe scribantur ad illud nomina, uti monstrat figura pag. iv. Proinde omnia hec predicta requisita debent preparari in novilunio in diebus Mercurii et Veneris horisque hisce Planetis propriis. Que autem sint hore Planetarum ex libris Astrologorum satis aliunde patet. Quinto formetur Sigillum sive titulus characteristicus illius Spiritus quem citare intendis: debet autem scribi cum sanguine corvi nigerini ad pellem capre nigre factam et appendatur ad baculum quoque abscissum corilo erigaturque ad margines circuli uti docet figura pag. v. Sexto Magister sive debet esse solus sive si velint esse plures sit numerus semper impar. Septimo requiritur locus securus absitus et solitudinarius quod si in domo fiat operacio habeat cubile aptum versus Orientem et relinquatur sive porta sive fenestra aperta; nec sint plures in domo persone quam que ad operacionem pertinent; quare semper melius et securius est ut experimenta fiant sub celo, in eremis, silvis, pratisque desertis nullorumque hominum conspectui et auditu obnoxiis. Octavo experimenta fiant in diebus Mercurii sive Veneris sive in prima hora noctis sive in sexta post solis occasum; de die autem debent fieri in ipsissimis horis Planetarum Veneris seu Mercurii. Nono Magister ante Operacionem bene deliberet quale negocium tractare velit cum spiritibus ne medio experimenti fiat confusio seu perturbacio. Magistrum itaque oportet esse virum gravem animosum, qui in lingua et pronunciacione non paciatur defectum. Socii omnes nec verbum loquantur sed solus Magister cum spiritibus tractare audeat. Hiis omnibus denique bene preparatis et ordinatis Magister adhibeat fumigia ex sequentibus speciebus:

R : Semen papaveris nigri
   Herba Cicuta
   Coriandrum
   Apium et crocus et hec in equali pondere.

Decimo si Magister rem habet quam Spiritus adimplere resisterent, accipiat baculum et cum eo feriat eorum Sigilla, sed si nimium pertinaces forent, appropinquet ea ad carbones cum quibus fumigatum est, faciat quasi assare et successive ardescere velit et statim eos obedientes habebit.

Circulum cum Sociis ingressurus dicat :

Harim Kasistacos Enet miram Baal Alisa mamutai arista Kappi Megiarath Sagisiya Suratbakar.

Sequuntur Citaciones Nomina et Sigilla Spirituum qui per hoc opus advocari et citari possunt.

Sigillum primi Principis vid. pag. viij.

Citacio primi Almuchabzar

Asib Hecon Anthios Rarapafta Kylim Almuchabzar alge Zorionoso Amilech Amias Segir Almetubele Halimasten Rarapafta Kylim O Almuchabzar horet Kylim.

Citacio secunda primi Principis

Aritepas Oulyri Hecon asib alperiga O Almuchabzar ! Rabet Almetubele Syrath alecla icarim alderez Aldemel met cadir Measdi Algir aleclar Ryia sothus Alchantum ioradio Ealusi Amilkamar Alenzod :

Citacio tercia Almuchabzar

Albantum alenzod Almuchabzar ! Hecon asip Amilcamar alperiga algir filastaros aleclar Syrath asyngarum berumistas legistas Ruppa sastaraya aronthas Baracasti hemla Omisyrath abdilbak Amilkamar alcubel taris Algir alasaff megastar Magin horet Karapatta Kylim O ! Almuchabzar.

Quam primum apparent Spiritus in forma humana visibili Magister eos interroget utrum isti sint qui ab eo fuerunt citati ? et si spiritus hoc iureiurando cum iureiurando (sic) cum imposicione manuum super baculum [qui ex circulo iis porrigi debet] confirm-

averint; salutet eos et sistat modo subsequenti in fine pag.
xv. et pag. xxxv. Hunc Principem vero modo sequenti :

Alkumkazar medidosta Asaristatos falusi algir abdilbak =
karis helotim latintos O Almuchabzar ! milasarintha iubarath
mimas Amka Solit karytos Faribai aliasi miron kylim arastaton
tyrantus Almuchabzar.

His dictis Spiritus ipsum interrogabunt quare fuerint vocati ?
etc. Magister illis negocium proponat et si adimpleverint
dimittat illos prout sequitur in fine pag. xv. et pag. xxx istum
vero specialiter sic :

Sarmistaros labyratha Asanta bartha Megimaia karapatta
horet kylim O Almuchabzar !

SIGILLUM ACHUNCHAB vid. pag. xi.

Citacio.

Asip hecon anthios karapatta kylim Achunchab Perificanthus
alasaff haram astarladip Megastar hagiasesta parit hemla pantus-
tata amagarim kalip kisolastar aleclar elgir altemel alperiga Horet
kylim O Achunchab !

SIGILLUM AGHIZIKKE vid. pag. xii.

Citacio.

Hamagit hecon asip Kampatta kylim Aghizikke sisalmaz
alenzod alcubel algir sarmistaros alasat Abdilbak Guscharasch
heam diadrasas dalasai Betaran herik iulem Megastar Helib istam
horet kylim O Aghizikke !

SIGILLUM BALTUZARAZ vid. pag. xiii.

Citacio.

Megaras Galim asip hecon kylim Baltuzaraz negyrus haleai
amith aresatos gimastas permasai alar aluhazi Hacub salataya
almetubeli algir Abilbak mirastatos Alenzod medagasti O Baltu-
zaras kylim horet.

Sequuntur alia adhuc sigilla aliquorum Spirituum qui per sub-
sequentem coniuracionem advocantur. Sigilla vide pag. xiiij.
Nomina eorum numeres secundum ordinem sigillorum a manu
dextra ad sinistram suntque sequentia :

KAPULIPH, SUHUB ; GALHABARI ET ALMISCHAK.

Citacio.

Mabgatusta berenata sarmistaros gorisgatba Helotim latintos
aciton Axagiatum amka iaribai artas gilgarkipka Selingarasch
alberalabon gimistas Kateraptas amogiorith miagastos Diadrasi
Radistar dalasa hagaigia Belzop hecon asip Karapatta kylim O
Suhub Galhabari O Almischak Kapuliph antios guschorasch

S

Alcubel alenzod algir Rabet almetubele Abdilbak mirastatos alasaff algir megastar ioradip faluli zorionoso alget kapkar imat Abdilbaim eralim fiascar albirastos perifiantus Berapkukagapharam Abdilbaim erasin Zakarip Aresatos Talmasten Karapatta kylim horet kylim.

INSTICIO SIVE CONSISTENCIA SPIRITUUM.

Harim kelit Amogar Bail namutai aristakappi Megiarath agualim Segirit beranabtar Cesastus megarustat amargim Bargastaton ioratkar Karistacao Alim Miron anasterisatos horet kylim.

VALEDICCIO SPIRITUUM.

Bedarit labyratha Asonta barda Meles kalas hemastar Bemtsstaras Bedarit Enet elmisistar Almiranthus.

Quando Magister cum Sociis egreditur circulo dicat hec sequentia verba vide pag. xvi.

Begarsten alengip Harim Gantalsa stai Becekym Dingiltas Mecarkayrup Hermagastus aganton Badaky Gragaim Bemdastoras Argint.

FINIS.

APPENDIX V

Regesta Vaticana, Tom. xii., fol. 136 vo., epist. 170.

. . . . archiepiscopo Cantuariensi sancte Romane ecclesie cardinali. De provisione dilecti filii magistri Michaelis Scoti, cuius eminentis sciencie titulus de ipso testimonium perhibet, quod inter litteratos alios dono vigeat sciencie singulari patris intimo cogitantes affectu, pro eo tibi, quod inter ceteros per orbem sciencia preditos eminenti litteratura et profundioris prerogativa doctrine coruscas, fiducialiter affectione plena dirigimus scripta nostra, firmam spem fiduciamque tenentes, quod probos clericos diligas et delecteris in illis ac per hoc ad providendum tante sciencie clerico promptus et facilis inveniri debeas per te (137ro.) ipsum. Quocirca fraternitati tue per apostolica scripta mandamus, quatinus tam liberaliter quam libenter predicto magistro infra provinciam tuam auctoritate nostra provideas in beneficio quod recipiente congruat et deceat providentem, ita quod ex hoc devocionem et diligenciam tuam in Domino commendare possimus et nos illud habeamus acceptum qui nollemus omnino quod dictus magister, qui maioribus dignus esset, gracie nostre, que reputatur ei debitum, frustraretur effectu, contradictores autem per censuras ecclesiasticas appellacione remota compescas. Dat. Lateran. xvii Kal. februar. anno octavo.

This extract, which has not hitherto been fully printed in any of the authorities (Pressutti, *Regesta Honorii Pape III.* vol. ii. pp. 194, 258; Bliss, *Calendar of Entries in the Papal Registers,* vol. i. pp. 94, 97) has reached me from the Vatican just before going to press. I owe it to the kindness of Monsignor Ehrle, the Prefect of the Bibliotheca Apostolica, and am glad to reproduce it here, not only because of the light it throws on the events mentioned in Chapter viii., but as a testimony to the opinion then held of Scot's attainments in science. Incidentally too, it places beyond question the fact mentioned on p. 14, namely, that he was in holy orders. With regard to the title

of 'Master,' here repeated, I may add that this would seem to
have been equivalent among the Regulars to that of 'Doctor'
among the secular clergy ; so that there is a further probability
that Scot belonged to one of the monastic orders. Should any
one still doubt that the 'M. Scotus' whom Honorius named for
Cashel is the same person as Michael Scot, this extract may
help to resolve the matter. Honorius evidently held Michael
in the highest esteem, and it will be difficult to find another
M. Scotus so likely to have been preferred by him in the very
same year.

INDEX

ERRATA

Page 55, line 11. *For* ' m⁰c⁰c⁰x,' *read* ' m⁰cc⁰x.'

Page 81, note 1. *For* 'The term had not been previously used in theology,' *read* 'The term seems not to
have been previously used in pure theology.'